D1823645

Palgrave Studies in Young People and Politics

Series Editors
James Sloam
Department of Politics and International Relations
Royal Holloway, University of London
Egham, UK

Constance Flanagan
School of Human Ecology
University of Wisconsin–Madison
Madison, WI, USA

Bronwyn Hayward
School of Social and Political Sciences
University of Canterbury
Christchurch, New Zealand

Over the past few decades, many democracies have experienced low or falling voter turnout and a sharp decline in the members of mainstream political parties. These trends are most striking amongst young people, who have become alienated from mainstream electoral politics in many countries across the world. Young people are today faced by a particularly tough environment. From worsening levels of child poverty, to large increases in youth unemployment, to cuts in youth services and education budgets, public policy responses to the financial crisis have placed a dispro-portionate burden on the young.

This book series will provide an in-depth investigation of the changing nature of youth civic and political engagement. We particularly welcome contributions looking at:

- Youth political participation: for example, voting, demonstrations, and consumer politics
- The engagement of young people in civic and political institutions, such as political parties, NGOs and new social movements
- The influence of technology, the news media and social media on young people's politics
- How democratic innovations, such as social institutions, electoral reform, civic education, can rejuvenate democracy
- The civic and political development of young people during their transition from childhood to adulthood (political socialisation)
- Young people's diverse civic and political identities, as defined by issues of gender, class and ethnicity
- Key themes in public policy affecting younger citizens – e.g. youth (un)employment and education
- Cross-cutting themes such as intergenerational inequality, social mobility, and participation in policy-making – e.g. school councils, youth parliaments and youth wings of political parties

The series will incorporate a mixture of pivot publications (25,000-50,000 words), full-length monographs and edited volumes that will analyse these issues within individual countries, comparatively, and/ or through the lenses of different case studies.

More information about this series at
http://www.palgrave.com/gp/series/15478

Julianne K. Viola

Young People's Civic Identity in the Digital Age

palgrave
macmillan

Julianne K. Viola
Centre for Higher Education Research and Scholarship
Imperial College London
London, UK

Palgrave Studies in Young People and Politics
ISBN 978-3-030-37404-4   ISBN 978-3-030-37405-1   (eBook)
https://doi.org/10.1007/978-3-030-37405-1

© The Editor(s) (if applicable) and The Author(s), under exclusive licence to Springer
Nature Switzerland AG 2020
This work is subject to copyright. All rights are solely and exclusively licensed by the
Publisher, whether the whole or part of the material is concerned, specifically the rights of
translation, reprinting, reuse of illustrations, recitation, broadcasting, reproduction on
microfilms or in any other physical way, and transmission or information storage and retrieval,
electronic adaptation, computer software, or by similar or dissimilar methodology now
known or hereafter developed.
The use of general descriptive names, registered names, trademarks, service marks, etc. in this
publication does not imply, even in the absence of a specific statement, that such names are
exempt from the relevant protective laws and regulations and therefore free for general use.
The publisher, the authors and the editors are safe to assume that the advice and information
in this book are believed to be true and accurate at the date of publication. Neither the
publisher nor the authors or the editors give a warranty, expressed or implied, with respect to
the material contained herein or for any errors or omissions that may have been made. The
publisher remains neutral with regard to jurisdictional claims in published maps and
institutional affiliations.

Cover illustration: franckreporter / Getty Images

This Palgrave Macmillan imprint is published by the registered company Springer Nature
Switzerland AG.
The registered company address is: Gewerbestrasse 11, 6330 Cham, Switzerland

For Mimsy,
who has always encouraged me to speak up,
and who always listens to me when I do.

PREFACE

When I set out to conduct the research presented in this book, the 2016 presidential election campaign in the United States had just kicked off, and many people around the world were following the candidates and their campaigns on social media. I had not intended to design my research around what would become such a pivotal moment in American history, wherein disinformation spread on social media like wildfire and apparently influenced the outcome of the election (events which all occurred after the interviews upon which this book is based). Rather, I set out to understand the lived civic experiences of young people growing up in today's digitally mediated world, as an effort to bring those experiences to light in the eyes of academics, educators, parents, and policymakers.

This book is the culmination of a qualitative investigation into these civic experiences and offers first-hand insight into what young people themselves think about their role in society and the ways in which they can be civically engaged in today's world. During the interviews and in subsequent conversations with participants, many participants revealed that no one—especially no adult—had ever asked them for their thoughts or opinions on these topics before. I was surprised and sad to hear this. This trend of neglecting the voices of those under 18 in the area of civic studies is evident in prior research, which tends to focus on older youth of voting age (Kahne & Sporte, 2008; Watkins, 2009; Weinstein, 2014; Weinstein, Rundle, & James, 2015; Youniss & Levine, 2009). In some cases, the research has put a spotlight on the most engaged people within that population (Weinstein, 2014).

Such research disregards the perspectives and experiences of young people before they reach voting age, a time in adolescent development when young people are developing their civic identity and discovering the ways in which they want to contribute to their communities. Importantly, research until now has not investigated how young people understand citizenship—a key personal and reflective component of civic identity. I believe that youth voices are paramount to research, and to shaping the future of society; as such, I took a qualitative and interpretivist approach to this project, which shares the voices of American youth so that academics and practitioners can best understand the position of young people in society, and their current and future potential as political actors.

Between 2015 and 2016, when I carried out the interviews with 46 young people between the ages of 14 and 17 years old in the cities of Boston and Cambridge, Massachusetts, the immigration debate dominated public discourse, especially on social media. In the years since, the immigration debate continues to maintain a place at the forefront of public consciousness, alongside the climate crisis and movement for stricter gun control. Young people are involved in—and indeed are often at the forefront of—campaigns in all of these areas, including the DREAMer movement to protect undocumented young people from deportation, the #FridaysForFuture #ClimateStrike to demand large-scale policy action to prevent further global warming, and the #NeverAgain movement for gun control. Several of these campaigns originated on social media with those hashtags, which young people continue to use for organising and publicising their advocacy and engagement on social media.

Contemporary society is often characterised by the ubiquitous use of technology, especially social media. It is therefore not surprising that we seem to be observing more young people engaging with these social and political issues: we can see their support for and engagement in the #ClimateStrike on their Twitter feeds, their images of the March For Our Lives on Instagram. Young people's lives in the developed world are digitally mediated, and the findings from the study presented in this book offer a number of perspectives on how this way of life has some influence over their experiences of their own identity, civic identity (which involves the experience and understanding of citizenship and civic engagement), and engagement in the political world:

1. In our digitally mediated world, young people are making more conscious decisions about how they express themselves, and which parts of themselves they wish to present to the public and which to keep private. In the public sphere, young people must consider what others in the community will think of them and the opinions that they express, and whether they will be heard based on who they are. This is particularly difficult for young people, because adults may look at young people and make the disempowering judgment that they are "too young" to have a serious concern about a specific issue.

2. Just as young people have very different lived perspectives from one another, they also have different experiences of lived citizenship. Young people have different understandings of what it means to be a citizen, and what it means to be civically engaged. Citizenship has always been an elusive concept, and there is also no single, agreed-upon definition of civic engagement. Young people experience these concepts—which collectively make up civic identity—in very different ways. These understandings and experiences are shaped by their position in society, and their digitally mediated lives. In particular, the immigration debate at the forefront of public discourse and young people's inability to vote played a strong role in shaping their civic identity, especially those who were children of immigrants, or those who were immigrants themselves.

3. Young people feel their voices are unheard, even with the uptake of social media for civic engagement, which is surprising. Social media does not always have the positive effect on youth voice that we might expect it to, and young people often choose to keep their political opinions, beliefs, and identities private, because they fear judgment from adults that they do not know enough, and they fear losing friendships over differing political viewpoints. This finding ought to be a wake-up call to parents and educators: just because young people have access to platforms on which they can share their lives and opinions does not meant they feel heard. While there are indeed new forms of digitally mediated civic engagement, young people need the support of their parents and educators to build their political voice and capacity for civic engagement.

Based on these findings, I was able to develop a new framework of civic identity that was informed directly by the experiences of the young people who participated in this research. This framework is designed to inform academics interested in youth civic and political identity and engagement, young people's experiences of contemporary society, and adolescent identity formation, and practitioners interested in transforming and developing civic education curriculum to be appropriate for the digital age. I hope this book will also reach parents and educators of young people, as young people consistently point to these adults as trusted and wise figures from whom they can learn, and who can educate and encourage them in their participation in wider society.

We must remember that the young people of today have an important place in shaping the future of society, culture, and politics around the world. The young people who were between the ages of 14 and 17 years old when I interviewed them are now aged 18 through 21. Many of the young people who did not feel heard several years ago now have the right to vote in the United States and will be voting in the 2020 presidential election. I will leave it to the readers to draw their own conclusions about the implications of these young people's lived experiences are for the future of the United States, and the world.

London, UK   Julianne K. Viola
December 2019

REFERENCES

Kahne, J., & Sporte, S. (2008). Developing Citizens: The Impact of Civic Learning Opportunities on Students' Commitment to Civic Participation. *American Educational Research Journal, 45*(3), 738–766.

Watkins, S. C. (2009). *The Young and the Digital: What the Migration to Social-Network Sites, Games, and Anytime, Anywhere Media Means for Our Future.* Boston, MA: Beacon Press.

Weinstein, E. (2014). The Personal Is Political on Social Media: Online Civic Expression Patterns and Pathways Among Civically Engaged Youth. *The International Journal of Communication, 8,* 210–233.

Weinstein, E., Rundle, M., & James, C. (2015). A Hush Falls Over the Crowd? Diminished Online Civic Expression Among Young Civic Actors. *International Journal of Communication, 9,* 84–105.

Youniss, J., & Levine, P. (2009). A "Younger Americans Act": An Old Idea for a New Era. In J. Youniss & P. Levine (Eds.), *Engaging Young People in Civic Life* (pp. 13–28). Nashville, TN: Vanderbilt University Press.

ACKNOWLEDGMENTS

I would first like to thank my doctoral supervisor, Rebecca Eynon, for her generous support of my ideas and endeavours throughout my career, and for her encouragement to write this book. Most of the work for this book was carried out whilst I was a doctoral researcher at the University of Oxford. Sincere thanks to my editors at Palgrave Macmillan, Ambra Finotello and Anne-Kathrin Birchley-Brun, and series editor James Sloam, for their support throughout the writing and publication process. Many thanks also for the thoughtful feedback I received from Chris Davies and Matt Henn, alongside the valuable comments from the reviewers at various stages of the writing process. Thank you to my colleagues and friends at Cornell University, the Harvard Graduate School of Education, the University of Oxford Department of Education, Linacre College, and Imperial College London's Centre for Higher Education Research and Scholarship, and my mentors, Hunter Gehlbach and Victoria Nash, who inspired and supported me at various stages throughout this work. Thank you especially to Geraldine Guillermin, Timothy Welsh, Greg Salvucci, Dan Hess, Susie VanBlaricum, Dora Lubin, Myra Sack, and Charlie Levinson for welcoming me into their schools and programs to help me organize interviews with their students.

I am especially grateful for the friends who have been by my side throughout the years of research upon which this book is based: Kate Barton, Jill Boggs, Edward Brooks, Frances Butcher, Caroline Clark, Silvia Cortes, Clive Drakeford, Lucy Ellis, Hilary Farley, Danielle Fitzpatrick, Adam Formica, Laura Godfrey, Arielle Graham, Powell Graham, Sarah Groh, Alissa Groisser, Claire Hoffman, Mandy Janusckiewicz, Anna Jungbluth,

Antje Lang, Suzana Markolovic, Kiron Neale, Maddy Pennington, Tom Pennington, Oscar Rahnama, John Redos, James Somerville, Maabur Sow, Brian Stockless, Megan Turnbull, and Joseph Woods.

Heartfelt thanks to my family: Jennifer and Robert Wolff, Eric, Jacqueline, Erin, and Scout Viola, Fiona Raso, and Joan and the late Maurice Bick for their steadfast support and love. And finally, this work would not have been possible without the young people who shared their voices and experiences in the study that informed this book; I am immensely grateful to all of them.

London, UK   Julianne K. Viola
December 2019

Praise for *Young People's Civic Identity in the Digital Age*

"In its innovative focus on the voices of young people regarding their civic engagement, this timely book addresses one of the most urgent issues of the day. Avoiding simplistic generalisations about young people's uses of new technologies, Julianne Viola's fascinating findings should encourage the adult world to pay serious attention to young people's understandings of civic matters."

—Chris Davies, *Emeritus Fellow, Kellogg College, University of Oxford, UK,* and co-author of *Teenagers and Technology* (with R. Eynon, 2013)

"Julianne Viola provides a timely and nuanced exploration of how young people in the United States understand and realise political citizenship and civic engagement in the digital age. Her preparedness to foreground the voices of young Americans is refreshing and illuminating. The book offers original insights into how new technologies and emerging digital civic spaces inform and shape youth civic identities and participation. This is essential reading for anyone seeking to better understand the attitudes and experiences of young citizens in America today."

—Andrew Mycock, *Reader in Politics, Department of Behavioural and Social Sciences, University of Huddersfield, UK*

CONTENTS

LIST OF FIGURES

LIST OF TABLES

CHAPTER 1

Introduction: The Need to Investigate the Civic Experiences of American Young People

1.1 MOTIVATION FOR RESEARCH

For better or worse, the contemporary society we live in is often characterized by widespread digital media use. Social media use is nearly universal among young people, with 97 percent of 13- to 17-year-olds active on at least one of seven major social media platforms, and 16 percent of 13- to 17-year-olds saying that social media is useful for accessing news and current events (Anderson & Jiang, 2018). A 2017 national survey of 10- to 17-year-olds in the United States found that among social media users, 76 percent turn to Facebook and YouTube for their news information (Robb, 2017). It is therefore not surprising that young people are receiving messages from people beyond their immediate social circles about their place in society as young people and how they might engage in the public sphere. In particular, young people's understandings of citizenship and their place in the world have been shaped by the messages they receive from the adults around them (that they are "just children" and that they should "stay out of politics") and the political messages they absorb through digital outlets, like Twitter (where anti-immigrant rhetoric has played the largest role).

Young people, particularly those between the ages of 14 and 17 years old, have a low sense of efficacy and feel that their voices will not be heard, because adults in their lives and politicians alike do not take young people seriously. Young people are often excluded from the political

© The Author(s) 2020
J. K. Viola, *Young People's Civic Identity in the Digital Age*,
Palgrave Studies in Young People and Politics,
https://doi.org/10.1007/978-3-030-37405-1_1

process because they are perceived as disengaged and disinterested (Pickard, 2019). However, a growing body of research demonstrates that young people care deeply about the hot-button issues (and crises) of the day (Pickard & Bessant, 2017), and wish to make a positive impact. Young people now have access to open source tools and social networking platforms, which they can use to address political and social issues directly (Benkler, 2006; Coleman, 2008). Young people now turn to more accessible forms of engagement (Delgado & Staples, 2007; Ginwright, 2009), which are often digitally mediated and accepted as non-traditional means of engagement (Henn & Foard, 2012). Rather than waiting until they reach voting age (Earl & Schussman, 2008; Kawashima-Ginsburg, 2011; Soep, 2015; Weinstein, Rundle, & James, 2015), young people find ways to demonstrate that they care about their communities (Kahne & Westheimer, 2006). Young people sign petitions, interact with elected officials on social media, access information from news alerts on their smartphones, and read blog posts on Tumblr to negotiate others' opinions and develop their own (Barrett & Zani, 2014).

This book is about young people's civic experiences in contemporary American society, and how young people navigate the political world in an age defined by experiences that are digitally mediated. Many contemporary studies focus on young voters (ages 18 through 25 or ages 18 through 30) in America and other democracies; this book draws on the experiences of young people in the United States before they have reached voting age, providing vital perspectives on citizenship and civic engagement by young people, who are so often overlooked or ignored by adults in their lives and in society. This book rests in the intersection where media studies, youth studies, and civic studies meet, and addresses the paucity of literature around the lived citizenship experiences of young people. By focusing on the experiences of young people living in the United States at a unique time in the nation's democratic history, this book is timely and relevant to the current political and social context in which young people are coming of age. This book not only highlights the changing nature of youth civic and political engagement, but it deeply explores the lived citizenship of young people.

In contemporary society, the meaning of citizenship and what it means to be civically engaged is shaped by individuals' experiences of citizenship. However, for decades, research on the meaning of citizenship has been based in theoretical understandings of adults' conceptualizations and experiences of citizenship, a concept that has always consisted of multiple meanings and understandings (Ellis, Hálfdánarson, & Isaacs, 2006). Citizenship includes legal and social components (Marshall & Bottomore, 1992; Osler & Starkey, 2006, 2018): the rights, duties, and privileges within a political collective (Olsen, 2012), and a sense of belonging (Flanagan, 2013) and the privilege connected with that belonging (Bellamy, 1998). These theories of understanding citizenship have led researchers to further develop models and styles of citizenship to include membership and participation (Bennett, 2008; Kerr & Cleaver, 2009; Thun, 2016).

Despite this widespread understanding that adults understand citizenship in these thematic areas, there is limited empirical research examining the themes and theories of citizenship as it is experienced and conceptualized by young people before they reach adulthood, especially in contemporary society. Today, young people are experiencing the world in a more digitally mediated manner than previous generations, and scholars have described changes in citizenship alongside how technology is involved in civic engagement (Bennett, 2008; Schudson, 1998). The most recent and relevant studies of the civic experiences of young people took place in the early 2000s (Bennett, Wells, & Freelon, 2011; Lister, Smith, Middleton, & Cox, 2003). Lister et al. (2003) conducted an empirical study of how young people in a British city perceive citizenship and their own transitions as citizens. Lister et al. (2003) presented a framework for understanding how young people between the ages of 16 and 23 conceptualize citizenship, but did not address civic engagement or technology; their study was conducted prior to the introduction of social media and other technologies into daily life. Contemporary society is marked by a culture of digitally sharing our lives and opinions with others (Watkins, 2009), and has been well documented (boyd, 2007; Ito et al., 2010; Lenhart et al. 2015; Xenos & Foot, 2008). While young people in the United States consume and create digital content (Coleman & Rowe, 2005; Lenhart & Madden, 2005), most often, young people are using technology to interact with their friends, with 72 percent of young people ages 13 through 17 communicating with their friends through social media (Lenhart, 2015).

With the understanding that experiences are increasingly digitally mediated, Bennett et al. (2011) conducted an analysis of United States-based web sites operated by a diverse set of civic and political organizations to assess styles of citizenship on civic websites (Bennett, 2008). Bennett et al.'s (2011) study focused on the investigation of youth-focused civic websites, their site traffic, and potential civic learning opportunities embedded in the sites, rather than focusing on the civic experiences of young people themselves. This provided me with the impetus to learn the experiences of young people through empirical research, which would contribute an up-to-date understanding of citizenship and civic engagement that includes the direct experiences of young people in contemporary society. As Lister et al.'s (2003) work is most closely related to this aim, I will draw on their work on citizenship throughout this book. Citizenship and civic engagement are the two key components of civic identity, which refers to how we share aspects of ourselves with others, and how we interact with each other and with political leaders. While there is no single agreed-upon definition of civic engagement, in this book its definition includes activities that are aimed at improving a community, in both digitally mediated and non-digitally mediated ways. These concepts of civic identity and civic engagement are the core of the theoretical motivation of this study, and will be addressed in depth throughout this book.

My own interest in this area of research in civic identity and civic engagement stems primarily from my personal involvement in youth civic organizations, especially the Junior State of America, which is the largest student-run and student-led organization in the United States (Junior State of America Foundation, 2018). Through after school programming, regional conventions, and summer programs for high school students, the Junior State of America fosters the development of leadership skills, civil debate, and civic engagement through volunteer and activism opportunities. My own participation in the Junior State of America summer programs as a secondary school student and, later on, as a tutor, led me to pursue postsecondary studies in government and politics. My curiosity about how the government works and how citizens participate in democracy led me to study civic education, investigating its link to voting behavior, and its prevalence in the missions of charter schools in the United States. Through a variety of research undertakings over the last decade, I have been surprised to find that civic education is lacking throughout the United States, and that research on the subject is often limited to populations over the age of 18, which is the legal voting age in the United States and in many other democracies.

As I investigated the state of civic education in the United States, technology continued to weave its way into my everyday life, and I began to wonder about the implications of the prevalence of new media and digital technologies in the lives of others around me. I became especially curious about how technology manifested itself in the lives of young people, because of the trends in young people gaining access to technology at younger ages. Such questions have fascinated me, and I sought to learn more about technology's implications for civic life, from the formation of civic identity, to civic education, and ways that people can engage civically. Understanding that there is no single definition of civic engagement, and no concrete definition of civic identity, led me to pursue this investigation.

As an educator and tutor, I worked closely with young people aged 11 through 18 in public schools, after school programs, and summer programs in the United States. I have always enjoyed interacting with and learning from young people in this life stage, and from my experiences, I learned that many of the young people I had worked with often desired to be engaged, and were excited to share their experiences and perspectives with those who asked. My collective experiences and interests led me to question the interaction between young people, technology, and civic engagement. I saw a great opportunity to learn whether and how young people felt they could engage in their community and their society through digitally mediated ways, and how I, as the researcher, could become a medium through which young people could share their experiences and perspectives.

1.2   Context of the Study that Informed This Book

1.2.1   *Perceived Disengagement of Young People*

Prior research in this area has focused on the perceived disengagement of young people. For decades, there has been a global debate about youth civic engagement and political participation, painting a mixed picture about whether and how young people are civically engaged. In the United States, explanations for the low turnout rates among young voters stem from research in social capital and political participation. Smith (1999) noted that this trend is correlated with a decline in participation among adolescents in extracurricular activities and volunteer organizations, and Putnam's (2000) work on the decline in social capital echoed this theory. Other scholars speculate that youth are disengaged due to broad social changes like job insecurity and neo-liberal ideology, which have alienated young people from the political process (Furlong & Cartmel, 2007;

Harris, Wyn, & Younes, 2010). Scholars also debate whether youth appear less concerned with economic, social, and political issues, due to the perception that the issues do not directly affect them (Galland, 2007), or if it is a myth that youth are self-absorbed and not concerned with public affairs (Youniss & Levine, 2009).

There has been an effort within the academic community to resolve this myth, and the focus on young people's disengagement is most likely due to research on youth engagement focusing on what young people are *not* doing, such as voting with high turnout rates (Pontes, Henn, & Griffiths, 2019), and therefore views and portrays them as inactive (Eden & Roker, 2002). Yet, as Youniss and Levine (2009) argue, there must be a shift in thinking to view youth as assets, rather than a population that has problems. When the focus shifts to what young people *are* doing, research demonstrates that young people are engaged in their communities, but in non-traditional ways (Lister, Smith, Middleton, & Cox, 2005). Young people now have access to open source tools and social networking platforms, which they can use to address political and social issues directly (Benkler, 2006; Coleman, 2008).

Young people are civically engaged, due in part to the affordances of technologies, as mentioned above, yet there are structures that must be in place within civic education for young people to become civically engaged most effectively. Most commonly, young people learn about means of civic engagement through civic education (Kahne & Westheimer, 2006; Levinson, 2010), and such an exposure to civic learning has been linked to later civic engagement (Kahne & Sporte, 2008; Keating & Janmaat, 2015). In the United States, where the study presented in this book takes place, education for democratic citizenship has been embedded in the educational culture of the nation, but has not been a priority in public education for several decades. Most recent reports released by the Center for American Progress indicate that no state currently provides sufficient and comprehensive civic education: only nine states and the District of Columbia require one year of U.S. government or civics, 31 states require only a half-year of civics or U.S. government education, and 10 states have no civics requirement (Shapiro & Brown, 2018). In the states that do have a civics curriculum, the curriculum narrowly focuses on civic knowledge, such as the history of the Constitution and Bill of Rights and instruction on state and local voting policies. However, those state curricula often lack experiential learning opportunities or local problem-solving components that would scaffold the skills and sense of agency that young people need for civic engagement (Shapiro & Brown, 2018). Civic education precipitates civic engagement, which can yield an increase in efficacy and development of political voice (Keating, Kerr, Benton, Mundy, & Lopes, 2010). In contemporary society, technology has many affordances to amplify voice, which is especially important for young people, who need their voices to be heard to make future contributions to the society that they live in. When they feel they are making a difference by being civically engaged—and receive positive reinforcement for that engagement—they will stay engaged (Bandura, 2008).

Today's youth have come of age in the time of digital technologies (Xenos & Foot, 2008), and now have a different kind of citizenship from their parents—it has become digitally mediated through blogging, social networking, civic gaming, podcasts, and online petitions (Bennett, Freelon, & Wells, 2010; Gerodimos & Ward, 2007). Young peoples' high level of engagement with technology has actually demonstrated young people to be more active participants in society. While high engagement with technology does not always equate to high engagement in civic life, the positive association between the two indicates that the myth that young people are completely disengaged ought to be reconsidered: references to youth disengagement are common, but in the digital era youth participation is "active and vibrant" (Xenos & Foot, 2008, p. 54). In their participation, young people have strayed away from traditional news media, and retrieve much of their news information through digital media sources (Hendricks & Frye, 2012; Poindexter, 2012), further emphasizing how daily activities have become digitally mediated in contemporary society.

1.2.2 New Forms of Engagement with Technology

In contemporary society, technology is an integral part of daily life. At present, technology is both a leisure activity—streaming televisions shows and movies on Netflix is one of young people's many favorite ways to relax—and is a way for young people to interact with others. It has been widely accepted for decades that social and educational factors influence the development of political identity (Gillman & Sofer, 1978), and today, these social and educational factors are mediated digitally. Social circles are now broadened through the connections made through social media and opinions that are read via online news outlets and alerts on smartphones. The quotidian use of technology and the Internet has influenced factors that contribute to one's civic identity, including how one shares aspects of the self with others, and interacts with others and with political leaders.

With the present study's focus on civic identity and civic engagement, it is also important to note how technology—especially the Internet—manifests itself in the public sphere. For many, the Internet "is the first port of call for finding information" (Livingstone, 2010, p. 3). People turn to the Internet and social media platforms to access news information, share their views, and encourage other people to act on issues that they support. The Internet can be used to mobilize groups that previously have not often participated in politics (Mesch & Coleman, 2007), and, in theory, social media also brings each user only one step away from political and social leaders, by Tweet or Direct Message, making these leaders appear more accessible and willing to use social media to interact with their constituents.

For example, throughout the 2008 Presidential Election campaign, social media allowed young people to connect and develop interest groups related to Barack Obama and his candidacy. Through those social media communities, people gathered and participated in the electoral process. With the university student-supported Barack Obama groups that were formed on Facebook, Obama became a very visible candidate that appealed to the age group that was using social media. Ultimately, he won the election, and many attribute the victory to the power of the Internet (Watkins, 2009). Furthermore, platforms like Twitter and Facebook afford users the opportunity to compose posts to share their beliefs and positions, and social media is also a place where people learn about what is going on in their communities, schools, and countries. The Internet has also afforded new styles of protest (Castells, 2007), marked recently by the Arab Spring (Hermida, Lewis, & Zamith, 2014; Howard et al., 2011) and the Black Lives Matter movement (Carney, 2016). Digital technologies and social networking websites and apps have provided more opportunities for people to shape their civic identity by interacting with content and people of different political perspectives, giving us the option to go outside of our geographical communities and into the wider world.[1] These digitally mediated interactions shape young people's daily lives, and how they see themselves fitting into and contributing to contemporary society.

---

[1] Previous research demonstrates that Facebook and similar sites keep us trapped in a bubble of our own worldview (Bakshy, Messing, & Adamic, 2015). This challenge will be explored further in Chapter 2.

While there is a host of literature related to youth engagement in contemporary society, this prior research has focused on the civic engagement of young voters between the ages of 18 and 25 (Kahne & Sporte, 2008; Watkins, 2009; Weinstein, 2014; Weinstein et al., 2015; Youniss & Levine, 2009). In some cases, the focus has homed in on the most engaged people within that population (Weinstein, 2014). This aforementioned research has left out the perspectives and experiences of young people before they reach voting age, a time in adolescent development wherein young people are developing their civic identity and understanding the ways in which they want to contribute to their communities. Furthermore, prior research has not investigated how young people understand citizenship—a key personal and reflective component of civic identity. The study presented in this book focuses on young people before they reach voting age in an effort to understand how people in this life stage think about how they see themselves fitting into and participating in contemporary society. This age group is at a crucial life stage (Pickard, 2019) at which to study how young people think about their identities and behaviors as citizens or members of the community before they are eligible to vote (Haste, 2005). There is much to be learned about civic activities beyond voting, which has been demonstrated by research into the non-traditional means of civic engagement experienced by young people (Earl & Schussman, 2008; Soep, 2015; Weinstein et al., 2015). Focusing on young people between the ages of 14 and 17 will provide a better understanding of the experiences and perspectives of young people before they are able to participate in their society by voting. Moreover, qualitative investigation into these experiences will explore what young people themselves think about their role in society and the ways in which they can be civically engaged in today's world. This book engages directly with the civic experiences of young people ages 14 through 17, and I have therefore deliberately focused the literature review in Chapter 2 on prior research that investigates young people before they reach voting age.

1.2.3   *Research Aims*

This study aims to understand the civic experiences of young people, ages 14 through 17, growing up in today's digital era to better understand how they are engaging in contemporary society, because the literature to date does not provide insight into how young people are thinking about citizenship and civic engagement in this digital era. Young people are in a unique stage of development, marked by the development of values and a belief system, and an identity (Sherrod, Torney-Purta, & Flanagan, 2010). This identity is informed by the experiences and interactions that young people have with others and the world around them. By learning how this age group thinks about how they present themselves to others, their civic identities, and their approaches to engaging in the political world, academics, educators, and policymakers can better understand the tools and skills that young people need in order to develop into contributing and responsible members of their communities and society. The research questions that guided this study are as follows:

1. **In what ways do young people, ages 14 through 17, present themselves to others in contemporary society?** The processes by which individuals undertake identity formation are not straightforward, and are particular to each person. Delving into the thought process behind young people's decisions about themselves and their identity is critical to understanding how young people present themselves to others, and how they perceive their place in the world. Erikson's (1968) theory of identity and Goffman (1959, 1978) and Schlenker's (1986, 2012) work on social interaction theory inform the findings that address this research question in Chapter 3.

2. **What are the mechanisms through which young people form their civic identity in this digital era, and how do young people understand citizenship and civic engagement?** Flanagan (2013) highlights that little is known about how this age group thinks about their own citizenship. Young people are in a critical life stage during which they are forming their own personal identities, and at this stage, they are simultaneously forming a civic identity. This age group is known to create online profiles and experiment with identity using online profiles (boyd, 2014; Gardner & Davis, 2013; Ito et al., 2010; Subrahmanyam & Šmahel, 2011). Therefore, it is important to understand how young people consider their civic identities in contemporary society, and how technology may inform this civic identity development. The processes by which young people form their civic identities and think about their communities are essential to understanding the factors that govern young people's civic engagement. Findings that address this research question will be the focus of Chapter 4.

3. **What are the means through which young people engage in the political world, and what factors contribute to this engagement?** Today, scholars debate whether young people appear less concerned about issues of public concern (Galland, 2007), or if this is a myth (Youniss & Levine, 2009). But what are young people's thoughts and reasoning for their own civic engagement, digitally mediated and more generally? Literature highlighting the distinctions between the private and public self will help to explain elements of this research question when it is addressed through the findings presented in Chapter 5.

1.2.4 *Methodology Overview*

This book endeavors to uncover the perspectives of young people, aged 14 through 17, growing up in today's digital era to better understand how civic identity is developed and how civic engagement activities are experienced among this age group in contemporary society. Previously, Buckingham (2000) observed that young people have been excluded from politics based on their perceived immaturity as an age group. But, in order for young people to be expected to be active citizens, others must believe them capable of doing so. As researchers, we must understand and perceive through a moral and political lens that young people have a position in the world, and that their experiences and perspectives matter (Greene & Hill, 2005). We must shift our thinking and view youth as assets, rather than a population that has problems, like dropping out of school and low voter turnout (Hart & Kirshner, 2009; Youniss & Levine, 2009).

Study Participants
This study included participants within this age group with the assumption that young people are capable of making decisions and informing themselves of issues of public concern, as well as engaging civically. If adults and researchers assume that young people are inadequate and incapable, we are at fault. This population of individuals has previously been excluded from studies about conceptions of citizenship and civic engagement, but research has demonstrated that young people use technology in a multitude of ways (Davies & Eynon, 2013), and civically engage in many ways (Pontes, Henn, & Griffiths, 2018). This study therefore investigates what young people experience and understand about their civic lives in contemporary society.

The study presented in this book intentionally included participants under the age of 18, as age 18 marks legal adulthood in the United States, and the age at which young people can vote, a widely recognized "key measure of active citizenship" (Coleman, 2007, p. 173). I was interested to learn about how this age group thinks about how they present themselves to others, their civic identities, and their approaches to engaging in the political world without the right to vote, to better understand the tools and skills that young people need—technology-based and otherwise—in order to develop into contributing and responsible members of their communities and society.

Schools retain the duty to educate future citizens, and schools may use the knowledge gathered from this study to inform civic education curriculum and best practices for civic engagement in contemporary society. I recruited most participants from schools in the cities of Cambridge and Boston, Massachusetts, United States of America serving students aged 14 through 17. My initial goal in this recruitment strategy was to ensure a high yield of participation agreements with traditional public schools and private schools, and a total of 46 young people were recruited to participate in this research. Appendix B contains brief descriptions of participants, including their pseudonym, age, and brief observations about them.

In-depth Interviews
In-depth interviews were deemed the most appropriate method for data collection for a study investigating such personal topics as identity and civic identity. Individual interviews are practical when the research investigates topics that focus on individual experiences (Beitin, 2012). I conceptualize interviews as guided conversations, and this orientation toward the research method allowed me as the researcher to develop a positive rapport with each participant to establish a "safe and comfortable" environment for sharing the interviewee's experiences (DiCicco-Bloom & Crabtree, 2006, p. 316). These interviews made it possible to discover the individual experiences that shape young people's identity, civic identity, and civic experiences. Meaning is constructed through young people's relationships and exchanges with their peers, social media, and their participation in this study; in-depth interviews afford the opportunity to construct meaning with the participants through follow-up questions and inquiry for further details when a participant shares their experiences and views. To best investigate the research questions, I set out to recruit

participants for two phases of in-depth interviews, gathering evidence from the experiences and perspectives of the young people themselves. Phase One explored the concepts of civic identity, community, citizenship, civic engagement, and technology, and Phase Two delved deeper into the key themes that emerged from the Phase One interviews.

The 46 young people who participated in this study were selected based on their relevance to the research aim and research questions (Schwandt, 2007). The research was conducted in the United States of America, where civic education has been a longstanding tradition in public education (Journell, 2010), specifically in the state of Massachusetts. Massachusetts was chosen as the sampling location because of my personal connections with school principals, teachers, and after school program leaders in the area to streamline the recruitment process. I sought a sample of young people who could speak to the range and variation of civic experiences that young people might have in a range of different backgrounds to allow for rich interviews that would help me learn a great deal about the "issues of central importance" to the study (Patton, 1990, p. 169). For example, it was important to achieve a sample of participants from a range of socioeconomic backgrounds, because, as discussed in Chapter 2, there is a discrepancy in civic engagement among those of a high socioeconomic background and low socioeconomic background (Flanagan & Levine, 2010; Hyman & Levine, 2008; Verba, Schlozman, & Brady, 1995). Moreover, socioeconomic background also influences whether the participants have access to technology (Middaugh & Kirshner, 2015). As the motivation for this study is the digitally mediated nature of daily life, it was important to recruit participants who would have a range of experiences with technology as well.

The research questions that are the focus of this study guided and informed the interview questions, and served as the core structure upon which the interview was based. My investigation centered on the concept of civic identity, so I set out to learn about how young people interpret citizenship, civic engagement, and community membership. As Bennett (2008) acknowledges, "the entire question of civic engagement is confounded by how one chooses to define citizenship itself" (p. 8). For this reason, I first invited conversation about citizenship with the participants before delving into the topics of technology use and civic engagement. As Pontes et al. (2018) address, the involvement of young people in choosing and explaining their own definitions is crucial to social research. Pontes et al. (2018) share that it is "not sufficient" for the researcher to offer a definition, but it is also not sufficient to use that definition with the population being studied. Therefore, I opted to allow each participant's preferred definition of civic engagement to frame the interview.

Table 1.1 illustrates demographic information,[2] and compares the sample to the averages across the Commonwealth of Massachusetts, the state in which the study took place. Rather than making claims of representativeness in this study, Table 1.1 provides a context for the study. Different regions in the United States of America have different distributions of race and wealth. For example, southern states, like New Mexico and California, tend to have a greater Hispanic and Latino population, and greater African American/ Black population than the northeast, where Massachusetts is situated (United States Census Bureau, 2011). The variation in the actual sample from the state averages infers that the urban area where the study took place is not entirely representative of the state, or northeast region, as a whole, but provides a context for understanding the experiences of young people in the study. The civic experiences of young people may be influenced by their background, as different groups of people are likely to have different experiences, particularly in consideration of race in individuals' lived experiences (Garcia, Sanchez, Sanchez-Youngman, Vargas, & Ybarra, 2015). A recent report from the Pew Research Center indicates a difference in perceptions on race and opportunity in the United States (Parker, Horowitz, & Mahl, 2016). Notably, African American/ Black individuals tend to be more disadvantaged, with Blacks more than twice as likely as whites to be living in poverty (Parker et al., 2016). Blacks experience failing schools, racial discrimination, and fewer job opportunities (Parker et al., 2016), which

---

[2] As you can observe in Table 1.1, the gender split in the study does not mirror that of the Commonwealth of Massachusetts. I found that both male and female participants shared similar civic experiences and concerns. For instance, Jackie (female) and Kenai (male) shared their frustration that adults had discouraged them from engaging politically, and Bibiana (female) and Joseph (male) both experience a tension between a sense of belonging in the United States and a legal status of citizenship. As Chapters 3, 4, and 5 will address, the civic experiences among the participants in this study related more to how adults treat them as "just kids," and the messages circulating in public discourse, particularly around immigration. The experiences that were discussed in this study were experienced by all genders, and therefore the uneven gender distribution did not impact the results of the study. However, given the current growth of feminist societies in schools (Kim & Ringrose, 2018) and growing collectivized feminism in public life (Retallack, Ringrose, & Lawrence, 2016), further research should be done to investigate gender identity and its relationship to civic identity.

influences their opportunities to improve their livelihoods and engage civically. Kahne and Middaugh (2009) found that African American/ Black students experienced fewer civic-oriented government classes and discussions about current events, compounding this civic empowerment gap (Levinson, 2010), as addressed in Section 2.5.

The participants' lived experiences influenced the issues of public concern that they cared to discuss in the interviews. For instance, the Black Lives Matter movement and issue of police brutality against black males was an important issue of public concern for the participants, particularly those who identified as African American/ Black. As noted in Table 1.1, there is a higher proportion of African American/ Black participants in this study compared to public schools across Massachusetts, which may explain why the Black Lives Matter issue was so prevalent. Overall, the

Table 1.1 Demographic information

	Number of participants	Percentage of participants	State averages[a]
Age			
14	10	22%	–
15	15	33%	–
16	13	28%	–
17	6	13%	–
18	2	4%	–
Gender			
Female	32	70%	49%
Male	14	30%	51%
Race			
African American/Black	17	30%	8%
Biracial/Multiracial	2	4%	3%
White/European / Caucasian Americans	18	39%	67%
Hispanic/Latino/ Latina	3	7%	16%
Asian American	4	9%	6%
Other	2	4%	–
School Type			
Public	27	59%	–
Private	17	37%	–
Unknown	2	4%	–
Total Number of Participants	46	100%	–

"–" indicates where data was unavailable

[a]State averages include data from public schools only (National Center for Education Statistics, 2015)

sample of participants demonstrates a range of backgrounds and experiences of the young people living in the Cambridge and Boston area. It can be inferred that young people in other parts of the state may have experiences different from those in the urban areas, as their communities are comprised of different backgrounds and lived experiences.

After interviewing 46 participants, I had achieved a strong sample of participants from each demographic group of interest, and at that point I found that participants' statements and views were overlapping and the data was theoretically saturated (Charmaz & Belgrave, 2012). As Beitin (2012) notes, there is no optimal sample size in qualitative research, and "theoretical saturation is becoming the most common approach to sample size" (p. 244). Following theoretical saturation, I devised an interview schedule for Phase Two to home in on the key themes that had arisen after Phase One. I employed an iterative data analysis process for this study, beginning with the field notes and transcriptions following each interview for both Phase One and Phase Two, and subsequently coding each transcript before moving into a method of analysis through writing.

In this particular study, there were six participants with whom I had conversations that were particularly memorable: some had shared stories or experiences that seemed particularly noteworthy, and others shared many personal details and beliefs with me. I decided that for each of these six participants, I would write a participant vignette, which would help me to construct a narrative to better understand each of these six participants by thoroughly reviewing their interview transcripts. While writing these vignettes, I reflected on the emerging themes of community, citizenship, technology, and life as a young person, and documented these themes as a mind map. As these themes emerged within and across each participant vignette, I referred back to my coding scheme in NVivo[3] and recognised that the codes I initially created were directly related to these emerging themes and the research questions. This process enabled me to look at correlations between themes, and reassess them as they correlate between other themes (Dey, 1993). I synthesized these findings and themes in tandem with a consultation of literature in each area, and developed a structure for the way in which I would reveal the study's findings in this book.

---

[3] NVivo is a computer assisted data analysis software. This tool helped me to store, code, and analyze the interview transcripts.

1.3   TERMINOLOGY

This study focuses on young people aged 14 through 17 in the United States and how they present themselves to others, and how they conceptualize and experience citizenship and civic engagement, within the context of civic education in the United States, and in an era characterized by technology use. This section will illustrate the use of each of these terminologies for the purpose of the study: *young people, identity, civic, civic identity, civic engagement, civic education,* and *technology*.

It is important to note that not all young people are the same, and that I do not intend to group all young people into one category (Pickard, 2019). Therefore, *young people* is the primary term I will use to discuss the population of individuals aged 14 through 17, about whom this study has been conducted. While this term is utilized to describe youth, adolescents, and teenagers in different disciplines, these terms have become a normative way to define this population of people, and may be used interchangeably throughout the book (Ito et al., 2010). The young people in this study were all between 14 and 17 years of age at the time of the Phase One interviews. These young people have grown up in a world characterised by rapid technological advances (Côté, 2018), and a daily life that is digitally mediated. Section 2.3 discusses this population in more detail with the relevant literature.

Identity is an individual and social experience (boyd, 2007) of defining oneself "based on our characteristics and attributes and the social context(s) of which we are part" (Davies & Eynon, 2013, p. 60). *Identity* is a process that develops through exposure to other people, ideas, and experiences (Erikson, 1968; Nagel, 1987). Section 2.3 discusses theories of identity and how individuals choose to present their identity to others.

Civic refers to activities related to the public sphere and community, including political activities and discourse (Levine, 2016). While there is not a single agreed-upon definition of *civic identity* or *civic engagement*, for the purposes of this study, *civic identity* includes two key components: a personal component and a collective component. The notion of civic identity has been modified for this study from Knefelkamp (2008) and prominent civic scholars Youniss and Yates (1997):

1. a broader sense of how an individual develops and situates oneself and one's beliefs within a broader group of people,

- and -

2. how that individual engages with others in the social, political, and economic structures within their society.

Section 2.4 will elaborate on the concept of civic identity.

Civic engagement will follow a combination of the following two definitions, which brings together ideas from scholars who incorporate technology into civic engagement, and those who do not. First, the definition of *civic engagement* as "participation in the public sphere through direct experience with online publishing, discourse, debate, co-creation of culture, and collective action" (Rheingold, 2008, p. 102), and second, as "any activity aimed at improving one's community" (Raynes-Goldie & Walker, 2008, p. 162). The justification for these two definitions will be further explained in Chapter 2.

There is a debate in the literature regarding a distinction between *engagement* and *participation*. While civic engagement has been broadly defined, as mentioned above, political participation tends to have a narrow definition focusing on electoral participation (Ekman & Amnå, 2012). The definition of political participation is slowly beginning to merge with the definition of civic engagement that I use in this book, which includes community-centered service and volunteer work (Ekman & Amnå, 2012), and can also include participation in formal political institutions through voting in participatory budgeting, for example. This definition has also expanded to include digitally mediated activities, including campaigning online, political groups organized on social media, and petitions that circulate through the Internet (Van Deth, 2016).

Pontes et al. (2018) distinguish between political engagement and political participation, and argue that political engagement is an exploratory phase of a person's political life, whereas political participation requires commitment to a political action, such as voting. Pontes et al. (2018) define political engagement as "having interest in, paying attention to, having knowledge or opinions about, being conscious of, proactive about and constantly informed about politics" (p. 13). In this book, I focus on *civic engagement* that includes both political and non-political activities. The term *civic participation* is used interchangeably with *civic engagement*, as in other studies that informed the study presented in this book (Hart & Kirshner, 2009; Keating et al., 2010; Livingstone, Couldry, & Markham, 2007; Vilchis, Scott, & Besaw, 2015). *Political participation* in particular is a *means* of civic engagement, as it has emerged in the findings presented in Chapter 4. In this study, civic engagement refers to all facets of civic life and improving one's community, through both political and non-political means. As discussed above, there is no widely agreed upon definition of "civic" amongst scholars, but the term commonly refers to public life. The definitions of civic engagement that I draw upon in this study reflect all activities aimed at improving one's community, digitally mediated and otherwise, and will be further justified in Chapter 2. Further research is necessary to explore the possible distinction between engagement and participation.

Civic education refers to how young people are educated to become citizens of a democratic society. The goal of civic education is to "develop competent citizens who have the knowledge, skills, and attitudes necessary to participate responsibly and effectively in the political and civic life of a democracy" (Patrick, 2003, p. 2). Civic education is also an opportunity to teach critical thinking, social analysis, and skills of deliberation (Westheimer, 2004). Formal education plays a significant role in the formation of civic ideals, and is considered the predominant indicator of political activity among individuals (Journell, 2010). Today, education is an important way in which individuals can fulfill the "ideals of citizenship," which Reuben (2005) defines as "communicating and debating changing values, translating ideas into expectations for behavior, and expressing beliefs in institutional forms" (p. 21).

Neil Selwyn (2016) defines *technology* as "how humans modify nature to meet their needs and wants… to improve existing forms of living" (p. 6). By Selwyn's (2016) definition, technology refers to more than machinery and tools, and can also include the human knowledge that surrounds the activities that utilize these machinery and tools (MacKenzie & Wajcman, 1985). In contemporary society, it is this understanding of technology as more than material artifacts that makes it possible to include the digital modifications humans have made to their everyday life, such as the Internet (Wessels, 2010), within the definition.

In this study, *technology* is "anything that you can do digitally… on a smartphone, computer, laptop, tablet, game console" (Davies & Eynon, 2013, p. 2). The definition of social media in this study will follow danah boyd's (2014) definition: "sites and services that emerged in the early 2000s, including social networking, blogging, and related sites that included tools for user created content" (p. 6). Digital spaces like Facebook, Twitter, Tumblr, Instagram, and Snapchat will be considered social media for the purposes of this study (Mihailidis, 2014). Chapter 2 will elaborate upon the backgrounds and uses of these social media, as they are the most frequently used sites among the participants in this study. Throughout the book, I argue that as people interact with technology in many ways in daily life, the digital world is an extension of that daily life. In other words, daily life is often mediated by the digital, and henceforth I will discuss activities and interactions being "digitally mediated." Other scholars argue that there is a difference between and a debate about what constitutes the online and offline worlds, particularly related to civic engagement activities, which will be addressed in Section 2.4.2.

The range of activities and processes represented by *technology* and the *digital* in this book are those experienced by the participants in this study. These activities include activities that can be done using a computer, tablet, and smartphone (in most instances), and normally include access to the Internet. Participants in this study discussed using technology to: communicate with their friends (i.e., sending text messages or commenting on social media posts), organize school groups (i.e., posting a notice about dance team try-outs on the school Facebook page), access the news (i.e., having notifications to Twitter turned on, receiving email news digests from online newspapers, watching television news at home), set reminders (i.e., setting an alarm on a smartphone to wake up in the morning, or have an automated reminder to take out the trash on a certain day of the week), complete homework (i.e., using Google Classroom to access school assignments), play video games (i.e., participating in multi player games using a PlayStation console), and stream movies and television programs (i.e., using Netflix and Hulu to catch up on their favorite series), among others.

1.3.1   Contributions

This study of young people's civic experiences in contemporary society in the United States offers several contributions. This qualitative study provides rich data from youth voices, which document both the unique individual experiences of each participant as well as shared patterns that originate significance from having emerged from these unique accounts (Patton, 1990), and also inform understanding of how young people form their civic identity in this digital era, and how educators might scaffold young people's civic experiences through civic education that is revitalized for today's digitally mediated world. By studying these experiences of young people using the methods outlined in the previous section, this study contributes to the development of existing literature and research about young people's civic experiences in contemporary society.

To date, a majority of previous research has focused on the deficits of young people, like low youth voter turnout, rather than the non-traditional forms of civic engagement that are possible at all ages, including participating in political demonstrations and blogging about salient political issues (Barrett & Zani, 2014). Prior research has also only scratched the surface of how young people understand and experience citizenship. Additionally, there has been limited research carried out that specifically addresses the civic experiences of young people before they reach voting age, and, consequently, there is a lack of an appropriate framework for understanding these experiences. Prior studies have examined the civic potential of technology (Lenhart et al., 2008) and the status of civic engagement among young people (Bennett, 2008; Velasquez & LaRose, 2015; Weinstein et al., 2015; Youniss & Levine, 2009; Youniss & Yates, 1997), but have not examined young people's own civic experiences as they come of age in the digital era. Therefore, this study shares young people's unique perspectives on citizenship and civic engagement, and contributes a framework for understanding civic identity in contemporary society. Prior frameworks focus on citizenship, and lack investigation into the digital features of young people's contemporary life (Lister et al., 2003) and a deep understanding of the experiences of young people themselves through qualitative inquiry (Bennett et al., 2011).

1.4   ORGANIZATION OF THE BOOK

Following the Introduction, the book begins with a critical review of literature in Chapter 2 to better situate this study. Chapter 2 begins with literature that highlights the digitally mediated nature of society, particularly civic applications of technology. The literature then turns to focus on conceptualizations of young people from the psychological perspective of Erikson (1968) and sociological perspectives of Goffman (1959, 1978) and Schlenker (1986, 2012). These perspectives inform the theory of presentation of the self, the theory of identity that guides this study of young people in today's world.

To introduce the concept of civic identity, Chapter 2 details how citizenship and civic engagement have previously been defined, especially through landmark research on young people's conceptualizations of citizenship by Lister et al. (2003, 2005). Lister et al.'s (2003, 2005) work resulted in a framework for understanding how young people conceptualize citizenship, which later informs the findings presented in this book in

Chapter 4. Chapter 2 also discusses the ways in which civic engagement activities have been digitally mediated in the digital era, which marks a time at which attention has turned to science, technology, engineering, and mathematics (STEM) education. Civic education is an important factor in later civic engagement, but has faced a decline around the world, especially in the United States, where a strong tradition for education for democratic citizenship has prevailed, yet in recent years has failed to be incorporated into formal curriculum. The literature review positions the study to investigate the ways in which the digital era and the civic sphere intersect for young people ages 14 through 17. Chapter 2 reveals the need for a reinvigoration of civic education, informed by a more appropriate framework of civic identity to understand the experiences of young people in today's world.

Chapters 3, 4, and 5 will present findings that address the research questions for this study, first focusing on identity formation among young people, then moving toward civic identity as experienced by young people in contemporary society. Chapter 3 will address the first research question, *In what ways do young people, ages 14 through 17, present themselves to others in contemporary society?* We must first appreciate young people's identity, as determined by their self-presentation, in Chapter 3. Presentation of the self is an even more difficult task for young people of color. This chapter highlights how identity and presentation of the self can be understood in contemporary society, providing a foundation for how young people might present themselves as citizens or members of society as well. The case of Martin, a young black male, helps to highlight how young people struggle with their presentation of self in today's digital era.

Chapter 4 will address the second research question, *What are the mechanisms through which young people form their civic identity in contemporary society? How do young people understand citizenship, and civic engagement?* Civic identity refers to the broader sense of developing and situating oneself and one's beliefs within a group of people, and how one engages with others in the social, political, and economic structures within their society. Conceptualizations of what it means to be a citizen and what it means to be civically engaged shape political and civic beliefs and what civic engagement looks like for young people. The data reveal that technology informs and shapes the *experiences* that young people have related to citizenship and civic engagement, but young people still hold traditional views of citizenship and civic engagement, despite this influence.

Chapter 5 will address the final research question, *What are the means through which young people engage in the political world, and what factors contribute to this engagement?* This chapter will illustrate civic identity in practice by describing how young people are engaging in and shaping their views of today's political world in digitally mediated ways. Technology is embedded within each of these areas and themes, and adds nuance to how young people present themselves and gather information about the world around them, and how they see themselves engaging politically. The data demonstrate that young people feel their voices and efficacy are restricted, despite their digitally mediated civic experiences.

Chapter 6 will conclude the book. Chapter 6 will discuss the implications of the findings presented in Chapters 3, 4, and 5. This concluding chapter will revisit the research questions presented in Chapter 1, and explain how the civic habits and experiences of young people are connected to their digitally mediated lives in contemporary society. Chapter 6 will also introduce the theoretical and educational contributions of the study, which include a new framework of civic identity in contemporary society, and recommendations for a reinvigoration of civic education to foster a greater sense of efficacy among young people.

References

Anderson, M., & Jiang, J. (2018). *Teens, Social Media & Technology.* Pew Research Center.

Bakshy, E., Messing, S., & Adamic, L. A. (2015). Exposure to Ideologically Diverse News and Opinion on Facebook. *Science, 348*(6239), 1130–1132.

Bandura, A. (2008). An Agentic Perspective on Positive Psychology. In S. Lopez (Ed.), *Positive Psychology: Expecting the Best in People.* New York: Praeger.

Barrett, M., & Zani, B. (2014). *Political and Civic Engagement: Multidisciplinary Perspectives.* London: Routledge.

Beitin, B. K. (2012). Interview and Sampling: How Many and Whom. In J. F. Gubrium, J. A. Holstein, A. B. Marvasti, & K. D. McKinney (Eds.), *The SAGE Handbook of Interview Research* (2nd ed., pp. 243–253). London: SAGE.

Bellamy, R. (1998). *Citizenship: A Very Short Introduction.* Oxford: Oxford University Press.

Benkler, Y. (2006). *The Wealth of Networks: How Social Production Transforms Markets and Freedom.* New Haven, CT: Yale University Press.

Bennett, W. L. (2008). Changing Citizenship in the Digital Age. In W. L. Bennett (Ed.), *Civic Life Online: Learning How Digital Media Can Engage Youth* (pp. 1–24). Cambridge, MA: The MIT Press.

Bennett, W. L., Freelon, D., & Wells, C. (2010). Changing Citizen Identity and the Rise of a Participatory Media Culture. In L. Sherrod, J. Torney-Purta, & C. Flanagan (Eds.), *Handbook of Research on Civic Engagement in Youth* (pp. 393–423). Hoboken, NJ: John Wiley & Sons.

Bennett, W. L., Wells, C., & Freelon, D. (2011). Communicating Civic Engagement: Contrasting Models of Citizenship in the Youth Web Sphere. *Journal of Communication, 61*(5), 835–856.

boyd, d. (2007). Socializing Digitally. *Vodafone Receiver Magazine,* 18.

boyd, d. (2014). *It's Complicated: The Social Lives of Networked Teens.* New Haven, CT: Yale University Press.

Buckingham, D. (2000). *After the Death of Childhood: Growing Up in the Age of Electronic Media.* Cambridge: Polity Press.

Carney, N. (2016). All Lives Matter, But So Does Race: Black Lives Matter and the Evolving Role of Social Media. *Humanity & Society, 40*(2), 180–199.

Castells, M. (2007). Communication, Power, and Counter-power in the Network Society. *International Journal of Communication, 1*(1), 238–266.

Charmaz, K., & Belgrave, L. L. (2012). Qualitative Interviewing and Grounded Theory Analysis. In J. F. Gubrium, J. A. Holstein, A. B. Marvasti, & K. D. McKinney (Eds.), *The SAGE Handbook of Interview Research* (2nd ed., pp. 347–366). London: SAGE.

Coleman, S. (2007). How Democracies have Disengaged from Young People. In B. D. Loader (Ed.), *Young Citizens in the Digital Age: Political Engagement, Young People and New Media* (pp. 166–185). London, England: Routledge.

Coleman, S. (2008). Doing IT for Themselves: Management versus Autonomy in Youth E-citizenship. In L. Bennett (Ed.), *Civic Life Online: Learning How Digital Media can Engage Youth* (pp. 189–206). Cambridge, MA: The MIT Press.

Coleman, S., & Rowe, C. (2005). *Remixing Citizenship: Democracy and Young People's Use of the Internet.* Carnegie Young People Initiative.

Côté, J. E. (2018). *Youth Development in Identity Societies: Paradoxes of Purpose.* New York: Routledge.

Davies, C., & Eynon, R. (2013). *Teenagers and Technology.* London: Routledge.

Delgado, M., & Staples, L. (2007). *Youth-led Community Organizing: Theory and Action.* New York, NY: Oxford University Press.

Dey, I. (1993). *Qualitative Data Analysis: A User Friendly Guide for Social Scientists.* New York: Routledge.

DiCicco-Bloom, B., & Crabtree, B. F. (2006). The Qualitative Research Interview. *Medical Education, 40,* 314–321.

Earl, J., & Schussman, A. (2008). Contesting Cultural Control: Youth Culture and Online Petitioning. In W. L. Bennett (Ed.), *Civic Life Online: Learning How Digital Media Can Engage Youth* (pp. 71–95). Cambridge, MA: The MIT Press.

Eden, K., & Roker, D. (2002). '... *Doing Something': Young People as Social Actors.* Leicester: Youth Work Press.

Ekman, J., & Amnå, E. (2012). Political Participation and Civic Engagement: Towards a New Typology. *Human Affairs, 22*, 283–300.

Ellis, S. G., Hálfdánarson, G., & Isaacs, A. (2006). Introduction. In S. G. Ellis, A. Isaacs, & G. Hálfdánarson (Eds.), *Citizenship in a Historical Perspective*. Pisa: Pisa University Press.

Erikson, E. H. (1968). *Identity: Youth and Crisis*. New York: W.W. Norton & Company.

Flanagan, C. (2013). *Teenage Citizens: The Political Theories of the Young*. Cambridge, MA: Harvard University Press.

Flanagan, C., & Levine, P. (2010). Civic Engagement and the Transition to Adulthood. *Future Child, 20*(1), 159–179.

Furlong, A., & Cartmel, F. (2007). *Young People and Social Change, New Perspectives* (2nd ed.). Berkshire: Open University Press.

Galland, O. (2007). *Boundless Youth: Stories in the Transition to Adulthood* (T. Matthews & P. Hamilton, Trans.). Oxford, UK: The Bardwell Press.

Garcia, J. A., Sanchez, G. R., Sanchez-Youngman, S., Vargas, E. D., & Ybarra, V. D. (2015). Race as Lived Experience: The Impact of Multi-dimensional Measures of Race/Ethnicity on the Self-reported Health Status of Latinos. *Du Bois Review: Social Science Research on Race, 12*(2), 349–373.

Gardner, H., & Davis, K. (2013). *The App Generation: How Today's Youth Navigate Identity, Intimacy, and Imagination in a Digital World*. New Haven, CT: Yale University Press.

Gerodimos, R., & Ward, J. (2007). Rethinking Online Youth Civic Engagement: Reflections on Web Content Analysis. In B. D. Loader (Ed.), *Young Citizens in the Digital Age: Political Engagement, Young People and New Media* (pp. 114–126). London, England: Routledge.

Gillman, S., & Sofer, E. G. (1978). Children, Adolescents, and Politics: A Selective Review. *Cambridge Journal of Education, 8*(2–3), 78–97.

Ginwright, S. (2009). *Black Youth Rising: Activism and Radical Healing in Urban America*. New York, NY: Teachers College Press.

Goffman, E. (1959). *The Presentation of Self in Everyday Life*. Garden City, NY: Doubleday Anchor Books.

Goffman, E. (1978). The Presentation of Self to Others. In J. G. Manis & B. N. Meltzer (Eds.), *Symbolic Interaction: A Reader in Social Psychology* (3rd ed., pp. 234–244). London: Allyn and Bacon.

Greene, S., & Hill, M. (2005). Researching Children's Experience: Methods and Methodological Issues. In S. G. Hogan (Ed.), *Researching Children's Experience: Approaches and Methods: Methods and Approaches* (pp. 1–22). SAGE.

Harris, A., Wyn, J., & Younes, S. (2010). Beyond Apathetic or Activist Youth: 'Ordinary' Young People and Contemporary Forms of Participation. *Young, 18*(1), 9–32.

Hart, D., & Kirshner, B. (2009). Civic Participation and Development Among Urban Adolescents. In J. Youniss & P. Levine (Eds.), *Engaging Young People in Civic Life* (pp. 102–120). Nashville, TN: Vanderbilt University Press.

Haste, H. (2005). *My Voice, My Vote, My Community: A Study of Young People's Civic Action and Inaction.* London: Nestle Social Research Programme.

Hendricks, J. A., & Frye, J. K. (2012). Social Media and the Millennial Generation in the 2010 Midterm Election. In H. S. Al-Deen & J. A. Hendricks (Eds.), *Social Media: Usage and Impact* (pp. 183–199). Plymouth: Lexington Books.

Henn, M., & Foard, N. (2012). Back on the Agenda and Off the Curriculum? Citizenship Education and Young People's Political Engagement. *Teaching Citizenship, 32*, 32–35.

Hermida, A., Lewis, S. C., & Zamith, R. (2014). Sourcing the Arab Spring: A Case Study of Andy Carvin's Sources on Twitter During the Tunisian and Egyptian Revolutions. *Journal of Computer-Mediated Communication, 19*(3), 479–499.

Howard, P. N., Duffy, A., Freelon, D., Hussain, M. M., Mari, W., & Maziad, M. (2011). *Opening Closed Regimes: What Was the Role of Social Media During the Arab Spring?* Project on Information Technology & Political Islam.

Hyman, J. B., & Levine, P. (2008). *Civic Engagement and the Disadvantaged: Challenges, Opportunities and Recommendations.* Medford, MA: The Center for Information and Research on Civic Learning and Engagement.

Ito, M., Baumer, S., Bittani, M., boyd, d., Cody, R., Herr-Stephenson, B., et al. (2010). *Hanging Out, Messing Around, and Geeking Out: Kids Living and Learning with New Media.* Cambridge, MA: The MIT Press.

Journell, W. (2010). Standardizing Citizenship: The Potential Influence of State Curriculum Standards on the Civic Development of Adolescents. *PS: Political Science and Politics, 43*(2), 351–358.

Junior State of America Foundation. (2018). *Who We Are.* Retrieved from JSA https://www.jsa.org/who-we-are/

Kahne, J., & Middaugh, E. (2009). Democracy for Some: The Civic Opportunity Gap in High School. In J. Youniss & P. Levine (Eds.), *Engaging Young People in Civic Life* (pp. 29–58). Nashville, TN: Vanderbilt University Press.

Kahne, J., & Sporte, S. (2008). Developing Citizens: The Impact of Civic Learning Opportunities on Students' Commitment to Civic Participation. *American Educational Research Journal, 45*(3), 738–766.

Kahne, J., & Westheimer, J. (2006). The Limits of Political Efficacy: Educating Citizens for a Democratic Society. *PS: Political Science & Politics, 39*(2), 289–296.

Kawashima-Ginsburg, K. (2011). *Understanding a Diverse Generation: Youth Civic Engagement in the United States.* Medford, MA: The Center for Information and Research on Civic Learning and Engagement.

Keating, A., & Janmaat, J. G. (2015). Education Through Citizenship at School: Do School Activities Have a Lasting Impact on Youth Political Engagement? *Parliamentary Affairs, 69*, 409–429.

Keating, A., Kerr, D., Benton, T., Mundy, E., & Lopes, J. (2010). *Citizenship Education in England 2001–2010: Young People's Practices and Prospects for the Future: The Eighth and Final Report from the Citizenship Education Longitudinal Study (CELS)*. Great Britain Department for Education.

Kerr, D., & Cleaver, E. (2009). Strengthening Education for Citizenship and Democracy in England: A Progress Report. In J. Youniss & P. Levine (Eds.), *Engaging Young People in Civic Life* (pp. 235–272). Nashville, TN: Vanderbilt University Press.

Kim, C., & Ringrose, J. (2018). "Stumbling upon Feminism": Teenage Girls' Forays into Digital and School-based Feminisms. *Girlhood Studies, 11*(2), 46–62.

Knefelkamp, L. L. (2008). Civic Identity: Locating Self in Community. *Diversity & Democracy: Civic Learning for Shared Futures, 11*(2), 1–3.

Lenhart, A. (2015). *Teens, Technology and Friendships: Video Games, Social Media and Mobile Phones Play an Integral Role in How Teens Meet and Interact with Friends*. Pew Research Center.

Lenhart, A., Duggan, M., Perrin, A., Stepler, R., Rainie, L., & Parker, K. (2015). *Teens, Social Media & Technology Overview 2015*. Pew Research Center.

Lenhart, A., Kahne, J., Middaugh, E., Macgill, A., Evans, C., & Vitak, J. (2008). *Teens, Video Games, and Civics: Teens' Gaming Experiences Are Diverse and Include Significant Social Interaction and Civic Engagement*. Pew Internet & American Life Project.

Lenhart, A., & Madden, M. (2005). *Teen Content Creators and Consumers*. University of Michigan School of Information. Pew Internet & American Life Project.

Levine, P. (2016, October 21). *A Definition of 'Civic'*. Retrieved from A Blog for Civic Renewal http://peterlevine.ws/?p=17532

Levinson, M. (2010). The Civic Empowerment Gap: Defining the Problem and Locating Solutions. In L. Sherrod, J. Torney-Purta, & C. Flanagan (Eds.), *Handbook of Research on Civic Engagement in Youth* (pp. 331–361). Hoboken, NJ: John Wiley & Sons.

Lister, R., Smith, N., Middleton, S., & Cox, L. (2003). Empirical Perspectives on Theoretical and Political Debate. *Citizenship Studies, 7*, 235–253.

Lister, R., Smith, N., Middleton, S., & Cox, L. (2005). Young People Talking About Citizenship in Britain. In N. Kabeer (Ed.), *Inclusive Citizenship: Meanings and Expressions* (pp. 114–131). New York: Zed Books.

Livingstone, S. (2010). Digital Learning and Participation Among Youth: Critical Reflections on Future Research Priorities. *International Journal of Learning and Media, 2*(2–3), 1–13.

Livingstone, S., Couldry, N., & Markham, T. (2007). Youthful Steps Towards Civic Participation: Does the Internet Help? In B. D. Loader (Ed.), *Young Citizens in the Digital Age: Political Engagement, Young People and New Media* (pp. 21–34). London: Routledge.

MacKenzie, D., & Wajcman, J. (1985). *The Social Shaping of Technology*. Milton Keynes: Open University Press.

Marshall, T. H., & Bottomore, T. (1992). *Citizenship and Social Class* (Vol. 2). London: Pluto Press.

Mesch, G. S., & Coleman, S. (2007). New Media and New Voters: Young People, the Internet and the 2005 UK Election Campaign. In B. D. Loader (Ed.), *Young Citizens in the Digital Age: Political Engagement, Young People and New Media* (pp. 35–47). London: Routledge.

Middaugh, E., & Kirshner, B. (2015). Educating Powerful Citizens in a Changing World. In E. Middaugh & B. Kirshner (Eds.), *#youthaction: Becoming Political in the Digital Age* (pp. 1–8). Charlotte, NC: Information Age Publishing, Inc.

Mihailidis, P. (2014). *Media Literacy and the Emerging Citizen: Youth, Engagement, and Participation in Digital Culture*. New York: Peter Lang, Inc.

Nagel, J. (1987). *Participation*. Englewood, NJ: Prentice-Hall.

National Center for Education Statistics. (2015). Retrieved March 2015 from GreatSchools.Org

Olsen, E. D. (2012). *Transnational Citizenship in the European Union: Past, Present and Future*. New York: Continuum Books.

Osler, A., & Starkey, H. (2006). Education for Democratic Citizenship: A Review of Research, Policy and Practice 1995–2005. *Research Papers in Education, 21*(4), 433–466.

Osler, A., & Starkey, H. (2018). Extending the Theory and Practice of Education for Cosmopolitan Citizenship. *Educational Review, 70*(1), 31–40.

Parker, K., Horowitz, J., & Mahl, B. (2016). *On Views of Race and Inequality, Blacks and Whites Are Worlds Apart*. Pew Research Center.

Patrick, J. J. (2003). *The Civic Mission of Schools: Key Ideas in a Research-Based Report on Civic Education in the United States. ERIC Digest*. ERIC Clearinghouse for Social Studies/Social Science Education. Bloomington: Education Resources Information Center (ERIC).

Patton, M. Q. (1990). *Qualitative Evaluation and Research Methods* (2nd ed.). Thousand Oaks, CA: SAGE.

Pickard, S. (2019). *Politics, Protest and Young People: Political Participation and Dissent in 21st Century Britain*. London: Palgrave Macmillan.

Pickard, S., & Bessant, J. (2017). Introduction. In S. Pickard & J. Bessant (Eds.), *Young People Re-Generating Politics in Times of Crises* (pp. 1–16). Cham: Palgrave Macmillan.

Poindexter, P. M. (2012). *Millennials, News, and Social Media*. New York: Peter Lang.

Pontes, A., Henn, M., & Griffiths, M. D. (2018). Towards a Conceptualization of Young People's Political Engagement: A Qualitative Focus Group Study. *Societies, 8*(1), 17.

Pontes, A. I., Henn, M., & Griffiths, M. D. (2019). Youth Political (Dis)
Engagement and the Need for Citizenship Education: Encouraging Young
People's Civic and Political Participation Through the Curriculum. *Education,
Citizenship and Social Justice, 14*(1), 3–21.

Putnam, R. (2000). *Bowling Alone: The Collapse and Revival of American
Community.* New York: Touchstone.

Raynes-Goldie, K., & Walker, L. (2008). Our Space: Online Civic Engagement
Tools for Youth. In W. L. Bennett (Ed.), *Civic Life Online: Learning How
Digital Media Can Engage Youth* (pp. 161–188). Cambridge, MA: The
MIT Press.

Retallack, H., Ringrose, J., & Lawrence, E. (2016). "Fuck Your Body Image":
Teen Girls' Twitter and Instagram Feminism in and Around School. In J.
Coffey, S. Budgeon, & H. Cahill (Eds.), *Learning Bodies: Perspectives on
Children and Young People* (Vol. 2, pp. 85–103). Singapore: Springer.

Reuben, J. A. (2005). Patriotic Purposes: Public Schools and the Education of
Citizens. In S. Fuhrman & M. Lazerson (Eds.), *Institutions of American
Democracy: The Public Schools* (pp. 1–24). New York: Oxford University Press.

Rheingold, H. (2008). Using Participatory Media and Public Voice to Encourage
Civic Engagement. In W. L. Bennett (Ed.), *Civic Life Online: Learning How
Digital Media Can Engage Youth* (pp. 97–118). Cambridge, MA: The
MIT Press.

Robb, M. B. (2017). *News and America's Kids: How Young People Perceive and
Are Impacted by the News.* San Francisco, CA: Common Sense Media.

Schlenker, B. (1986). Self-identification: Toward an Integration of the Private and
Public Self. In *Public Self and Private Self* (pp. 21–62). New York: Springer.

Schlenker, B. (2012). Self-Presentation. In M. R. Leary & J. P. Tangney (Eds.),
Handbook of Self and Identity (2nd ed., pp. 542–570). New York: Guilford Press.

Schudson, M. (1998). *The Good Citizen: A History of American Civic Life.*
New York: The Free Press.

Schwandt, T. A. (2007). Sampling Logic. In T. A. Schwandt (Ed.), *The SAGE
Dictionary of Qualitative Inquiry* (pp. 270–272). Thousand Oaks, CA: SAGE.

Selwyn, N. (2016). *Education and Technology: Key Issues and Debates.* London:
Bloomsbury Publishing.

Shapiro, S., & Brown, C. (2018, February). *The State of Civic Education.* Retrieved
from Center for American Progress https://www.americanprogress.org/issues/
education-k-12/reports/2018/02/21/446857/state-civics-education/

Sherrod, L., Torney-Purta, J., & Flanagan, C. (2010). *Handbook of Research on
Civic Engagement in Youth.* Hoboken, NJ: John Wiley & Sons.

Smith, E. (1999). The Effects of Investments in the Social Capital of Youth on
Political and Civic Behavior in Young Adulthood: A Longitudinal Analysis.
Political Psychology, 20(3), 553–580.

Soep, E. (2015). Phones Aren't Smart Until You Tell Them What To Do. In E. Middaugh & B. Kirshner (Eds.), *#youthaction: Becoming Political in the Digital Age* (pp. 25–41). Charlotte, NC: Information Age Publishing, Inc.

Subrahmanyam, K., & Šmahel, D. (2011). *Digital Youth: The Role of Media in Development*. New York, NY: Springer.

Thun, V. (2016). *Liberal, Communitarian or Cosmopolitan? The European Commission's Conceptualization of EU Citizenship*. University of Oslo, ARENA Centre for European Studies. Oslo: ARENA.

United States Census Bureau. (2011). *The Hispanic Population: 2010*. Census Brief.

Van Deth, J. (2016). Political Participation. In G. Maxxoleni, K. G. Barnhurst, K. Ikeda, R. Maia, & H. Wessler (Eds.), *The International Encyclopedia of Political Communication*. Chichester: Wiley Blackwell.

Velasquez, A., & LaRose, R. (2015). Youth Collective Activism Through Social Media: The Role of Collective Efficacy. *New Media & Society, 17*(6), 899–918.

Verba, S., Schlozman, K., & Brady, H. (1995). *Voice and Equality: Civic Voluntarism in American Politics*. Cambridge, MA: Harvard University Press.

Vilchis, M., Scott, K., & Besaw, C. (2015). COMPUGIRLS Speak: How We Use Social Media for Social Movements. In E. Middaugh & B. Kirshner (Eds.), *#youthaction: Becoming Political in the Digital Age* (pp. 59–79). Charlotte, NC: Information Age Publishing, Inc.

Watkins, S. C. (2009). *The Young and the Digital: What the Migration to Social-Network Sites, Games, and Anytime, Anywhere Media Means for Our Future*. Boston, MA: Beacon Press.

Weinstein, E. (2014). The Personal Is Political on Social Media: Online Civic Expression Patterns and Pathways Among Civically Engaged Youth. *The International Journal of Communication, 8*, 210–233.

Weinstein, E., Rundle, M., & James, C. (2015). A Hush Falls Over the Crowd? Diminished Online Civic Expression Among Young Civic Actors. *International Journal of Communication, 9*, 84–105.

Wessels, B. (2010). *Understanding the Internet*. Basingstoke: Palgrave Macmillan.

Westheimer, J. (2004). Introduction – The Politics of Civic Education. *PS: Political Science and Politics, 37*(2), 231–234.

Xenos, M., & Foot, K. (2008). Not Your Father's Internet: The Generation Gap in Online Politics. In W. L. Bennett (Ed.), *Civic Life Online: Learning How Digital Media Can Engage Youth* (pp. 51–70). Cambridge, MA: The MIT Press.

Youniss, J., & Levine, P. (2009). A "Younger Americans Act": An Old Idea for a New Era. In J. Youniss & P. Levine (Eds.), *Engaging Young People in Civic Life* (pp. 13–28). Nashville, TN: Vanderbilt University Press.

Youniss, J., & Yates, M. (1997). *Community Service and Social Responsibility in Youth*. Chicago: University of Chicago Press.

CHAPTER 2

Where Technology, Youth, and Civics Meet: A Springboard for Understanding Civic Identity

2.1 Overview

Buckingham (2000) observed that young people have been excluded from politics "on the basis of arguments about their essential inadequacies," (p. 169) like maturity and political knowledge. Such perceptions about young people have pervaded public discourse for years, but a growing body of research now recognizes that young people are civically engaged before they reach voting age (Earl & Schussman, 2008; Kawashima-Ginsburg, 2011; Soep, 2015; Weinstein, Rundle, & James, 2015), and they are therefore engaged in non-traditional ways (Henn & Foard, 2012). Young people care about their communities and society at large, but feel their voices are not heard (Kahne & Westheimer, 2006).

The Internet has become embedded in daily life (Bakardjieva, 2005) and prior research demonstrates that young people use technology in myriad ways, and use the Internet more than older people do (Hirzalla & Van Zoonen, 2011; Kim, Russo, & Amnå, 2017). The Internet has provided a new medium for young people to express themselves and interact with others about issues of personal and public concern, including political and social issues. While scholars have investigated this civic potential of technology through quantitative methods (Lenhart et al., 2008), there is a need to qualitatively examine the civic experiences of adolescents with the belief that young people are capable of making decisions and informing

© The Author(s) 2020
J. K. Viola, *Young People's Civic Identity in the Digital Age*,
Palgrave Studies in Young People and Politics,
https://doi.org/10.1007/978-3-030-37405-1_2

themselves about issues of public concern, and that they may do so in digitally mediated ways.

Young people are in a unique life stage in which they are discovering who they are, and who they wish to be (Erikson, 1968) through their interactions with others (Goffman, 1959; Schlenker, 2012). This life stage is marked by the development of a sense of self and a system of values and beliefs (Sherrod, Torney-Purta, & Flanagan, 2010), which makes this a critical period to investigate young people's civic identity, which is developed through internal and societal factors (Haste, 2004), including education.

The International Association for the Evaluation of Educational Achievement (IEA) conducted several studies of civic education around the world (1999, 2009) to measure and compare the status of curriculum and civic knowledge for students in Year 9. While the 1990s saw a growing interest throughout the world in developing civic education curriculum, the education tradition of the United States was founded on the belief that education should prepare young people for their role as citizens in a democracy. Civic education has been a longstanding tradition in the United States, compared to other nations, such as the United Kingdom, where formal civic education came later, after the Crick Report (1998; McLaughlin, 2000; Pickard, 2019).

Throughout the past two and a half centuries since the founding of the United States, this tradition of civic education has prevailed. Marquette and Mineshima (2002) detail significant developments in United States civic education throughout history, starting with the Founding Fathers of the United States, including George Washington, John Adams, James Madison, Benjamin Franklin, and Alexander Hamilton, who believed in a free public education for all, such that all members of society would be educated for participation in their new democracy. During the nineteenth century, waves of immigration from Europe provided educators with the opportunity to embrace acculturation. Such attitudes toward enriching young people's understanding of other cultures gradually made its way into history curriculum, which also included lessons on the government institutions of the United States. In the early twentieth century, John Dewey (1916) made significant contributions to civic education, and saw young people not just as future participants in political activity, such as voting, but as young members of society, who must be taught how to think critically to engage in society. In the 1980s, the United States public education system adopted the term "social studies" for a new school subject that would encompass history, civics, geography, economics, and political science. The United States developed national standards for civic education curriculum, but the 2010 National Assessment of Educational Progress (NAEP) report card demonstrated that "levels of civic knowledge in U.S. have remained unchanged or even declined over the past century" (National Center for Education Statistics, 2011).

This book takes a holistic approach to the literature, because the study addresses the gap within the literature at the nexus of media studies, youth studies, and civic studies, as depicted by the asterisk in Figure 2.1 below. These fields have made some contributions to the understanding of young people's experiences in contemporary society, including: technology use in daily life, young people's engagement with technology, theories of identity formation and expression, youth civic engagement habits and

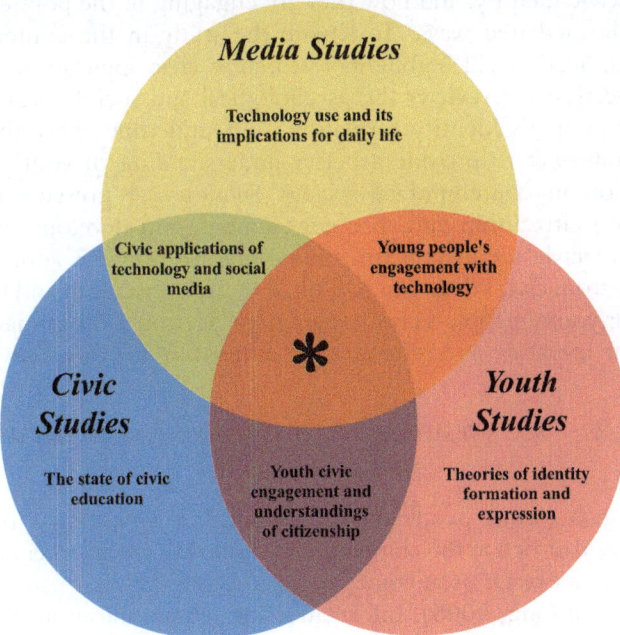

Fig. 2.1 The present study's position in the literature and potential contributions. This study addresses the gap in the literature around youth civic identity, and is situated where media studies, youth studies, and civic studies intersect, marked by the asterisk in this figure

models of citizenship, the state of civic education, and civic applications of technology. However, there is much to be explored at the nexus of media studies, youth studies, and civic studies: young people's civic identity in contemporary society. The study presented in this book will illustrate how the themes outlined in the following sections intersect to inform our understanding of what young people experience in their civic lives in contemporary society, and will address how this study fills the gaps in the literature in these three areas.

The literature review will address these key areas in each field that contribute to an understanding of the unique present era in which young people are finding themselves as they mature toward adulthood. The literature review highlights previous research that is most applicable to the research questions presented in Chapter 1. This study aims to build upon this previous research to understand how young people are forming their civic identity, and how they are engaging in the political world in digitally mediated ways. To situate the study in the contemporary digital era, Section 2.2 highlights research in civic applications of technology. Section 2.3 reviews the psychological and sociological theories of young people's identity formation, and underlines how these two theories intersect to provide a better understanding of youth identity presentation in contemporary society. Section 2.4 presents previous research on citizenship and civic engagement, and develops an understanding of civic identity in this digital era. Section 2.5 addresses the shift away from civic education in United States curriculum and its implications for young people's civic experiences. Section 2.6 summarizes the gaps in the literature and reiterates the motivation for this study.

2.2   Contemporary Society: An Era Marked by Technology

To understand young people in today's world, it is necessary to explore the features that define the contemporary time. We live in an era in which technology can reach us anytime, any place, at a very fast pace (Selwyn, Gorard, & Furlong, 2006). Information and communications technologies (ICTs) have pervaded society (Castells, 1996) for over forty years. Today, technologies most commonly used are laptops, personal computers (PCs), smartphones, tablets, and video game consoles. The vast majority of Americans—95 percent—use mobile phones, and 77 percent of

Americans own smartphones, up from just 35 percent in 2011 (Pew Research Center, 2018).

Not only does technology intersect with activities in our everyday life (Livingstone, 2010), but technology has become *embedded* in daily life (Bakardjieva, 2005), from the moment we wake up to the alarm that rings from our smartphones, to the news alerts that flash across our computer and phone screens, to the messaging services we use to communicate with others. Throughout the book, I argue that as people interact with technology in many ways in daily life, the digital mediates our interactions and experiences of daily life. Other scholars argue that there is a difference between and a debate about what constitutes the online and offline worlds, particularly related to civic engagement activities, which will be addressed in Section 2.4.2.

Cultural norms are shifting as a result of technology's pervasiveness in much of the developed world's culture: it is acceptable to be constantly connected, and for many, it is the norm (Turkle, 2011). Technology will be discussed throughout this book and refers to "anything that you can do digitally... on a smartphone, computer, laptop, tablet, game console" (Davies & Eynon, 2013, p. 2). Furthermore, the technology that features in contemporary society primarily refers to digital devices, such as smartphones, that can connect people to the Internet, which is "pervasively incorporated" into our everyday life (Haythornthwaite & Wellman, 2002, p. 7).

2.2.1   The Internet and Social Media: An Overview

Civics scholar Helen Haste (2010) finds that the Internet affords opportunities for individuals to assess, modify, and disseminate information. Moreover, the Internet is a place where people can talk, exchange ideas, and form communities (Turkle, 1995). Technology, especially the Internet, can provide the means to bring together individuals into groups (Servaes, 2003). One such technology is social networking websites, which is one of the common and mainstream uses of technology by young people (Davies & Eynon, 2013). Social networking developed out of the human need to connect and relate to others, and enables interactivity by removing barriers between the public and private spheres of communication (Fenton, 2012). Social networking websites first emerged in the early 2000s, and include blogging websites as well as related websites that feature tools for user-created content (boyd, 2014). On social networking websites, individuals can create a public or semi-public profile, make visible their social networks, and view the connections that others have (boyd & Ellison, 2007).

Many social networking websites have moved beyond the webpage platform to applications, or "apps," which are software programs designed for mobile devices like smartphones and tablets (Gardner & Davis, 2013). Apps allow people to be connected to their social media without the constraint of being connected to a computer with a web browser, and allow people to share aspects of their lives every moment of the day. Apps can be a gateway to social networking sites and tools: for example, Facebook, Twitter, and Tumblr are all social networking websites, but can also be accessed through an app. Collectively, social media are "new media that enable social interaction between participants, often through the sharing of media" (Ito et al., 2010, p. 28), and include social networking websites, collaborative spaces, and apps such as Facebook, Twitter, Tumblr, Instagram, and Snapchat (Mihailidis, 2014). These websites and their corresponding apps are designed in such a way that encourages users to experiment with their self-expression (Gardner & Davis, 2013), a theme that will be further explored in Chapter 3.

Several popular social networking websites that feature as apps and are commonly used by young people, especially in the United States, include Facebook, Twitter, Tumblr, Instagram, and Snapchat. Social media is not a "one size fits all" model, and young people tend to use each social media site for a different purpose (boyd, 2014; Weinstein et al., 2015). Appendix A outlines the key features and affordances of each of these aforementioned social media. Appendix A also highlights the potential implications of these apps for civic identity formation, which are briefly outlined below.

Facebook has a unique "Events" feature, which allows users to create events, or find out about events happening in their area that they might be interested in. Young people may learn about protests (i.e., a school walkout) through a Facebook Event. Twitter's re-Tweet feature "empowers a user to spread information of their choice beyond the reach of the original Tweet's Followers" (Kwak, Lee, Park, & Moon, 2010). This allows the dissemination of information beyond the intended audience, broadening the reach of individual voices. Moreover, Twitter (theoretically) allows users to directly connect to anyone with an account, from their best friend to the President of the United States. Twitter news alerts on smartphones and tablets keep young people informed about political affairs and current events at the international, national, and local level.

Tumblr users can customize their blogs with various fonts, colors, layouts, and usernames. Unlike Facebook, Tumblr allows for people to explore with their username and maintain an anonymous identity if they wish. Some users may use this anonymity to explore their political opinions and beliefs that they might not feel comfortable sharing with their friends and family, and others who know them. While anonymity in content sharing is sought on Tumblr, a more public platform is sought on Instagram. Social media blurs the lines between producer and consumer, allowing for people to become active participants and content creators in digital spaces, rather than passive recipients (Gosa, 2012). One of the most well-known content creation apps is Instagram, which focuses on user-produced photography. Often, young people take to Instagram to post selfies[1] and share photos from their daily lives. Young people can take to Instagram to share a selfie with a caption indicating a political message (i.e., "Black Lives Matter"), and can learn about current events by Following politicians' and news outlets' Instagram pages.

The key feature of Snapchat that distinguishes it from the rest is that the photos or videos that are shared in individual messages disappear after the recipient views the message. This feature is most appealing to young people who wish to ensure privacy of their conversations with their peers: parents or teachers cannot read the message once the recipient has opened it. Young people can use Snapchat as a medium to communicate with their friends about current events.

Diversity of Young People's Engagement with Technology
Public discourse has assumed generational thinking, the idea that people born after a certain date have different experiences from other age groups (Hoover, 2009), and misrepresented young people of this digital era by referring to them collectively as digital natives (Bayne & Ross, 2011). Although evidence points to great numbers of young people engaging with technology, we cannot assume that all young people are a homogenous group with access to technology, and that all young people possess the know-how to and interest in using technology, even if the pervasive discourse suggests otherwise (Selwyn, 2003). While technology is present in daily life, its presence alone does not mean it is a part of every young

[1] Selfie is defined by Oxford Dictionaries as "a photograph that one has taken of oneself, typically one taken with a smartphone or webcam and shared via social media" (Oxford University Press, 2018).

person's daily life, or that it is a part of daily life in the same ways for each person. Young people differ in their levels of interest, motivation, and skills for technology use that might have others label them as "digital natives," suggesting variation among young people's digital experiences (White & Le Cornu, 2011). While many young people are constantly connected to the world through their digital devices and social media (Watkins, 2009), it is misleading to think that all young people use technology all of the time and that all young people have been *transformed* by their experiences with technology (Davies & Eynon, 2013). In fact, certain factors (i.e., socioeconomic status) influence whether young people have access to technology at all, and whether they use technology in similar ways (Middaugh & Kirshner, 2015).

While the digital divide may be shrinking over time, it still exists (Gosa, 2012; Haythornthwaite & Wellman, 2002). With technology, young people of all socioeconomic backgrounds could become connected to the wider world and "experiences and opportunities beyond their immediate environments" (Gardner & Davis, 2013, p. 89). However, certain groups experience limited access to technology and the aforementioned experiences, emphasizing the digital divide: limited access groups are predominantly from low socioeconomic strata, and tend to seek alternative access to the Internet, such as using school or library computers, or going to internet cafés (Davies & Eynon, 2013; Kent & Facer, 2004). The lack of access to information and communication technologies prohibits young people from these lower socioeconomic strata from directly experimenting with the technology in ways that would benefit them (Davies & Eynon, 2013). This disparity in access to quality Internet connection and technology was at first one of the only factors of the digital divide (Goode, 2010). In time, the digital divide has moved from a simplistic definition of who does and does not have access, towards a more complex definition that explores inequalities in skills, usage, and engagement (Loader, 2007; van Dijk & Hacker, 2003). The digital divide has implications for using the Internet for civic engagement: advantaged groups that already dominated the political participation arena before the advent of the Internet still use the Internet for political participation more than other populations (Schlozman, Verba, & Brady, 2010). However, despite the acknowledgement that the digital divide exists, even people who do not use the Internet themselves benefit indirectly from message exchanges between friends, international communication between family members, web searches for shopping information or information about how the world works

(Haythornthwaite & Wellman, 2002). In this study, it is important to acknowledge that technology may play a role in the civic experiences of some young people but not others, for all of the reasons listed above. While the contemporary time is marked by digitally mediated life, each young person experiences daily life differently.

While the majority of young people have used technology as a part of their daily lives, such use has been viewed both positively and negatively: it can "create new forms of community and civic life" and offer resources for "empowerment," but it can also lead to privacy concerns and commercial exploitation (Buckingham, 2013, p. 31). Moreover, young people do not take up these opportunities equally (Livingstone & Bober, 2004). While there are indeed risks and concerns associated with technology and internet use, this book takes a critical perspective on the generally positive applications of technology, especially its civic applications, which are promising resources for young people who have not yet reached voting age, and will be outlined in the following section.

Civic Applications of Technology

The digital world we live in informs our presentations of our selves and our interactions with others. In this sense, the Internet has the potential to "increase social capital, civic engagement, and develop a sense of belonging to a community" (Quan-Haase, Wellman, Witte, & Hampton, 2002, p. 319). Social media offers young people new ways to share and learn about political ideas, raise funds, mobilize others to protest, vote, and make progress on public issues (Kahne, Middaugh, & Allen, 2014). This section will illustrate the ways in which people use social media to consume and share information about themselves and the world around them and actively share their personal beliefs and experiences.

Exposure to diverse perspectives is key to democratic society (Hodgin, 2016; Kahne, Middaugh, Lee, & Feezell, 2012), and can help young people develop their perspective-taking skills. The ability to understand different perspectives is important, as experience with diversity can give young people exposure to people with perspectives different from their own (Serriere, 2014). Perspective taking (Selman, 1971) plays into civic behavior: if it is possible to put oneself in another's shoes, one can better advocate for that other person (Tynes & Monterosa, 2015). Literature points to the Internet and social media as mechanisms through which people are connected to each other and exposed to a diversity of cultures, information, and ideas (Kahne et al., 2014). In such interactions, individuals may reassess their own opinion upon discovering that the other person's opinion differs from theirs (Huckfeldt & Sprague, 1995). The Internet and social media have the potential to provide opportunities for young people to learn about issues, access news information, share their point of view and learn those of others, and take action for change (Hodgin, 2016; Tapscott, 1998). This study will demonstrate the links between technology and identity presentation further in Chapter 3.

Individuals can learn from their peers in their immediate social circles through the posts and news headlines they share on their profiles, but people can also gain exposure to others with whom they previously might have had little contact. Technology is blurring traditional social and institutional hierarchies (Friedman, 2005), which is evident in contemporary society as people connect to public officials on Twitter and other platforms. For example, politicians are harnessing the power of social media, with 80 percent of members of U.S. Congress having their own YouTube channels to interact with their constituents (NPR, 2009). Social media has now become a way for candidates for political office to connect with their constituents (Hendricks & Frye, 2012). Even individuals running for public office at the local level run campaign websites, which enable people to learn about the candidate's platform, make campaign donations, and engage in web-based political actions (Xenos & Foot, 2008).

But, while social networking sites were thought to bring about a platform for dialogue and exposure to differing political ideas, in some cases it has been easier for individuals to find and connect with other like-minded individuals and groups, thereby enhancing an individual's own political opinions (Bakshy, Messing, & Adamic, 2015; Fenton, 2012). Young people have embraced technology to connect with people whose values and interests they share (Quan-Haase & boyd, 2011), and because of this, technology can also constrain people from exposure to diverse perspectives (Kahne, Ullman, & Middaugh, 2011). Social media connects people through friend networks, which are notable influences on political opinions. Research on voting behavior and social media use indicates that Facebook messages between friends in the 2010 midterm elections in the United States influenced users' political self-expression and real-world voting (Bond et al., 2012). In some cases, friend networks are the most important factor limiting the cross-cutting content individuals are exposed to, and when there is friend overlap within social networks, many within those networks hear and read the same opinions (Bakshy et al., 2015; boyd, 2008). Moreover, social media is not vetted by any authority, which is both positive—because that allows anyone, including young people, to post content—and negative, because misinformation can also be spread more easily (Middaugh & Kirshner, 2015).

The link between news consumption and civic engagement is well documented in political communications research (McLeod et al., 1996; McLeod, Scheufele, & Moy, 1999; Prior, 2007). Young people have a different relationship to news information than previous generations (Buckingham, 2002). In the digital era, young people are reliant on social media for communication as well as gathering news information (Hendricks & Frye, 2012; Poindexter, 2012), and share and consume media that are individually relevant to them (Linton, 2015). The use of social media is positively associated with promoting material related to and sharing opinions about issues of public concern, and encouraging others to vote or take action on an issue (Rainie, Smith, Schlozman, Brady, & Verba, 2012). The Internet—especially social media and news outlets with social media accounts or websites—is often a primary source of information about issues of public concern. Today, many young people turn to Facebook, Twitter, and alerts from news apps on their smartphones in order to access their news information, and learn about issues that might be of concern to them.

Young people synthesize the information that surrounds them on television, the Internet, and on news alert apps, and as they form their beliefs and opinions, young people may be compelled to engage in political discussions, which can motivate them to both learn more and act (Middaugh, 2016). When it comes time to share opinions of their own, technology and digital media "enable young people to have political voice and influence without being 18, having money, or even being a citizen" (Kahne et al., 2014). Social media can serve as a platform for posting one's personal thoughts and opinions, and such a platform can even be seen as a "bullhorn" that lets them reach many more people (boyd, 2008, p. 114). Young people can also re-Tweet or re-post articles from news outlets that they engage with digitally as a way to illustrate or amplify their opinion on a given issue (Garcia & Middaugh, 2015). Furthermore, young people can share their voice by signing a petition on the Internet, an action that has increased because of the low cost to creating and signing them (Earl & Kimport, 2009; Earl, Kimport, Prieto, Rush, & Reynoso, 2010). These petitions can be linked and shared to social media profiles to exponentially increase the number of people who view—and sign—the petition.

Many young people are constantly connected to each other and to the wider world through the technologies of the digital era. The Internet and social media afford new opportunities for young people to be connected to others, and to learn about issues of public concern. There remains, however, a need to investigate young people's use of technology and social media for civic engagement *before* they reach voting age. It is critical to examine this because young people between ages 14 and 17 are in an important life stage wherein they are developing their own beliefs—which may very well be informed by the opinions and news information that the read through the digital sources that are accessible to them. Learning about the experiences of young people aged 14 through 17 is critical to helping academics and educators to understand how young people in this life stage interact with technology, each other, and their communities. Understanding this bigger picture is made possible by first understanding how young people are connecting themselves to the wider world through their presentations of self, the way that identity is most often expressed.

2.3   Conceptualizations of Young People

Young people, particularly teenagers, are the most frequent users of the Internet (boyd, 2007; Ito et al., 2010; Lenhart et al., 2015; Xenos & Foot, 2008), and are established users of technology for civic purposes, as described in the previous section. Despite this knowledge, as the previous section addressed, often studies look at young people between the ages of 18 and 25 years old (Kahne & Sporte, 2008; Watkins, 2009; Weinstein, 2014; Weinstein et al., 2015; Youniss & Levine, 2009). This ignores an entire population of people from study, and leaves a gap in understanding of this particular age group's relationship to technology and the world around them. This section aims to elaborate on the conceptualizations of young people, and describe the theories of identity most applicable in contemporary society to better understand the experiences of this particular group of people. This section will illustrate the terminology applied to people in this age group, and describe the relevant psychological and sociological theories of identity, which will help to address the first research question when the findings are presented in Chapter 3. An understanding of this life stage will inform the knowledge we have about how this age group use social media, and, potentially, whether young people embrace its civic applications.

First, it is necessary to address that the terminology applied to people in this age group—adolescents, youth, and young people—are all terms that originate in psychology and sociology. When considering this age group, scholars, journalists, and parents often group them together as "adolescents" or "teenagers." It must be remembered, however, that such terms are a socially constructed identity we put on these people (Holloway & Valentine, 2003). We make these distinctions as a way to help ourselves understand the life stage in which these individuals are situated, a stage marked by transformations in and development of a unique identity. In order to fully appreciate this life stage, we ought to look at both the psychological and sociological perspectives that apply to this population, and their identity formation—as understood by presentations of the self—which will help us to know how young people see themselves fitting into the world, and their place in it as citizens.

Psychologists use the term "adolescents," to describe people in this life stage, while sociologists utilize the terms "young people" or "youth." I utilize these terms to refer to the same group of people, but in previous studies on youth in the civic sphere involve young people ages 18 through 25 years old.[2] Adolescence is a transition phase between childhood and adulthood, with no clear start and end (Muuss, 1996). Most significantly, adolescence is a critical period in which individuals experiment with and seek to find an identity, and when youth begin to think about their future lives as adults (Erikson, 1968; Kahne & Sporte, 2008). Identity is a process that develops through exposure to other people, ideas, and experiences (Erikson, 1968; Nagel, 1987). I view identity as Davies and Eynon (2013) have defined it: the individual and social experience of "how we define ourselves, based on our characteristics and attributes and the social context(s) of which we are part" (p. 60). This notion that identity is both a psychological and social process (boyd, 2007) is important, because it reflects the experiences of young people today, who often combat stereotypes, such as being individuals who have "identity crises" because "they are not cognitively developed; they are not sufficiently individuated; and they all act alike" (Lesko, 1996, p. 466). Adolescents are often stuck in a socially constructed definition and connotation of their age group

[2] The vast majority of research on youth civic engagement to date has focused on people who have reached adulthood, between 18 and 25 years of age. Similarly, many studies investigating social media use also focus on the 18–25 or 18–29 year old population because they are the heaviest users of social media (Yamamoto, Kushin, & Dalisay, 2015).

(Holloway & Valentine, 2003), as age grounds many social practices, such as voting (Lesko, 1996). Adolescents struggle for autonomy and independence in this life stage (Muuss, 1996), which is made more difficult as they are reduced to the aforementioned stereotypes by adults in their lives, and lack autonomy and independence.

When young people reach age 18, they are often perceived as independent. This is because 18 years old is the perceived age of maturation: in the field of human development, the age of 18 is the accepted point in the human life as the cut-off point between adolescence and adulthood. By the age of 18, adolescents have achieved biological maturation, but not social maturation at the level of typical adults (Berk, 2009). During adolescence, young people develop the underlying qualities for political participation, including communication, perspective taking, and development of political attitudes (Sherrod et al., 2010). The age of 18 is also the accepted point in most democratic cultures where young people are granted full legal rights for political participation (Finlay, Wray-Lake, & Flanagan, 2010; Stepick, Stepick, & Labissiere, 2008). Young people under the age of 18 are experiencing a critical period in life: they are not yet legally recognized as adults with the right to vote, but they are mature enough to cognitively and emotionally conceptualize what it means to be a member of a community, hold values and beliefs, and form an identity of their own. With this knowledge, it is paramount to understand the transitions and shifts in identity that occur throughout adolescence to better understand how young people may reach this point in their civic identity.

To understand these transitions and shifts in identity, it is helpful to first understand theories of identity from both psychological and sociological perspectives. Many studies of adolescents rely on Erik Erikson's (1968) theory of identity (Arnett, 2004; Berzonsky, 2003; Davis, 2010; Davis & Weinstein, 2017; Markus & Nurius, 1986; McAdams, 1996). However, when investigating young people's civic identity in contemporary society, it has become clear that there are sociological factors at play, best presented by the work of Erving Goffman (1959, 1978) and Barry Schlenker (1986). We must view the identity formation process through both psychological and sociological perspectives simultaneously because this psychological and sociological interaction is precisely what young people themselves are experiencing in nuanced and digitally mediated ways in contemporary society. Psychologically, young people are deciding who they are, but then sociologically they are connecting to others using technology, and social media in particular, to try out these different identities and situate themselves within society.

2.3.1   *Psychological Construction of Identity*

When examining psychological influences on identity, Erik Erikson's (1968) theory is the most applicable. During adolescence, an individual has the "prerequisites in physiological growth, mental maturation, and social responsibility" (p. 91) to experience and pass through an identity crisis, the key stage in Erikson's (1968) identity theory. This stage refers to the point at which individuals are preoccupied with managing others' impressions of them, compared with who they feel they are internally (Erikson, 1968). I draw on Erikson's (1968) work to argue that young people are in a unique life stage wherein the development of identity is central to how they present themselves to and interact with others and their communities. Erikson's (1968) point that different circumstances and settings require individuals to display different aspects of the self is especially useful to this book as it allows us to consider what young people are experiencing psychologically as they are engaging in society, developing their civic identity and political views, and potentially sharing those views with others. To this end, Erikson's (1968) conceptualization of identity is generative for grasping how young people are forming their identity in contemporary society, when portrayals of identity often take place in digitally mediated ways. It is here also that Erikson's (1968) attention to adolescence as a turning point in life in which identity is developed is of value for informing why it is critical to examine this age group and their civic experiences, which are often not investigated until after young people reach voting age.

Erikson's (1968) theory has informed psychologists and human development scholars throughout the twentieth century, including James Youniss and Miranda Yates's (1997) landmark study on civic engagement, which grounds the literature on civic identity and engagement. Recently, Davis and Weinstein (2017) found through their qualitative research with young adults that attitudes and beliefs change over time as one matures, and that one might call into question the identity that they present to others, resulting in the removal of old posts from one's social media accounts that one no longer feels represent their present identity. This notion of thinking about what to present to others builds upon social interaction theory, which will be addressed in the following section.

2.3.2   Sociological Construction of Identity

Scholars agree that identity is a function of both internal and social factors (Côté & Levine, 2002; Davies & Eynon, 2013; Deutsch, 2005; Livingstone, 2009). Young people take aspects of their environment (Hasebrink & Paus-Hasebrink, 2007), social relationships, and interactions with others to construct their identities (Côté & Levine, 2002; Flanagan, 2013). Erikson (1968) noted that technological developments impact identities; today, digital technologies afford adolescents additional opportunities to play with, explore, and share different aspects of themselves with different audiences (Turkle, 2011). To this point, it is possible that young people may portray different identities or aspects of themselves on different social media sites (Ito et al., 2010) as a way to maneuver through various social contexts and conversations and acting accordingly (boyd, 2014). Identity is both digitally and socially mediated in contemporary society, which highlights the need to explore the social theories of identity.

Key to understanding the sociological construction of identity is the possible distinction and dynamics between the private self and the public self, most notably presented by Erving Goffman (1959, 1978), and, later, by Barry Schlenker (1986), alongside other social interaction theorists. The crux of social interaction theory is that people come to view themselves through the role they play in public and how others react to those presentations (Schlenker, 2012). People are considering who they would like to be, and who they feel they can be in a particular social context (Schlenker, 1985). Goffman's (1959) theory of the presentation of the self alludes to Shakespeare's *As You Like It*: "All the world's a stage, And all the men and women merely players" (Shakespeare, 2004 [1623]). Goffman (1959) contended that social life is a series of performances in which people project their identities to others. People want to present themselves favorably (Brown, 1998; Williams & Gilovich, 2008), and want to control others' impressions of them, and will therefore consider the audience before revealing which self to present to the public. Interaction with others is part of this consideration: in any given interaction, how will the other person react to what information one is sharing about oneself through voice, language, appearance?

Considering these impressions of others and how they shape the presentation of the self, Schlenker (1986) elaborated on Goffman's theory to distinguish further between the private self and the public self. The private self is the "core of one's inner being" (Schlenker, 1986, p. 21), the part that only one knows and keeps to the self without sharing with others. In contrast, the public self is displayed in social settings (Schlenker, 1986), which conveys to others certain aspects of the self that one feels comfortable sharing. Literature concerning self-presentation shows that when asked to describe the self, most people offer positive descriptions (Paulhus & Trapnell, 2008; Schlenker, 2012), but people tend to be more modest among friends or others with whom a level of emotional comfort exists (Schlenker, 2012). When one is in such a comfortable setting, automaticity is likely to occur, because the individual feels secure and is thinking less about how others perceive them (Schlenker, 2012). Other automatic processes include the chameleon effect, which describes the unconscious mimicry of others' expressions and mannerisms (Chartrand & Bargh, 1999). Considerations of presentations of the self can also include presentations of the self within conscious awareness, such as deciding to wear designer clothes to impress a group of wealthy socialites (Schlenker, 2012).

Davies and Eynon (2013) note that when young people consider their digital presence, they do so with a sense of their audience, and make conscious decisions about what to share and with whom. The following section will describe the applications of Erikson's (1968) theory of identity and Goffman's (1959, 1978) theory of the presentation of the self to the contemporary time, wherein people must determine which pieces of the self to share with others on social media.

2.3.3 Presentations of the Self in Contemporary Society: The Intersection of the Psychological and Sociological Theories of Identity

In this digital era, presentations of the self are digitally mediated, marking an illustration of the psychological and sociological approaches to understanding identity that were described in the previous sections. Schlenker (2012) concludes that in the digital world, people create identities that tend to be self-flattering, but presentations of the self vary depending on which social networking—or dating, or roleplaying—websites the individual is using to interact with others. It may be easier to stretch the truth about one's height, for example, if the individual is interacting with others on a website and there is little likelihood that they will meet in person. Literature illustrates that young people frequently use the Internet (Hirzalla & Van Zoonen, 2011; Kim et al., 2017), and often, Internet use is for the purpose of using social networking sites, which allow the creation of profiles and opportunities to present the self in different ways. Sites like Facebook and Instagram enable young people to communicate with their widening social circles and break down barriers between the public and private spheres of communication (Fenton, 2012; Livingstone, 2009). With technology and social media profiles embedded within daily life, it becomes easier for young people to explore and expand their identity through their social media profiles. Young people are deciding which aspects of the self they wish to keep private, and which to bring to the public eye.

Erikson (1968) explained that young people experience confusion as they experiment with different values and goals, leading them to experiment with different identities. In the digital era, young people can interact with new content and opinions that they might not have been exposed to otherwise, yielding them more opportunities to try out alternative identities, values, and beliefs (Turkle, 2011). Technology—and social media in particular—allows young people to have a new space to express themselves, separate from authority and control that they face in other aspects of their lives at home and school (Davies & Eynon, 2013). As Meyrowitz (1985) noted fifteen years before social media arrived, new media have impacted the social stages on which people present themselves. Applying this knowledge and Goffman's (1959) theory to contemporary society, social media is a new stage on which young people may present themselves to others. Interacting with digital media, especially through social media profile creation, has become a part of how today's young people are constructing their identities and sense of self, and presenting themselves to others.

Most social media profiles are designed in a way to provide information about what type of person the user is to other people and to the world (Livingstone, 2009). Some young people portray different identities or aspects of themselves on different social networking sites, but that may not necessarily reflect a change in identity. Rather, it reflects how young people act according to the social context in which they are situated (boyd, 2014). Furthermore, the anonymity of the Internet may allow for more identity experimentation, but not everyone chooses to remain anonymous or present an identity that differs much from one's identity that is presented offline (Subrahmanyam & Šmahel, 2011). As young people identify themselves with others through social networking sites, some choose to identify with others by *not* creating a social networking profile (Davies & Eynon, 2013).

On social networking and blogging websites such as Snapchat, Instagram, and Tumblr, young people typically establish their identity to others through the use of self-presentation tools like usernames, which may convey an individual's gender or interests. Association with popular music is also a known way of how adolescents present their identity (Davies & Eynon, 2013; Subrahmanyam & Šmahel, 2011). Social media apps and the Internet can enable people to approach identity formation in a more thoughtful way, connect with others who share similar views and values, and create new identities and technologies (boyd, 2014; Gardner & Davis, 2013; Ito et al., 2010; Subrahmanyam & Šmahel, 2011). Many social networking websites, such as Facebook and Twitter, incorporate a customizable profile feature, which allows young people to experiment with how they present themselves to the world through their self-identified interests and goals (Subrahmanyam & Šmahel, 2011). As youth create different social networking profiles, a few websites, like Facebook, ask that users put in their age, location, and gender. Many teenagers play with these mandatory fields, and often invent a name that includes a last name of a celebrity or friend. danah boyd (2014) notes that these young people are "refusing to play by the rules of self-presentation" (p. 46), which are defined by social media sites and instead, are creating their own rules as they create their own identities.

While young people create their own rules for self-presentation as they explore their identities, some young people are creating more than one profile on the same social networking platform as an effort to manage others' impressions of them (Rui & Stefanone, 2013), particularly by deleting one profile and creating a new one to mark a new identity. While young people are still able to present themselves in traditional ways through social media—for example, they can show their networks their new hairstyle through an updated profile picture—in the digital era, there is a new consideration that what is shared digitally is there to stay, and that there are different audiences within each network. For example, young people might have friends, family members, and teachers within their social networks (Rui & Stefanone, 2012), and each of these audiences might expect young people to present a different image. The new hairstyle may have felt exciting for some time, but it is possible that the young person may change their mind and does not want to be immortalized by that photograph and known for that particular hairstyle. Even when content is deleted from one's Facebook profile, some content still remains on Facebook servers (Facebook, 2018). As young people continue to grow and develop their identities, this may lead some young people into creating new social media profiles to mark their transformation.

Specific goals, such as pursuing approval, can prime individuals to present themselves in such a way that helps them to achieve those goals (Dijksterhuis & Aarts, 2010). In the digital era, this phenomenon is observed when young people post photographs of themselves to pursue approval in the form of Likes and comments from their friends. This presentation of the self for approval is a proxy for how young people see themselves in society, which sheds light on how young people see themselves as part of a group as citizens or community members (Gecas & Burke, 1995). The overall wellbeing of a group depends on people being able to count on one another to "do what they say they will do and be what they claim to be" (Schlenker, 2012, p. 551). Identity is central to civic identity: how one sees oneself fitting into and contributing to a group or larger society impacts the self they present to that group, and, consequently, the self that is presented is the self that the group expects the person to be (Schlenker, 2012). Young people are in a life stage that is marked by the development of a sense of self and a values and a belief system (Tapscott, 1998), making this a critical period to investigate young people's civic identity.

2.4   CIVIC STUDIES: DEVELOPING AN UNDERSTANDING OF CIVIC IDENTITY

Young people come to develop a sense of self, and situate themselves within society, but at the same time, they are becoming aware of issues of public concern and forming opinions about those issues. Young people are developing their understanding of themselves and their beliefs within their communities and how they can responsibly engage in those communities; they are developing their civic identity. This section will develop the definition of civic identity for this book by reviewing the literature on citizenship and civic engagement.

Civic scholars refer to civic identity as a concept that comprises personal and moral values, and includes a sense of connection and belonging to a community, and agency and responsibility for that community (Bers, 2008; Nasir & Kirshner, 2003; Youniss, McLellan, & Yates, 1997). Like identity, civic identity is individually and socially constructed (Haste, 2004). Civic identity emerges from participation in informal and formal activities that develops a sense of agency and social responsibility (Youniss et al., 1997), as well as through engaging in conversations with others, to learn from different perspectives (Knefelkamp, 2008). Adelson (1968) and Adelson and O'Neil (1966) were among the first to study the civic development of young people, and linked political understanding to cognitive development. Their work demonstrated that young people's understanding of citizenship expands in adolescence, making young people between the ages of 14 and 17 an ideal population to investigate.

Some scholars see civic identity as a "precondition" for civic engagement. Dahlgren and Olsson (2007) argue that one must feel empowered in such a way that engaging civically is meaningful. Understanding one's place in the community and society can help one determine the most impactful way for one to engage in the community. However, other scholars note that it could be the other way around: participation in civic activities—engaging civically—also aids in the formation of a civic identity (Knefelkamp, 2008; Nasir & Hand, 2008). This book will provide a better understanding of the relationship between citizenship, civic engagement, and civic identity. The following sections will distinguish between the components of civic identity, which, in addition to a personal component, includes a collective component (Youniss et al., 1997), specifically related to family influence. Young people learn about democracy and participation first from their families, by observing the civic actions of the adults around them (Hartmann, Carpentier, & Cammaerts, 2007). Discussions about current events and politics with family and friends can impact the process of civic identity formation (Flanagan, 2013).

As civic scholars broadly define civic identity to include personal and collective components, I have modified the notion of civic identity from Knefelkamp (2008) and Youniss and Yates (1997). These scholars refer to a personal reflection component related to citizenship, and a civic engagement component:

1. a broader sense of how an individual develops and situates oneself and one's beliefs within a broader group of people,
   - and -
2. how that individual engages with others in the social, political, and economic structures within their society.

While there are existing frameworks of conceptualizations of citizenship, a similar framework does not exist for civic engagement—and, most importantly, no framework exists which acknowledges these two components to form a single framework of civic identity. The sections that follow will illustrate these two components of civic identity in further detail to illustrate the need for a civic identity framework that addresses both of these components. Presentation of the self is central to civic identity: how one decides to present oneself as part of a group or larger society impacts how one acts in that civic setting (Schlenker, 2012). For example, if an individual is a member of a local Young Republicans group, others in the group and in the wider community may expect that young person to be active in the political party, especially by joining a campaign to canvas for Republican candidates until that young person is eligible to vote for those candidates. This study will shed light on how young people perceive society's expectations of them, and how they in turn choose to present themselves as members of society.

2.4.1   Citizenship

The first key component of civic identity, a personal component, refers to how young people think of themselves as citizens (Hall, Williamson, & Coffey, 1998) belonging to a political community (Mouffe, 1992), and the second component, a collective component, refers to the ways young people think about and participate in civic engagement. Citizenship is an elusive concept (Ignatieff, 1995), but its meanings are guided in "socially-inspired norms" (Linton, 2015, p. 193). For most, citizenship is a birth right (Dudley & Gitelson, 2002), but it is often depicted as a capability based on knowledge and skills, and most often understood in terms of responsibility (Pontes, Henn, & Griffiths, 2019), with citizenship as an ideal and a goal (Ireland, Kerr, Lopes, Nelson, & Cleaver, 2006; Nelson & Kerr, 2006; Ross, 2008).

Notably, Bennett (2008) identified two styles of citizenship: dutiful citizens, who believe their obligation is to participate in government, with voting as the "core democratic act," and actualized citizens, who have a higher sense of individual purpose, and view other forms of engagement as more valuable and meaningful than voting. The person that Bennett (2008) refers to as a dutiful citizen may be a voter, campaign donor, or political party member, and an actualized citizen may find democratic fulfillment in organizing a protest (Loader, 2007). Similarly, Flanagan (2013) defines a citizen as a person who feels a part of something bigger than the self, and is a member of a political community.

Community membership, and one's sense of what it means to be a citizen, is a central element of civic identity, and has been studied in adult populations. Many young people recognize citizens as people with rights and duties who are part of a community and contribute to the community (Dias & Menezes, 2014). There are different ways of conceptualizing a community (Annette, 2008), including community as a place, and community as a sense of belonging. Community can also be based on the "construction of cultural identities" (Annette, 2008, p. 393), interest, and political ideals. Brint (2001) defines community as an "aggregate of people who share common activities and/or beliefs and who are bound together principally by relations of affect, loyalty, common values, and/or personal concern" (p. 8). Research on the understanding of a sense of community goes back to the 1960s, 1970s, and 1980s, and still applies today. Social bonding and connection is a notable element of a sense of community, as studied by Riger and Lavrakas (1981). This bonding leads to a feeling of membership, influence and sense of mattering, integration and fulfillment of needs, and shared emotional connection with others (McMillan & Chavis, 1986). This fraternalism and mutual support (Brint, 2001) yields desires for communities to serve as spaces offering opportunities to facilitate civic values, education, experiences, and action (Camino & Zeldin, 2002).

The concept of citizenship raises questions regarding young people and their significance in society (Pickard, 2019), and Flanagan's (2013) aforementioned idea of citizenship as a socio-political stance and sense of belonging can help young people to better understand and participate in democracy. Within the context of a growing public concern about the perceived apathy and disengagement among young people, Lister, Smith, Middleton, and Cox (2003, 2005) conducted a study of young people aged 16–23 in the United Kingdom to understand how they view their transitions to citizenship, which is one of few studies examining this concept with this age group. Other, limited, research focuses on children between the ages of 5 and 14 (Dias & Menezes, 2014). From Lister et al.'s (2003, 2005) research, five themes of citizenship emerged, involving young people's perceptions of citizenship to include the following themes:

1. *Universal Status*—feeling like one belongs, including all people in a community as citizens;

2. *Social Contract*—abiding by the rights and duties that are governed by the law;
3. *Respectable Economic Independence*—having waged employment, paying taxes, having a house and a family;
4. *Constructive Social Participation*—being an active citizen contributing to and helping the community;
5. *The Right to a Voice*—feeling that one has a voice and is heard, with voting as a symbolic action of this theme of citizenship.

Lister et al.'s (2003, 2005) model is the most recent model of how young people conceptualize citizenship, and the most applicable to the study presented in this book. While the above model presents five distinct themes, in this model there is an absence of technology and its possible role in these understandings of citizenship, and the civic engagement experiences of young people. Bennett, Wells, and Freelon's (2011) work assessed styles of citizenship present within United States-based civic organizations' websites. However, this study focused primarily on the websites, site traffic, and potential civic learning opportunities embedded in the sites, rather than how young people experienced citizenship. The study presented in this book seeks to address these gaps to provide a more nuanced understanding of how young people conceptualize citizenship in contemporary society.

Views about rights and responsibilities, and participation experiences, contribute to young people's own political theories and civic identity (Flanagan, 2013; Youniss et al., 1997). Developments in young people's own lives tend to determine the extent to which they identify as citizens (Lister et al., 2005), which the study presented in this book sought to discover. The concept of *lived citizenship*, the meaning and experience of citizenship in everyday lives (Hall & Williamson, 1999), is of particular interest in contemporary society because it can include the digital, which is present in the lives of many young people. *Lived citizenship* is not to be confused with *digital citizenship*. The term *digital citizenship* most often refers to the ability to make sense of and navigate the digital world (Hargittai, 2002; Seale & Dutton, 2012), particularly the skills involved in conducting one's behavior with digital tools (Lenhart et al., 2011). Cyberbullying, sexting, and copyright infringement are among the behaviors that are discouraged, while exercising caution for one's own privacy and the privacy of others (Ohler, 2011), and ethically accessing and using information and helping others to do the same (Thomas, 2018) are behaviors that are encouraged. Moreover, other scholars use the term *digital citizenship* to describe access to digital tools as a right of citizens (Journell, 2007; Oyedemi, 2015).

Emejulu and McGregor (2016) advocate for digital citizenship to move beyond these skills-based and rights-based interpretations to include the ability of individuals and groups to think critically about the socio-political, economic, and environmental impact of technology on everyday life and to collectively improve technology and digital practices. Further investigations into this type of alternative view of digital citizenship range from digital media's implications for civic culture (Couldry et al., 2014), to how citizenship behaviors are changing in an era where technology has made surveillance capabilities easier (Polat & Pratchett, 2014).

Digital citizenship, as it is often used, vaguely conceptualizes the interplay between citizenship and the digital, and is not a helpful term when investigating the conceptualizations of citizenship in contemporary society, when so many interactions are digitally mediated. It is therefore important to think beyond this term of digital citizenship, and instead consider the notion of *lived citizenship* and how young people fit into and participate in their communities and contemporary society in their everyday lives, which can involve sentiments and behaviors that are mediated by technology. I aimed to do this in this study through in-depth interviews with young people to focus on their lived experiences as young people in today's world.

The literature presented in this section has demonstrated that there is a need to investigate the nuances in understanding of citizenship and how it develops in this digital era. While the models presented by Lister et al. (2003, 2005) encompass a variety of conceptualizations of citizenship, they address citizenship as experienced by an age group that includes people of voting age, and do not deeply consider the lived citizenship of young people. The ways in which young people between the ages of 14–17 understand citizenship may differ from older populations, especially because young people do not have the same opportunities for engagement as adults—primarily because they cannot vote—and they have varying levels of efficacy in accordance with their prior civic experiences and current place in society. Contemporary society expects young people to either be apathetic and disengaged politically, or engaged in politics through digital means.

2.4.2   Civic Engagement of Young People

The second component of civic identity is civic engagement: how an individual engages with others in the social, political, and economic structures
within their society with the aim to improve them. While there is no single,
widely agreed upon definition of civic engagement (Adler & Goggin,
2005), the term encompasses activities like community associations and
involvement (Milner, 2009). A recent Google search of "*civic engagement*"
found over 177,800,000 citations for the term.[3] Definitions vary,
particularly pertaining to: the concepts of knowledge versus action;
whether the national or global scale is emphasized; whether engagement
pertains to citizens engaging with each other or with institutions; the
importance of ethics; how it is tied to democracy; and desired social and
political outcomes (Levine, 2012). Definitions of engagement most often
fall into categories such as community service, collective action, political
involvement, and social change (Adler & Goggin, 2005).

After evaluating conceptualizations of civic engagement set forth by
civic scholars (Delli Carpini, 2000; Kahne & Middaugh, 2009; Levinson,
2010; Putnam, 2000; Raynes-Goldie & Walker, 2008; Rheingold, 2008),
I determined that the definitions of civic engagement set forth by
Rheingold (2008) and Raynes-Goldie and Walker (2008) are most relevant to young people's lived citizenship in today's world. These definitions
allow for both digitally mediated and broad interpretations of civic engagement. With the understanding of lived citizenship, the definition of civic
engagement *should* be broad to include what is civic in the everyday lives
of young people (Bell, 2005). To this end, the most appropriate definitions of *civic engagement* will follow a combination of the following two
definitions. First, the definition of civic engagement as "participation in
the public sphere through direct experience with online publishing, discourse, debate, co-creation of culture, and collective action" (Rheingold,
2008, p. 102), and second, as "any activity aimed at improving one's community" (Raynes-Goldie & Walker, 2008, p. 162). The digital is embedded in everyday lives, and therefore it is necessary to consider how it might
be embedded within civic activities. Civic activities include service-oriented
endeavors, political participation, and "activism activities in which youth
engage to improve their worlds" (Weinstein, 2014, p. 212).

[3] Google search conducted on 31 May 2019. Note that the number of search results has
doubled from 84,800,000 results in a search of the same term conducted one year prior, on
30 May 2018.

The literature and policy debate has primarily focused on the disengagement of young voters in politics. Some believe this disengagement is a result of a decline in social capital (Putnam, 2000; Smith, 1999), others say that young people are excluded from the process, and lack traditional forms of participation. Because young people lack access to traditional forms of participation, such as voting, they may be drawn toward more accessible forms of engagement (Delgado & Staples, 2007; Ginwright, 2009). But, there is more to civic engagement than voter turnout rates (Dudley & Gitelson, 2002), and despite the persistent view that young people are disengaged, recent literature suggests that young people are interested in politics and are civically engaged, just in non-traditional ways (Henn & Foard, 2012). For example, Barrett and Zani (2014) argue that non-traditional forms of engagement include signing petitions, participating in political demonstrations, and writing political posts on blogs, among other means.

The focus on young people's disengagement is a result of the debate about young people focusing on what young people are *not* doing, such as voting in high turnout rates (Pontes et al., 2019), and therefore views and portrays them as deficient citizens (Eden & Roker, 2002). When the focus shifts to what young people *are* doing, the picture becomes different, and shows young people engaged in their communities (Lister et al., 2005). While young voters have lower voter turnout rates than their older counterparts, and often exhibit disenchantment with politics, young people are politically engaged (Pontes, Henn, & Griffiths, 2018). Roughly 40 percent of young people engage in at least one act of politics (Cohen, Kahne, Bowyer, Middaugh, & Rogowski, 2012). We cannot say there is a decline in civic engagement if we are considering digitally mediated civic engagement to be included in that term (Earl & Schussman, 2008). Today's young people are engaged in civic life (Kawashima-Ginsburg, 2011), but their efforts no longer have to be tied to formal institutions (Soep, 2015), and can be done digitally.

Societal changes can be achieved with the civic engagement and activism of young people (Teruelle, 2012) and their voices. When many voices come together, collective action benefits. Peter Levine (2008) highlights that "institutions work better when many people participate" (p. 120), that social justice results from equitable participation, and that people—not just legislation—can directly address some public problems. Young people today are interested in issues of public concern (Pontes et al., 2018). Teruelle (2012) draws parallels between contemporary youth and the young people in the 1960s and 1970s who were active in civil rights, social justice, women's rights, and the anti-war movement. Young people today and 50 years ago were passionate and motivated by issues that had a direct or personal impact on their lives (Teruelle, 2012). While young people are motivated by these issues and concerns, many young people feel that their concerns are not being represented or heard, which may dissuade them from civic engagement in the future (Mesch & Coleman, 2007). There is speculation—even hope—that young people will turn to the Internet to engage and share their voices, so it is important to address the debate among scholars regarding the impact of the Internet on civic engagement behaviors.

Digitally Mediated Civic Engagement

There is an ongoing debate among scholars regarding the impact of the Internet on daily lives, as well as on civic engagement. Prominent media scholar danah boyd (2007) argues that the "digital does not replace the physical," while Don Tapscott (1998) argues that the digital world reflects the physical world. I will argue further that the digital experience of the self and civic engagement is an extension of and an addition to the physical experiences, as growing evidence points to young people taking advantage of the opportunities to engage with politics through digital means (Jennings & Zeitner, 2003; Mossberger, Tolbert, & McNeal, 2008; Schlozman et al., 2010).

Many scholars have made distinctions between what online and offline engagement look like (Kahne & Bowyer, 2018). For some, online engagement means engaging in Jenkins's (2009) participatory politics activities on the Internet: creating content, connecting with others, collaborating with others, and circulating content; offline engagement includes attending political events, donating money to political campaigns, taking part in protests, and working on election campaigns. While some scholars argue there is a difference, I do not believe a distinction is necessary. Anything that Jenkins (2009) believes you can do using the Internet is possible without it. Similarly, in contemporary society, it is possible to do traditionally offline activities in digitally mediated ways. For example, people learn about political events through Facebook, and can watch them via Live Streaming. As Kahne and Bowyer (2018) identify in their work, campaign donations can be made using apps and candidate websites, and there is a significant part of campaigning now done through social media. I do not distinguish between civic engagement online and offline, and instead view civic engagement as digitally mediated. There are hypothesized differences between online and offline civic engagement, which will be discussed below.

There are four hypotheses for how online and offline political participation could be related. First, the *independence hypothesis* depends on the argument that online and offline spheres are independent of each other (Emmer, Wolling, & Vowe, 2012). Sometimes, this is because of the perceived amount of resources required for participation in either sphere. Some argue that online participatory activities require fewer resources (Hirzalla & Van Zoonen, 2011); sharing an article or post on Facebook condemning racism does not cost as much time as joining a Black Lives Matter march. Second, the *spill over hypothesis* posits that offline political actors utilize online tools to further their influence (Delli Carpini & Keeter, 2002; Krueger, 2002; Norris, 2001; Quan-Haase et al., 2002). Relatedly, Norris's (2000) mobilization thesis further posits that the Internet will only mobilize those who are already engaged, as do a host of other scholars (Bimber, 1999; Bonfadelli, 2002; Hendriks Vettehen, Hagemann, & Van Snippenburg, 2004; Krueger, 2002; Norris, 2001; Polat, 2005; Weber, Loumakis, & Bergman, 2003). Third, the *gateway hypothesis* is derived from the proposition that online participation gives way to subsequent offline participation (Conroy, Feezell, & Guerrero, 2012; Livingstone, 2007; Velasquez & LaRose, 2015). Internet use could therefore mobilize politically inactive populations (Barber, 2001; Delli Carpini, 2000; Krueger, 2002; Ward, Gibson, & Lusoli, 2003; Weber et al., 2003), including young people, who are the age group most likely to be online (Delli Carpini, 2000). Finally, the *reciprocity hypothesis* suggests that online and offline political activities mutually affect each other (Nam, 2012; Vissers & Stolle, 2014).

Despite the aforementioned distinctions between online and offline engagement, the lines between these types of civic engagement continue to be blurred as technology becomes more entwined in daily life. I subscribe to the reciprocity hypothesis, and question whether it is meaningful to separate the online and offline spheres, as it is possible that the online sphere mirrors or enhances what is already happening offline. The distinction between online and offline may no longer be necessary, as the digital world is very much a part of everyday reality for young people in contemporary society, and interactions and daily life are often digitally mediated. This book aims to discover how young people are experiencing civic engagement, and demonstrate that the reciprocity hypothesis is most applicable for the participants in this study. Similarly, this debate between online versus offline motivates the investigation into the role of technology in how young people decide to present themselves to others in contemporary society.

2.5   THE SIGNIFICANCE OF CIVIC EDUCATION FOR CIVIC ENGAGEMENT

Literature demonstrates that education, especially civic education, is an important factor in civic and political participation (Kahne & Middaugh, 2009; Levinson, 2010). Embedded within the United States public education tradition is the notion that education should prepare young people for their role as citizens to contribute to the nation's democratic way of life. Research has demonstrated that exposure to civic learning opportunities through education is a strong predictor of later civic engagement (Kahne & Sporte, 2008; Keating & Janmaat, 2015), and can also provide young people with a sense of purpose and efficacy, enhance political equality, and increase the likelihood of participation in adult civic life (Flanagan, 2013; Kahne & Sporte, 2008; Levine & Youniss, 2009). Civic characteristics and skills of adolescents include moral character, confidence, caring, contributing to the community, respectful argumentation, debate, and information literacy (Bers, 2008). Overall, these skills and capabilities are overwhelmingly positive (Benton et al., 2008), and can be developed through civics curriculum, which can also serve as an opportunity to teach critical thinking, social analysis, and skills of deliberation (Westheimer, 2004).

The United States of America has had a longstanding tradition of education for democracy, which still prevails. Civic republicanism—the ideal of cooperation among citizens and government, civic participation, and patriotism—is the national ethos that has pervaded the United States throughout the upbringing of today's young people aged 14 through 17 (Journell, 2010). Despite this national ethos, and presumed importance of civic education, a decline in resources in school systems has led to a lack of civic education curriculum since the 1960s (Levinson, 2010). In 2003, federal expenditures on civic education totaled less than half of one percent of the overall United States Department of Education budget (Westheimer, 2004). In contemporary society, 71 percent of school districts have reported decreasing time on subjects like civics to make more space for mathematics instruction (Kahne & Sporte, 2008). Furthermore,

the amount and scope of civic education curriculum has decreased, starting seventeen years ago. In 2003, Shelley Berman, former superintendent
of schools in Hudson, Massachusetts, noted that Massachusetts "significantly de-emphasized civics in the state standards" (Miller, 2004, p. 4).
Nystrand, Gamoran, and Carbonaro (2001) found that political discussions only take place in 10 percent of classrooms. Nearly a decade later
still, Journell (2010) found that in schools, "conversations about citizenship rarely extend beyond one's right to vote" (p. 351).

What was once commonplace in American schools has now become a
rare component of curriculum: as of 2016, the Education Commission of
the States in the United States found that most states do not include civics
as a part of their accountability systems (Railey & Brennan, 2016). For
those states that do have standards for civics curriculum, those standards
include: demonstrating the rights and responsibilities of citizenship, what
it means to participate civically and responsibly, understanding democratic
beliefs and principles, and political and legal processes, appreciation for
diversity and commitment to the common good (Railey & Brennan,
2016). While citizenship education is sometimes supported through state
standards and local school board missions, policymakers and education
advocates are concerned that "public education's function of training
young people for democratic citizenship is being pushed aside" (Miller,
2004, p. 1). Curriculum across the United States has all but dismantled
civics (Lithwick, 2018), with a majority of schools failing to provide civic
education (Kirshner, 2004; Larson, 2000).

The state of civic education in the United States has been transformed
from a robust civics curriculum in the 1950s and 1960s to barely existent
today. Recently, funding for civic education has been cut in favor of invest-
ing more into science, technology, engineering, and mathematics (STEM)
courses (Keating, Kerr, Benton, Mundy, & Lopes, 2010). The realloca-
tion of funding suggests that United States public schools are preparing
for an increasingly digital world, where young people would need to be
equipped with more knowledge about STEM subjects than about active
citizenship. This focus on STEM has become problematic because it has
left civic education in decline. Young people are receiving less civic education as a result, which has been unfortunate for the status of civic engagement as well: civic education begets civic engagement, which informs
one's civic identity and can yield an increase in development of political
voice (Keating et al., 2010).

Howard Rheingold (2008) defines voice as a "unique style of personal expression that distinguishes one's communications from those of others... [voice] can help connect young people's involvement in identity formation with their potential engagement with society as citizens" (p. 101). Voice is related to civic identity because voice gives individuals a means of presenting and expressing themselves to others. Voice yields personal efficacy, which is the belief that one can produce desired effects by their actions (Bandura, 2008). Associated with civic engagement, internal political efficacy refers to one's perception of their own ability to effectively participate in the political process (Balch, 1974) and has a positive relationship to one engaging in political activity (Wollman & Stouder, 1991). External political efficacy refers to perceptions of how the government and related institutions respond to citizens' needs (Kahne & Westheimer, 2006). When one's voice is heard, individuals receive affirmation of their political and social beliefs, and a greater sense of efficacy can be achieved. How one sees oneself in relation to others impacts their sense of efficacy: if an individual is comfortable sharing their identity with others and being a member of a group or society, they will perceive greater social support from that group (Guan & So, 2016) and, in turn, feel that their voice will be heard.

Individuals have different purposes for their voices, as they have different values (Bandura, 2008). When values differ, so does motivation to participate in civic engagement, and the sense of efficacy that one has with these civic actions. While differences in values result in different levels of efficacy, socioeconomic status can reveal differences in efficacy and voice as well. Verba, Schlozman, and Brady (1995) found that there is a discrepancy in civic engagement among those of high socioeconomic status and low socioeconomic status. Higher income earners (over $75,000 per year), in comparison to lower income earners (under $15,000 per year) are twice as likely to contact an elected official or engage in a protest. Higher income earners are also nearly three times more likely to participate in informal community activities, and over four times more likely to work on a campaign compared to lower earners (Verba et al., 1995). Discrepancies in socioeconomic status demonstrate that the ability to discuss and deliberate is not equal. In the political culture in the United States, some citizens who are already underrepresented—like those of lower socioeconomic status—become even more underrepresented by those who are better at articulating their arguments—those from higher socioeconomic status and education levels—thereby making the underrepresented voices even less powerful (Hess & McAvoy, 2015). Technology may deepen this inequality: previous research indicates that that the Internet increases levels of civic engagement, particularly among those who are socioeconomically advantaged and who already have an interest in becoming civically engaged (Oser, Hooghe, & Marien, 2013). The discrepancy in civic engagement that Verba et al. (1995) discovered refers to what Levinson (2010) calls the *civic empowerment gap*: individuals from wealthier backgrounds are more likely to engage in civic activities, because they have had more experiences and resources to empower them to do so. This study seeks to examine the civic experiences of young people, and how young people perceive their place in society and efficacy to engage civically to best inform the practices needed to reinvigorate civic education.

2.6 SUMMARY

The themes presented in this chapter all intersect where they meet the concepts of civic identity and civic engagement in the digital era. Technology in contemporary society could be a way to amplify voice, which is especially important for young people, who need their voices to be heard to make future contributions to the society that they live in. When they feel they are making a difference by being civically engaged— and receive positive reinforcement for that engagement—they will stay engaged (Bandura, 2008). Civic identity—one's conceptualization of citizenship and civic engagement—directly impacts how one perceives their own ability to make a difference. If sharing one's voice is an integral part of being an active citizen (Lister et al., 2005), then voice is a key component of civic identity. Civic education is what ties all of these elements together, by providing young people with a space to develop their own voice through learning how to discuss issues of public concern with others.

While previous studies have each explored one or more of these aforementioned themes, this critical review of academic literature has found that few studies have investigated the ways in which contemporary society and the civic sphere intersect for young people ages 14 through 17. Previous research in civic studies has examined young people's understandings of political participation (Sant, 2014), citizenship (Ataman, Çok, & Şener, 2012), and behaviors associated with political engagement (Sveningsson, 2016), but have not investigated citizenship and civic engagement together to understand civic identity. Some studies focus on only the most engaged young people (Weinstein et al., 2015), and still further studies in the civic and youth studies spheres consider young people over the age of 18 (Kahne & Sporte, 2008; Watkins, 2009; Weinstein, 2014; Weinstein et al., 2015; Youniss & Levine, 2009). Moreover, while there is a plethora of research on civic engagement, there a paucity of qualitative research examining civic identity and its components (Lister et al., 2005). Pontes et al. (2018) conducted the first study that specifically considers young people's conceptualization of political engagement, and the study presented in this book seeks to add to the growing body of research in this area, addressing civic identity as experienced by young people aged 14 through 17 growing up in contemporary society.

The study presented in this book considers young people under the age of 18 in the United States, and inquires about the participants' understandings of citizenship and civic engagement. The United States lends itself well as the social and educational context for this study, as the tradition of education for democratic citizenship is embedded in public schooling. Civic education has been a longstanding value of the United States public education system, and evidence points to its significance for later civic engagement (Kahne & Sporte, 2008). As I have demonstrated in this chapter, there has been a lack of empirical research on contemporary civic experiences that focuses on young people between the ages of 14 and 17 years old, who have yet to reach voting age. Prior research has contributed a model to illustrate how young people have conceptualized citizenship (Lister et al., 2003, 2005), but this model does not consider technology and its implication in these conceptualizations of citizenship. In this rapidly changing world, a first step in addressing these gaps is a study to gather rich qualitative data from 14 through 17 year olds considering their own perspectives on identity, citizenship, and civic engagement in contemporary society.

REFERENCES

Adelson, J. (1968). *Adolescent's Perspective on Law and Government*. Washington, DC: American Psychological Association.

Adelson, J., & O'Neil, R. P. (1966). Growth of Political Ideas in Adolescence: The Sense of Community. *Journal of Personality and Social Psychology, 4*(3), 295–306.

Adler, R. P., & Goggin, J. (2005). What Do We Mean By "Civic Engagement"? *Journal of Transformative Education, 3*(3), 236–253.

Annette, J. (2008). Community Involvement, Civic Engagement, and Service Learning. In J. Arthur, I. Davies, & C. Hahn (Eds.), *The SAGE Handbook of Education for Citizenship and Democracy* (pp. 388–398). London: SAGE.

Arnett, J. (2004). *Emerging Adulthood: The Winding Road from the Late Teens Through the Twenties.* New York: Oxford University Press.

Ataman, A., Çok, F., & Şener, T. (2012). Understanding Civic Engagement Among Young Roma and Young Turkish People in Turkey. *Human Affairs, 22,* 419–433.

Bakardjieva, M. (2005). *Internet Society: The Internet in Everyday Life.* London: SAGE.

Bakshy, E., Messing, S., & Adamic, L. A. (2015). Exposure to Ideologically Diverse News and Opinion on Facebook. *Science, 348*(6239), 1130–1132.

Balch, G. (1974). Multiple Indicators in Survey Research: The Concept 'Sense of Political Efficacy'. *Political Methodology, 1,* 1–43.

Bandura, A. (2008). An Agentic Perspective on Positive Psychology. In S. Lopez (Ed.), *Positive Psychology: Expecting the Best in People.* New York: Praeger.

Barber, B. (2001). The Uncertainty of Digital Politics: Democracy's Uneasy Relationship with Information Technology. *Harvard International Review, 23,* 42–48.

Barrett, M., & Zani, B. (2014). *Political and Civic Engagement: Multidisciplinary Perspectives.* London: Routledge.

Bayne, S., & Ross, J. (2011). 'Digital Native' and 'Digital Immigrant' Discourses: A Critique. In R. Land & S. Bayne (Eds.), *Digital Difference: Perspectives on Online Learning* (pp. 159–169). Boston, MA: Sense Publishers.

Bell, B. (2005). *Children, Youth, and Civic (Dis)Engagement: Digital Technology and Citizenship.* CRACIN Working Paper, Canadian Research Alliance for Community Innovation and Networking.

Bennett, W. L. (2008). Changing Citizenship in the Digital Age. In W. L. Bennett (Ed.), *Civic Life Online: Learning How Digital Media Can Engage Youth* (pp. 1–24). Cambridge, MA: The MIT Press.

Bennett, W. L., Wells, C., & Freelon, D. (2011). Communicating Civic Engagement: Contrasting Models of Citizenship in the Youth Web Sphere. *Journal of Communication, 61*(5), 835–856.

Benton, T., Cleaver, E., Featherstone, G., Kerr, D., Lopes, J., & Whitby, K. (2008). *Citizenship Education Longitudinal Study: Sixth Annual Report. Young People's Civic Participation In and Beyond School: Attitudes, Intentions and Influences.* Slough: National Foundation for Educational Research.

Berk, L. (2009). *Development Through the Life Span* (5th ed.). Boston, MA: Allyn & Bacon.

Bers, M. U. (2008). Civic Identities, Online Technologies: From Designing Civics Curriculum to Supporting Civic Experiences. In W. L. Bennett (Ed.), *Civic Life Online: Learning How Digital Media Can Engage Youth* (pp. 139–159). Cambridge, MA: The MIT Press.

Berzonsky, M. (2003). Identity Style and Well-being: Does Commitment Matter? *Identity, 3*(2), 131–142.

Bimber, B. (1999). The Internet and Citizen Communication with Government: Does the Medium Matter? *Political Communication, 16,* 409–429.

Bond, R. M., Fariss, C. J., Jones, J. J., Kramer, A., Marlow, C., Settle, J., et al. (2012). A 61-Million-Person Experiment in Social Influence and Political Mobilization. *Nature, 489,* 295–298.

Bonfadelli, H. (2002). The Internet and Knowledge Gaps: A Theoretical and Empirical Investigation. *European Journal of Communication, 17*(1) 65–84.

boyd, d. (2007). Socializing Digitally. *Vodafone Receiver Magazine,* 18.

boyd, d. (2008). Can Social Network Sites Enable Political Action? In A. Fine, M. Sifry, A. Rasiej, & J. Levy (Eds.), *Rebooting America* (pp. 112–116). Creative Commons.

boyd, d. (2014). *It's Complicated: The Social Lives of Networked Teens.* New Haven, CT: Yale University Press.

boyd, d., & Ellison, N. (2007). Social Network Sites: Definition, History, and Scholarship. *Journal of Computer-Mediated Communication, 13*(1), 210–230.

Brint, S. (2001). Gemeinschaft Revisited: A Critique and Reconstruction of the Community Concept. *Sociological Theory, 19*(1), 1–23.

Brown, J. D. (1998). *The Self.* New York: McGraw-Hill.

Buckingham, D. (2000). *After the Death of Childhood: Growing Up in the Age of Electronic Media.* Cambridge: Polity Press.

Buckingham, D. (2002). *The Making of Citizens: Young People, News and Politics.* London: Routledge.

Buckingham, D. (2013). *Beyond Technology: Children's Learning in the Age of Digital Culture.* Cambridge: John Wiley & Sons.

Camino, L., & Zeldin, S. (2002). From Periphery to Center: Pathways for Youth Civic Engagement in the Day-to-day Life of Communities. *Applied Developmental Science, 6*(4), 213–220.

Castells, M. (1996). *The Information Age: Economy, Society and Culture. Volume I: The Rise of the Network Society.* Oxford: Blackwell.

Chartrand, T. L., & Bargh, J. A. (1999). The Chameleon Effect: The Perception–Behavior Link and Social Interaction. *Journal of Personality and Social Psychology, 76,* 893–910.

Cohen, C. J., Kahne, J., Bowyer, B., Middaugh, E., & Rogowski, J. (2012). *Participatory Politics: New Media and Youth Political Action.* YPP Research Network.

Conroy, M., Feezell, J., & Guerrero, M. (2012). Facebook and Political Engagement: A Study of Online Political Group Membership and Offline Political Engagement. *Computers in Human Behavior, 28*(5), 1535–1546.

Côté, J. E., & Levine, C. G. (2002). *Identity Formation, Agency, and Culture: A Social Psychological Synthesis.* Mahwah, NJ: Lawrence Erlbaum Associates.

Couldry, N., Stephansen, H., Fotopoulou, A., MacDonald, R., Clark, W., & Dickens, L. (2014). Digital Citizenship? Narrative Exchange and the Changing Terms of Civic Culture. *Citizenship Studies, 18*, 615–629.

Crick, B. (1998). *Education for Citizenship and the Teaching of Democracy in Schools: Final Report of the Advisory Group on Citizenship.* London: Qualifications and Curriculum Authority.

Dahlgren, P., & Olsson, T. (2007). Young Activists, Political Horizons and the Internet: Adapting the Net to One's Purposes. In B. D. Loader (Ed.), *Young Citizens in the Digital Age: Political Engagement, Young People and New Media* (pp. 68–81). London: Routledge.

Davies, C., & Eynon, R. (2013). *Teenagers and Technology.* London: Routledge.

Davis, K. (2010). Coming of Age Online: The Developmental Underpinnings of Girls' Blogs. *Journal of Adolescent Research, 25*(1), 145–171.

Davis, K., & Weinstein, E. (2017). Identity Development in the Digital Age: An Eriksonian Perspective. In M. F. Wright (Ed.), *Identity, Sexuality, and Relationships Among Emerging Adults in the Digital Age* (pp. 1–17). Hershey, PA: IGI Global.

Delgado, M., & Staples, L. (2007). *Youth-led Community Organizing: Theory and Action.* New York: Oxford University Press.

Delli Carpini, M. (2000). Gen.com: Youth, Civic Engagement, and the New Information Environment. *Political Communication, 17*, 341–350.

Delli Carpini, M., & Keeter, S. (2002). The Internet and an Informed Citizenry. In D. Anderson & M. Cornfield (Eds.), *The Civic Web: Online Politics and Democratic Values* (pp. 129–153). Lanham, MD: Rowman & Littlefield Publishers.

Deutsch, N. L. (2005). "I like to Treat Others as Others Would Treat Me": The Development of Prosocial Selves in an Urban Youth Organization. *New Directions for Youth Development, Special Issue: Doing the Right Thing: Ethical Development Across Diverse Environments, 2005* (108), 89–105.

Dewey, J. (1916). *Democracy and Education.* Mineola, NY: Dover Publications.

Dias, T. S., & Menezes, I. (2014, June 2). Children and Adolescents as Political Actors: Collective Visions of Politics and Citizenship. *Journal of Moral Education, 43*, 250–268.

Dijksterhuis, A., & Aarts, H. (2010). Goals, Attention, and (Un)Consciousness. *Annual Review of Psychology, 61*, 467–490.

Dudley, R. L., & Gitelson, A. R. (2002). Political Literacy, Civic Education, and Civic Engagement: A Return to Political Socialization? *Applied Developmental Science, 6*(4), 175–182.

Earl, J., & Kimport, K. (2009). Movement Societies and Digital Protest: Fan Activism and Other Nonpolitical Protest Online. *Sociological Theory, 27*(3), 220–243.

Earl, J., Kimport, K., Prieto, G., Rush, C., & Reynoso, K. (2010). Changing the World One Webpage at a Time: Conceptualizing and Explaining Internet Activism. *Mobilization: An International Journal, 15*(4), 425–446.

Earl, J., & Schussman, A. (2008). Contesting Cultural Control: Youth Culture and Online Petitioning. In W. L. Bennett (Ed.), *Civic Life Online: Learning How Digital Media Can Engage Youth* (pp. 71–95). Cambridge, MA: The MIT Press.

Eden, K., & Roker, D. (2002). '... *Doing Something': Young People as Social Actors.* Leicester: Youth Work Press.

Emejulu, A., & McGregor, C. (2016). Towards a Radical Digital Citizenship in Digital Education. *Critical Studies in Education, 60,* 1–17.

Emmer, M., Wolling, J., & Vowe, G. (2012). Changing Political Communication in Germany: Findings from a Longitudinal Study on the Influence of the Internet on Political Information, Discussion, and the Participation of Citizens. *Communications, 37*(3), 233–252.

Erikson, E. H. (1968). *Identity: Youth and Crisis.* New York: W.W. Norton & Company.

Facebook. (2018). *What Happens to Content (Posts, Pictures) That I Delete from Facebook?* Retrieved from Facebook.com https://www.facebook.com/help/356107851084108?helpref=uf_permalink

Fenton, N. (2012). The Internet and Social Networking. In J. Curran, N. Fenton, & D. Freedman (Eds.), *Misunderstanding the Internet* (pp. 123–148). London: Routledge.

Finlay, A., Wray-Lake, L., & Flanagan, C. (2010). Civic Engagement During the Transition to Adulthood: Developmental Opportunities and Social Policies at a Critical Juncture. In L. Sherrod, J. Torney-Purta, & C. Flanagan (Eds.), *Handbook of Research on Civic Engagement in Youth* (pp. 277–206). Hoboken, NJ: John Wiley & Sons.

Flanagan, C. (2013). *Teenage Citizens: The Political Theories of the Young.* Cambridge, MA: Harvard University Press.

Friedman, T. L. (2005). *The World Is Flat: A Brief History of the Twenty-first Century.* New York: Penguin.

Garcia, A., & Middaugh, E. (2015). Lost, Sweaty, and Engaged in Dialogue: The Civic Opportunities of Geospatial Play. In E. Middaugh & B. Kirshner (Eds.), *#youthaction: Becoming Political in the Digital Age* (pp. 107–125). Charlotte, NC: Information Age Publishing.

Gardner, H., & Davis, K. (2013). *The App Generation: How Today's Youth Navigate Identity, Intimacy, and Imagination in a Digital World.* New Haven, CT: Yale University Press.

Gecas, V., & Burke, P. (1995). Self and Identity. In K. Cook, G. Fine, & J. House (Eds.), *Sociological Perspectives on Social Psychology* (pp. 41–67). Boston, MA: Allyn & Bacon.

Ginwright, S. (2009). *Black Youth Rising: Activism and Radical Healing in Urban America*. New York: Teachers College Press.

Goffman, E. (1959). *The Presentation of Self in Everyday Life*. Garden City, NY: Doubleday Anchor Books.

Goffman, E. (1978). The Presentation of Self to Others. In J. G. Manis & B. N. Meltzer (Eds.), *Symbolic Interaction: A Reader in Social Psychology* (3rd ed., pp. 234–244). London: Allyn and Bacon.

Goode, J. (2010). The Digital Identity Divide: How Technology Knowledge Impacts College Students. *New Media & Society, 12*(3), 497–513.

Gosa, T. L. (2012). Black Youth, Social Media, and the 2008 Presidential Election. In *Social Media: Usage and Impact* (pp. 219–233). Plymouth: Lexington Books.

Guan, M., & So, J. (2016). Influence of Social Identity on Self-Efficacy Beliefs Through Perceived Social Support: A Social Identity Theory Perspective. *Communication Studies, 67*(5), 588–604.

Hall, T., & Williamson, H. (1999). *Citizenship and Community*. Leicester: Youth Work Press.

Hall, T., Williamson, H., & Coffey, A. (1998). Conceptualizing Citizenship: Young People and the Transition to Adulthood. *Journal of Education Policy, 13*(3), 301–315.

Hargittai, E. (2002). Second-level Digital Divide: Differences in People's Online Skills. *First Monday, 7*(4).

Hartmann, M., Carpentier, N., & Cammaerts, B. (2007). Democratic Familyship and the Negotiated Practices of ICT Users. In P. Dahlgren (Ed.), *Young Citizens and New Media: Learning for Democratic Participation* (pp. 167–186). New York: Routledge.

Hasebrink, U., & Paus-Hasebrink, I. (2007). Young People's Identity Construction and Media Use: Democratic Participation in Germany and Austria. In P. Dahlgren (Ed.), *Young Citizens and New Media: Learning for Democratic Participation* (pp. 81–101). New York: Routledge.

Haste, H. (2004). Constructing the Citizen. *Political Psychology, 25*, 413–439.

Haste, H. (2010). Citizenship Education: A Critical Look at a Contested Field. In L. R. Sherrod, J. Torney-Purta, & C. A. Flanagan (Eds.), *Handbook of Research on Civic Engagement in Youth* (pp. 161–188). Hoboken, NJ: John Wiley & Sons.

Haythornthwaite, C., & Wellman, B. (2002). The Internet in Everyday Life: An Introduction. In B. Wellman & C. Haythornthwaite (Eds.), *The Internet in Everyday Life* (pp. 1–41). Oxford: Blackwell Publishing.

Hendricks, J. A., & Frye, J. K. (2012). Social Media and the Millennial Generation in the 2010 Midterm Election. In H. S. Al-Deen & J. A. Hendricks (Eds.), *Social Media: Usage and Impact* (pp. 183–199). Plymouth: Lexington Books.

Hendriks Vettehen, P., Hagemann, C., & Van Snippenburg, L. (2004). Political Knowledge and Media Use in the Netherlands. *European Sociological Review, 20*, 415–424.

Henn, M., & Foard, N. (2012). Back on the Agenda and Off the Curriculum? Citizenship Education and Young People's Political Engagement. *Teaching Citizenship, 32,* 32–35.

Hess, D., & McAvoy, P. (2015). *The Political Classroom: Evidence and Ethics in Democratic Education.* New York: Routledge.

Hirzalla, F., & Van Zoonen, L. (2011). Beyond the Online/Offline Divide: How Youth's Online and Offline Civic Activities Converge. *Social Science Computer Review, 29*(4), 481–498.

Hodgin, E. (2016, June 27). Educating Youth for Online Civic and Political Dialogue: A Conceptual Framework for the Digital Age. *Journal of Digital and Media Literacy, 4*(1–2).

Holloway, S. L., & Valentine, G. (2003). *Cyberkids: Children in the Information Age.* London: RoutledgeFalmer.

Hoover, E. (2009). The Millennial Muddle: How Stereotyping Students Became a Thriving Industry and a Bundle of Contradictions. *The Chronicle of Higher Education.*

Huckfeldt, R., & Sprague, J. (1995). *Citizens, Politics, and Social Communication: Information and Influence in an Election Campaign.* New York: Cambridge University Press.

Ignatieff, M. (1995). The Myth of Citizenship. In R. Beiner (Ed.), *Theorizing Citizenship* (pp. 66–72). New York: State University of New York Press.

International Association for the Evaluation of Educational Achievement. (1999). *IEA Civic Education Study.* Ann Arbor, MI: Inter-university Consortium for Political and Social Research.

International Association for the Evaluation of Educational Achievement. (2009). *International Civic and Citizenship Education Study 2009.* International Association for the Evaluation of Educational Achievement.

Ireland, E., Kerr, D., Lopes, J., Nelson, J., & Cleaver, E. (2006). *Active Citizenship and Young People: Opportunities, Experiences and Challenges in and Beyond School Citizenship Education. Longitudinal Study: Fourth Annual Report.* London, England: DfES.

Ito, M., Baumer, S., Bittani, M., boyd, d., Cody, R., Herr-Stephenson, B., et al. (2010). *Hanging Out, Messing Around, and Geeking Out: Kids Living and Learning with New Media.* Cambridge, MA: The MIT Press.

Jenkins, H. (2009). *Confronting the Challenges of Participatory Culture: Media Education for the 21st Century.* Cambridge, MA: MIT Press.

Jennings, M., & Zeitner, V. (2003). Internet Use and Civic Engagement: A Longitudinal Analysis. *Public Opinion Quarterly, 67,* 311–334.

Journell, W. (2007). The Inequities of the Digital Divide: Is E-learning a Solution? *E-Learning and Digital Media, 4*(2), 138–149.

Journell, W. (2010). Standardizing Citizenship: The Potential Influence of State Curriculum Standards on the Civic Development of Adolescents. *PS: Political Science and Politics, 43*(2), 351–358.

Kahne, J., & Bowyer, B. (2018). The Political Significance of Social Media Activity and Social Networks. *Political Communication, 35*(3), 470–493.

Kahne, J., & Middaugh, E. (2009). Democracy for Some: The Civic Opportunity Gap in High School. In J. Youniss & P. Levine (Eds.), *Engaging Young People in Civic Life* (pp. 29–58). Nashville, TN: Vanderbilt University Press.

Kahne, J., Middaugh, E., & Allen, D. (2014). *Youth, New Media, and the Rise of Participatory Politics*. The University of Chicago Press.

Kahne, J., Middaugh, E., Lee, N., & Feezell, J. (2012). Youth Online Activity and Exposure to Diverse Perspectives. *New Media & Society, 14*(3), 492–512.

Kahne, J., & Sporte, S. (2008). Developing Citizens: The Impact of Civic Learning Opportunities on Students' Commitment to Civic Participation. *American Educational Research Journal, 45*(3), 738–766.

Kahne, J., Ullman, J., & Middaugh, E. (2011). Digital Opportunities for Civic Education. Paper Prepared for the American Enterprise Institute Conference *Civics 2.0: Citizenship Education for a New Generation* October 20, 2011.

Kahne, J., & Westheimer, J. (2006). The Limits of Political Efficacy: Educating Citizens for a Democratic Society. *PS: Political Science & Politics, 39*(2), 289–296.

Kawashima-Ginsburg, K. (2011). *Understanding a Diverse Generation: Youth Civic Engagement in the United States*. Medford: The Center for Information and Research on Civic Learning and Engagement.

Keating, A., & Janmaat, J. G. (2015). Education Through Citizenship at School: Do School Activities Have a Lasting Impact on Youth Political Engagement? *Parliamentary Affairs, 69*, 409–429.

Keating, A., Kerr, D., Benton, T., Mundy, E., & Lopes, J. (2010). *Citizenship Education in England 2001–2010: Young People's Practices and Prospects for the Future: The Eighth and Final Report from the Citizenship Education Longitudinal Study (CELS)*. Great Britain Department for Education.

Kent, N., & Facer, K. (2004). Different Worlds? A Comparison of Young People's Home and School ICT Use. *Journal of Computer Assisted Learning, 20*(6), 440–455.

Kim, Y., Russo, S., & Amnå, E. (2017). The Longitudinal Relation Between Online and Offline Political Participation Among Youth at Two Different Developmental Stages. *New Media & Society, 19*(6), 899.

Kirshner, B. (2004). *Democracy Now: Activism and Learning in Urban Youth Organizations*. Stanford, CA: Stanford University Press.

Knefelkamp, L. L. (2008). Civic Identity: Locating Self in Community. *Diversity & Democracy: Civic Learning for Shared Futures, 11*(2), 1–3.

Krueger, B. (2002). Assessing the Potential of Internet Political Participation in the United States: A Resource Approach. *American Politics Research, 30*, 476–498.

Kwak, H., Lee, C., Park, H., & Moon, S. (2010, April). What Is Twitter, a Social Network or a News Media? In *Proceedings of the 19th International Conference on World Wide Web* (pp. 591–600).

Larson, R. W. (2000). Toward a Psychology of Positive Youth Development. *American Psychologist, 55*(1), 170–183.

Lenhart, A., Duggan, M., Perrin, A., Stepler, R., Rainie, L., & Parker, K. (2015). *Teens, Social Media & Technology Overview 2015.* Pew Research Center.

Lenhart, A., Kahne, J., Middaugh, E., Macgill, A., Evans, C., & Vitak, J. (2008). *Teens, Video Games, and Civics: Teens' Gaming Experiences Are Diverse and Include Significant Social Interaction and Civic Engagement.* Pew Internet & American Life Project.

Lenhart, A., Madden, M., Smith, A., Purcell, K., Zickuhr, K., & Rainie, L. (2011). *Teens, Kindness and Cruelty on Social Network Sites: How American Teens Navigate the New World of "Digital Citizenship".* Washington, DC: Pew Research Center Internet & American Life Project.

Lesko, N. (1996). Past, Present, and Future Conceptions of Adolescents. *Educational Theory, 46*(4), 453–472.

Levine, P. (2008). A Public Voice for Youth: The Audience Problem in Digital Media and Civic Education. In W. L. Bennett (Ed.), *Civic Life Online: Learning How Digital Media Can Engage Youth* (pp. 119–138). Cambridge, MA: The MIT Press.

Levine, P. (2012, December 11). *What Is the Definition of Civic Engagement?* Retrieved from http://peterlevine.ws/?p=10357

Levine, P., & Youniss, J. (2009). Policy for Youth Civic Engagement. In J. Youniss & P. Levine (Eds.), *Engaging Young People in Civic Life* (pp. 1–9). Nashville, TN: Vanderbilt University Press.

Levinson, M. (2010). The Civic Empowerment Gap: Defining the Problem and Locating Solutions. In L. Sherrod, J. Torney-Purta, & C. Flanagan (Eds.), *Handbook of Research on Civic Engagement in Youth* (pp. 331–361). Hoboken, NJ: John Wiley & Sons.

Linton, A. (2015). Politically Engaged and Alienated Youth: Reevaluating 2010 UK Student Protests. In E. Middaugh & B. Kirshner (Eds.), *#youthaction: Becoming Political in the Digital Age* (pp. 191–207). Charlotte, NC: Information Age Publishing, Inc.

Lister, R., Smith, N., Middleton, S., & Cox, L. (2003). Empirical Perspectives on Theoretical and Political Debate. *Citizenship Studies, 7,* 235–253.

Lister, R., Smith, N., Middleton, S., & Cox, L. (2005). Young People Talking About Citizenship in Britain. In N. Kabeer (Ed.), *Inclusive Citizenship: Meanings and Expressions* (pp. 114–131). New York: Zed Books.

Lithwick, D. (2018, February 28). They Were Trained for This Moment: How the Student Activists of Marjory Stoneman Douglas High Demonstrate the Power of a Comprehensive Education. *Slate.*

Livingstone, S. (2007). Youthful Experts? A Critical Appraisal of Children's Emerging Literacy. In R. Mansell, C. Avgerou, D. Quah, & R. Silverstone (Eds.), *Oxford Handbook on ICTs* (pp. 494–513). Oxford: Oxford University Press.

Livingstone, S. (2009). *Children and the Internet: Great Expectations, Challenging Realities.* Cambridge: Polity Press.

Livingstone, S. (2010). Digital Learning and Participation Among Youth: Critical Reflections on Future Research Priorities. *International Journal of Learning and Media, 2*(2–3), 1–13.

Livingstone, S., & Bober, M. (2004). Taking Up Online Opportunities? Children's Uses of the Internet for Education, Communication and Participation. *E-Learning, 1*(3), 395–419.

Loader, B. D. (2007). Young Citizens in the Digital Age: Disaffected or Displaced? In B. D. Loader (Ed.), *Young Citizens in the Digital Age: Political Engagement, Young People and New Media* (pp. 1–17). London: Routledge.

Markus, H., & Nurius, P. (1986). Possible Selves. *The American Psychologist, 41*(9), 954–969.

Marquette, H., & Mineshima, D. (2002). Civic Education in the United States: Lessons for the UK. *Parliamentary Affairs, 55*(3), 539–555.

McAdams, D. (1996). Personality, Modernity, and the Storied Self: A Contemporary Framework for Studying Persons. *Psychological Inquiry, 74*(4), 295–321.

McLaughlin, T. H. (2000). Citizenship Education in England: The Crick Report and Beyond. *Journal of Philosophy of Education, 34*(4), 541–570.

McLeod, J. M., Daily, K., Guo, Z., Eveland Jr., W. P., Bayer, J., Yang, S., et al. (1996). Community Integration, Local Media Use and Democratic Processes. *Communication Research, 23*, 179–209.

McLeod, J. M., Scheufele, D. A., & Moy, P. (1999). Community, Communication, & Participation: The Role of Mass Media and Interpersonal Discussion in Local Political Participation. *Political Communication, 16*, 315–336.

McMillan, D., & Chavis, D. (1986). Sense of Community: A Definition and Theory. *Journal of Community Psychology, 14*(1), 6–23.

Mesch, G. S., & Coleman, S. (2007). New Media and New Voters: Young People, the Internet and the 2005 UK Election Campaign. In B. D. Loader (Ed.), *Young Citizens in the Digital Age: Political Engagement, Young People and New Media* (pp. 35–47). London: Routledge.

Meyrowitz, J. (1985). *No Sense of Place: The Impact of Electronic Media on Social Behavior.* Oxford: Oxford University Press.

Middaugh, E. (2016, August 26). Social Media and Online Communities Expose Youth to Political Conversation, But Also to Incivility and Conflict. *USApp–American Politics and Policy Blog.* London School of Economics.

Middaugh, E., & Kirshner, B. (2015). Educating Powerful Citizens in a Changing World. In E. Middaugh & B. Kirshner (Eds.), *#youthaction: Becoming Political in the Digital Age* (pp. 1–8). Charlotte, NC: Information Age Publishing, Inc..

Mihailidis, P. (2014). *Media Literacy and the Emerging Citizen: Youth, Engagement, and Participation in Digital Culture.* New York: Peter Lang, Inc..

Miller, J. (2004). *Citizenship Education Policy at the School District Level.* Issue Paper. Education Commission of the States.

Milner, H. (2009). Youth Electoral Participation in Canada and Scandinavia. In J. Youniss & P. Levine (Eds.), *Engaging Young People in Civic Life* (pp. 187–218). Nashville, TN: Vanderbilt University Press.

Mossberger, K., Tolbert, C. J., & McNeal, R. S. (2008). *Digital Citizenship: The Internet, Society and Participation.* Cambridge, MA: MIT Press.

Mouffe, C. (1992). Citizenship and Political Identity. *October, 61,* 28–32.

Muuss, R. E. (1996). *Theories of Adolescence.* London: McGraw-Hill.

Nagel, J. (1987). *Participation.* Englewood, NJ: Prentice-Hall.

Nam, T. (2012). Dual Effects of the Internet on Political Activism: Reinforcing and Mobilizing. *Government Information Quarterly, 29*(S1), S90–S97.

Nasir, N. S., & Hand, V. (2008). From the Court to the Classroom: Opportunities for Engagement, Learning, and Identity in Basketball and Classroom Mathematics. *Journal of the Learning Sciences, 17,* 143–179.

Nasir, N. S., & Kirshner, B. (2003). The Cultural Construction of Moral and Civic Identities. *Applied Developmental Science, 7,* 138–147.

National Center for Education Statistics. (2011). *The Nation's Report Card: Civics 2010 (NCES 2011–466).* Washington, DC: Institute of Education Sciences, U.S. Department of Education.

Nelson, J., & Kerr, D. (2006). *Active Citizenship in INCA Countries: Definitions, Policies, Practices and Outcomes: Final Report.* London, England: Qualification and Curriculum Authority.

Norris, P. (2000). *A Virtuous Circle: Political Communications in Postindustrial Societies.* New York: Cambridge University Press.

Norris, P. (2001). *Digital Divide: Civic Engagement, Information Poverty, and the Internet Worldwide.* New York: Cambridge University Press.

NPR. (2009, December 27). *Republican Politicians Make a Social Media Push.* Retrieved from http://www.npr.org/templates/story/story.php?storyId=121891988

Nystrand, M., Gamoran, A., & Carbonaro, W. (2001). On the Ecology of Classroom Instruction: The Case of Writing in High School English and Social Studies. In P. Tynjala, L. Mason, & K. Lonka (Eds.), *Writing as a Learning Tool* (pp. 57–81). Norwell, MA: Kluwer Academic Publishers.

Ohler, J. (2011). Digital Citizenship Means Character Education for the Digital Age. *Kappa Delta Pi Record, 47,* 25–27.

Oser, J., Hooghe, M., & Marien, S. (2013). Is Online Participation Distinct from Offline Participation? A Latent Class Analysis of Participation Types and Their Stratification. *Political Research Quarterly, 66*(1), 91–101.

Oyedemi, T. (2015). Internet Access as Citizen's Right? Citizenship in the Digital Age. *Citizenship Studies, 19*(3–4), 450–464.

Paulhus, D. L., & Trapnell, P. D. (2008). Self-presentation of Personality: An Agency-communion Framework. In O. John, R. Robins, & L. Pervin (Eds.), *Handbook of Personality Psychology* (3rd ed., pp. 492–517). New York: Guilford Press.

Pew Research Center. (2018, February 5). *Mobile Fact Sheet*. Retrieved from Pew Research Center: Internet and Technology http://www.pewinternet.org/fact-sheet/mobile/

Pickard, S. (2019). *Politics, Protest and Young People: Political Participation and Dissent in 21st Century Britain*. London: Palgrave Macmillan.

Poindexter, P. M. (2012). *Millennials, News, and Social Media*. New York: Peter Lang.

Polat, R. K. (2005). The Internet and Political Participation: Exploring the Explanatory Links. *European Journal of Communication, 20*, 435–459.

Polat, R. K., & Pratchett, L. (2014). Citizenship in the Age of the Internet: A Comparative Analysis of Britain and Turkey. *Citizenship Studies, 18*(1), 63–80.

Pontes, A., Henn, M., & Griffiths, M. D. (2018). Towards a Conceptualization of Young People's Political Engagement: A Qualitative Focus Group Study. *Societies, 8*(1), 17.

Pontes, A. I., Henn, M., & Griffiths, M. D. (2019). Youth Political (Dis)Engagement and the Need for Citizenship Education: Encouraging Young People's Civic and Political Participation Through the Curriculum. *Education, Citizenship and Social Justice, 14*(1), 3–21.

Prior, M. (2007). *Post-broadcast Democracy: How Media Choice Increases Inequality in Political Involvement and Polarized Elections*. New York: Cambridge University Press.

Putnam, R. (2000). *Bowling Alone: The Collapse and Revival of American Community*. New York: Touchstone.

Quan-Haase, A., & boyd, d. (2011). Teen Communities. In G. A. Barnett (Ed.), *Encyclopedia of Social Networks* (Vol. 1). SAGE.

Quan-Haase, A., Wellman, B., Witte, J. C., & Hampton, K. N. (2002). Capitalizing on the Net: Social Contact, Civic Engagement, and Sense of Community. In B. Wellman & C. Haythornthwaite (Eds.), *The Internet in Everyday Life* (pp. 291–324). Oxford: Blackwell Publishing Lt.

Railey, H., & Brennan, J. (2016). *Education Trends Companion Report: 50-State Comparison: Civic Education*. Education Commission of the States.

Rainie, L., Smith, A., Schlozman, K. L., Brady, H., & Verba, S. (2012). *Social Media and Political Engagement*. Washington, D.C.: Pew Research Center Internet & American Life Project.

Raynes-Goldie, K., & Walker, L. (2008). Our Space: Online Civic Engagement Tools for Youth. In W. L. Bennett (Ed.), *Civic Life Online: Learning How Digital Media Can Engage Youth* (pp. 161–188). Cambridge, MA: The MIT Press.

Rheingold, H. (2008). Using Participatory Media and Public Voice to Encourage Civic Engagement. In W. L. Bennett (Ed.), *Civic Life Online: Learning How Digital Media Can Engage Youth* (pp. 97–118). Cambridge, MA: The MIT Press.

Riger, S., & Lavrakas, P. (1981). Community Ties: Patterns of Attachment and Social Interaction in Urban Neighborhoods. *American Journal of Community Psychology, 9*, 55–66.

Ross, A. (2008). Organizing a Curriculum for Active Citizenship Education. In J. Arthur, I. Davies, & C. Hahn (Eds.), *The SAGE Handbook of Education for Citizenship and Democracy* (pp. 492–505). London, England: SAGE.

Rui, J., & Stefanone, M. A. (2012). Strategic Self-presentation Online: A Cross-cultural Study. *Computers in Human Behavior, 29*, 110–118.

Rui, J., & Stefanone, M. A. (2013). Strategic Image Management Online. *Information, Communication & Society, 16*(8), 1286–1305.

Sant, E. (2014). What Does Political Participation Mean to Spanish Students? *Journal of Social Science Education, 13*(4), 11–25.

Schlenker, B. (1985). Identity and Self-identification. In B. R. Schlenker (Ed.), *The Self and Social Life* (pp. 65–99). New York: McGraw-Hill.

Schlenker, B. (1986). Self-identification: Toward an Integration of the Private and Public Self. In *Public Self and Private Self* (pp. 21–62). New York: Springer.

Schlenker, B. (2012). Self-Presentation. In M. R. Leary & J. P. Tangney (Eds.), *Handbook of Self and Identity* (2nd ed., pp. 542–570). New York: Guilford Press.

Schlozman, K., Verba, S., & Brady, H. (2010). Weapon of the Strong: Participatory Inequality and the Internet. *Perspectives on Politics, 8*, 487–509.

Seale, J., & Dutton, W. (2012). Empowering the Digitally Excluded: Learning Initiatives for (In)visible Groups. *Research in Learning Technology, 20*(4).

Selman, R. (1971). Taking Another's Perspective: Role-taking Development in Early Childhood. *Child Development, 42*, 1721–1734.

Selwyn, N. (2003). 'Doing IT for the Kids': Re-examining Children, Computers and the 'Information Society'. *Media, Culture, & Society, 25*(3), 351–378.

Selwyn, N., Gorard, S., & Furlong, J. (2006). *Adult Learning in the Digital Age: Information Technology and the Learning Society*. London: Routledge.

Serriere, S. C. (2014). The Role of the Elementary Teacher in Fostering Civic Efficacy. *The Social Studies, 105*(1), 45–56.

Servaes, J. (2003). Digital Citizenship and Information Inequalities: Challenges for the Future. In J. Servaes (Ed.), *The European Information Society: A Reality Check* (pp. 231–238). Bristol: Intellect Books.

Shakespeare, W. (2004 [1623]). *As You Like It*. Cambridge University Press.

Sherrod, L., Torney-Purta, J., & Flanagan, C. (2010). *Handbook of Research on Civic Engagement in Youth*. Hoboken, NJ: John Wiley & Sons.

Smith, E. (1999). The Effects of Investments in the Social Capital of Youth on Political and Civic Behavior in Young Adulthood: A Longitudinal Analysis. *Political Psychology, 20*(3), 553–580.

Soep, E. (2015). Phones Aren't Smart Until You Tell Them What To Do. In E. Middaugh & B. Kirshner (Eds.), *#youthaction: Becoming Political in the Digital Age* (pp. 25–41). Charlotte, NC: Information Age Publishing, Inc.

Stepick, A., Stepick, C., & Labissiere, C. (2008). South Florida's Immigrant Youth and Civic Engagement. *Applied Developmental Science, 12*(2), 57–65.

Subrahmanyam, K., & Šmahel, D. (2011). *Digital Youth: The Role of Media in Development.* New York: Springer.

Sveningsson, M. (2016). 'I Wouldn't Have What It Takes': Young Swedes' Understandings of Political Participation. *Young, 24*(2), 139–156.

Tapscott, D. (1998). *Growing Up Digital.* New York: McGraw-Hill.

Teruelle, R. (2012). Social Media and Youth Activism. In H. S. Al-Deen & J. A. Hendricks (Eds.), *Social Media: Usage and Impact* (pp. 201–217). Plymouth: Lexington Books.

Thomas, S. N. (2018). Promoting Digital Citizenship in First-year Students: Framing Information Literacy as a Tool to Help Peers. *College & Undergraduate Libraries, 25*(1), 52–64.

Turkle, S. (1995). *Life on the Screen: Identity in the Age of the Internet.* New York: Simon & Schuster.

Turkle, S. (2011). *Alone Together: Why We Expect More from Technology and Less from Each Other.* New York: Basic Books.

Tynes, B., & Monterosa, V. (2015). The Making of a Global Citizen: A Model Supporting Civic Learning Opportunities Among Urban Latino Youth. In E. Middaugh & B. Kirshner (Eds.), *#youthaction: Becoming Political in the Digital Age* (pp. 169–189). Charlotte, NC: Information Age Publishing, Inc.

van Dijk, J., & Hacker, K. (2003). The Digital Divide as a Complex and Dynamic Phenomenon. *The Information Society: An International Journal, 19*, 315–326.

Velasquez, A., & LaRose, R. (2015). Youth Collective Activism Through Social Media: The Role of Collective Efficacy. *New Media & Society, 17*(6), 899–918.

Verba, S., Schlozman, K., & Brady, H. (1995). *Voice and Equality: Civic Voluntarism in American Politics.* Cambridge, MA: Harvard University Press.

Vissers, S., & Stolle, D. (2014). Spill-over Effects Between Facebook and On/Offline Political Participation? Evidence from a Two-wave Panel Study. *Journal of Information, Technology, and Politics, 11*(3), 259–275.

Ward, S., Gibson, R., & Lusoli, W. (2003). Online Participation and Mobilisation in Britain: Hype, Hope and Reality. *Parliamentary Affairs, 56*, 652–668.

Watkins, S. C. (2009). *The Young and the Digital: What the Migration to Social-Network Sites, Games, and Anytime, Anywhere Media Means for Our Future.* Boston, MA: Beacon Press.

Weber, L., Loumakis, A., & Bergman, J. (2003). Who Participates and Why? An Analysis of Citizens on the Internet and the Mass Public. *Social Science Computer Review, 21*, 26–42.

Weinstein, E. (2014). The Personal Is Political on Social Media: Online Civic Expression Patterns and Pathways Among Civically Engaged Youth. *The International Journal of Communication, 8*, 210–233.

Weinstein, E., Rundle, M., & James, C. (2015). A Hush Falls Over the Crowd? Diminished Online Civic Expression Among Young Civic Actors. *International Journal of Communication, 9*, 84–105.

Westheimer, J. (2004). Introduction – The Politics of Civic Education. *PS: Political Science and Politics, 37*(2), 231–234.

White, D. S., & Le Cornu, A. (2011). Visitors and Residents: A New Typology for Online Engagement. *First Monday, 16*(9).

Williams, E. F., & Gilovich, T. (2008). Do People Really Believe They Are Above Average? *Journal of Experimental Social Psychology, 44*, 1121–1128.

Wollman, N., & Stouder, R. (1991). Believed Efficacy and Political Activity: A Test of the Specificity Hypothesis. *Journal of Social Psychology, 131*(4), 557–567.

Xenos, M., & Foot, K. (2008). Not Your Father's Internet: The Generation Gap in Online Politics. In W. L. Bennett (Ed.), *Civic Life Online: Learning How Digital Media Can Engage Youth* (pp. 51–70). Cambridge, MA: The MIT Press.

Yamamoto, M., Kushin, M. J., & Dalisay, F. (2015). Social Media and Mobiles as Political Mobilization Forces for Young Adults: Examining the Moderating Role of Online Political Expression in Political Participation. *New Media & Society, 17*(6), 880–898.

Youniss, J., & Levine, P. (2009). A "Younger Americans Act": An Old Idea for a New Era. In J. Youniss & P. Levine (Eds.), *Engaging Young People in Civic Life* (pp. 13–28). Nashville, TN: Vanderbilt University Press.

Youniss, J., McLellan, J. A., & Yates, M. (1997). What We Know About Engendering Civic Identity. *The American Behavioral Scientist, 40*(5), 620–631.

Youniss, J., & Yates, M. (1997). *Community Service and Social Responsibility in Youth*. Chicago: University of Chicago Press.

CHAPTER 3

Presentations of the Adolescent Self in Contemporary Society

"Tell me a little bit about yourself." I began each interview with this open-ended statement; I intended to invite an open discussion about each participant's own unique experiences as a young person in today's world. I sought to learn what factors influence each participant's identity, and the aspects of themselves they chose to share with me in the interview setting. This chapter focuses on the first research question that motivated this study.

It can be difficult to describe oneself in a few minutes during an extended interview, and it is especially challenging to ask young people to talk about themselves, particularly because adolescence is a critical time during which identity is fluid (Erikson, 1968). Martin, a humble 15-year-old, found it difficult to talk about himself when asked. Martin said that he prefers to *not* talk about himself. He shared that his mother, grandparents, and uncles taught him "morals and to be selfless" and to treat others as he would want to be treated. While Martin struggled to describe himself because he dislikes talking about himself, other young people struggle to describe themselves as they are still discovering whom they are. In my first conversation with Tanesha, aged 16, she said, "I don't know who I am" and that she does not like putting herself "into a box, because if I set a box, then I feel like that's trying to force myself into it...I feel like I don't know who I am yet. I'm still growing. I'm only 16." Tanesha expressed her desire for freedom to discover herself, and express herself as she gets older. Madeline, aged 17, echoed this

© The Author(s) 2020

J. K. Viola, *Young People's Civic Identity in the Digital Age*,
Palgrave Studies in Young People and Politics,
https://doi.org/10.1007/978-3-030-37405-1_3

acknowledgement of personal development when she said, "I'm still try-ing to figure out who I am."

Erikson's (1968) theory of identity formation in adolescence is a valu-able framework to understanding identity development in contemporary society, and how it is that young people "figure out" who they are, and who they want to be. Erikson's (1968) theory was a significant contribu-tion to the work of psychologists throughout the twentieth century, and researchers studying adolescents in contemporary society have found it applicable today (Davis & Weinstein, 2017). While Erikson (1968) asserts that identity formation is a lifelong process, it is central to the develop-ment of adolescents, who experience a conflict between identity synthesis and identity confusion, suspended in a psychosocial moratorium, during which adolescents try on different identities (Erikson, 1968). This para-digm of identity synthesis versus identity confusion shows that the stron-ger one's sense of identity synthesis, the more aware he/she/they are of his/her/their own uniqueness, strengths, and weaknesses (Luyckx, Gandhi, Bijttebier, & Claes, 2015). In practice, the psychosocial morato-rium stage of development involves creating and testing out new identities through varying means of self-expression. In contemporary society, social media provide many opportunities for creating and exploring different identities: selfies on Instagram and Snapchat and status updates on Facebook are just a few modern ways of expressing oneself (Davis & Weinstein, 2017). Different circumstances and settings require individuals to present different aspects of themselves, and express themselves in differ-ent ways (Erikson, 1968). Theorists Goffman (1959) and Schlenker (1986) provide a deeper insight into these distinctions, and will be addressed in Section 3.2.

This chapter addresses the first research question in this study: *In what ways do young people, ages 14 through 17, present themselves to others in con-temporary society?* Young people establish connections to others, and sometimes distinguish between a public and private self, which influences the ways in which they like to express themselves. These factors will be addressed throughout this chapter to help explain what it means to be a typical teenager in today's world, and will provide the scaffolding of iden-tity that supports civic identity, which will be addressed in Chapter 4. The presentations of the self that are presented in this chapter may influence how young people engage in the political world, which will be discussed in Chapters 5 and 6.

3.1   CONNECTION TO OTHERS

Adolescents are experiencing a life stage in which they are beginning to develop and understand their sense of self, which is influenced by a multitude of factors, including their relationship to others, and how they experience those relationships in digitally mediated ways. I sought to understand each participant's unique view of him or herself, and to inquire about these distinctive identities, I asked each participant to describe themselves, the activities they enjoy doing, and their other likes and interests. I found that the young people in this study often describe and present themselves in relation and connection to others, whether in relation to a school, sports team, country of origin, or position in the family. This section details these findings.

At age 14, many young people describe themselves through their likes and interests—often involving their extracurricular or sports activities outside of school. For example, Jane, a newcomer to her school, introduced herself to me by saying, "My name is Jane, I'm 14… I play softball, soccer, volleyball, basketball." Participation in sports teams is common among American young people during their high school years. Often, parents and teachers encourage young people to participate as a way to build leadership skills, exercise, and make new friends. It is very common for these high school sports teams and extracurricular groups to have their own Facebook pages and groups, so members and supporters can Follow and be aware of the next match or team dinner, and other events happening in the group. Imani, also aged 14, just started high school, and does "a lot programs, so I know a lot of people." Imani demonstrates her membership to her cohort by referring to the group as "we"—and speaking on the collective behalf of the group, she explains that everyone is "connected," and experiencing the transition to high school. Imani is involved in many programs, and interacts with groups of different people, allowing her to not feel like a stranger in her large high school. Imani and other participants discussed their membership in their sports team or after school club Facebook pages, where they interact with other members of those groups and find out about upcoming sports matches and events. This sense of knowing others and feeling connected and supported on teams or in school groups can be reassuring. For some, it is easy to identify this support as a positive influence on one's life: Damon—a very hardworking, determined 14-year-old—says that his family and friends have shaped his identity because "everybody wants to support me and help me become successful in life." At age 14, young people are at the start of adolescence, and are just beginning to understand themselves and how the people around them might impact their lives.

This importance of connection to others through shared interests carries through adolescence, and around ages 16 and 17, individuals' conceptions of themselves become more complex, and qualified with personal values and philosophies related to their connection with others—especially family and community. For example, Kali considers herself to be a "respectful person: we all come from different walks of life, so I can't tell somebody how to live their life, nobody can tell me how to live mine. And just, respecting where people come from, that's what you need to do in this life to get anywhere." Kali exhibits some of her personal values, philosophy, and understanding of the world around her in her description of herself, compared to the younger participants in this study. She highlights her compassion for others and reflected on where this comes from. Kali shared that her younger sister was shot and paralyzed at age 3, and their mother started a not-for-profit organization that focuses on "outreach for victims of violence." Kali has been strongly influenced by her own life experience living in what she refers to as "the inner city," and how her mother has coped with difficult situations. She feels a strong connection to her peers in the summer program that served as a recruitment pool and backdrop for our interview: all of the young people in the program share the same "inner city" background, and "don't have all of the materials that we need." This academic summer program offers scholarships to students every summer for 3 years, and if they successfully complete the 3-year program, they are awarded $3000 in scholarship funds to use toward their education at a college or university of their choice. Kali, evidently, feels humbled to be in this program, and senses a bond with her peers in the group because of their shared background.

Similarly, Peter, aged 17, described himself as "trustworthy" and highlights this quality of himself with what he views as a responsible job working in a preschool: he has "a lot of responsibility" and ensures that the children "don't get injured or anything." But, not all 16- and 17-year-olds hold these views, or choose to describe themselves while hinting at their values. Some continue the trend of describing themselves based on their sports teams or extracurricular activities and interests like the 14- and 15-year-olds in this study. This signifies that while young people see and describe themselves in different ways at different ages, age does not necessarily mark a specific stage in identity development. Identity development is unique to each individual, and goes beyond connecting to others through shared likes and interests with peers. While this connection is indeed a social mechanism through which one is able to gain an understanding of oneself and how one chooses to present aspects of the self to others, it is because of these connections that young people share certain likes and interests. The following section will describe the distinction between the public self and private self, as experienced by the teenagers in this study.

3.2   PRIVATE VS. PUBLIC SELF

Identity can be seen as a social process, dependent on the situation and perceived audience: we choose what pieces of ourselves to present to the world, and with whom to share those pieces (boyd, 2007b). Young people do think about how others view them, and how they represent themselves to others—a public self. In adolescence, young people begin to make the distinction between the private self and the public self, known only to each individual, and maybe to a select few close family and friends. This distinction can sometimes be explored using social media, and sometimes later manifests itself in one's decision to share one's civic identity and discuss political and social issues with others, such as friends, family, and teachers, which will be discussed in Chapter 5. The findings presented in the following section draw on social interaction theory: how identities are constructed through relations to and interactions with others (Goffman, 1978). It is not uncommon to make a distinction between the private self and the public self (Schlenker, 1986, 2012), whether this decision to make the distinction is conscious or not. For the young people in this study, many decisions about how to present themselves to the world could be easily articulated, and often demonstrated a connection to an audience. Audiences for young people could be parents, siblings, teachers, friends, and even strangers. These audiences represent the many opportunities for young people to share certain aspects of the self to others. Young people choose to share aspects of themselves and their identities in different ways, depending on their audience, and negotiate their displays of self for the benefit of themselves and others.

In public, 15-year-old Kevin expresses himself as a cheerful person who likes to crack jokes. During our interview, when I asked if there is anyone he looks up to as a role model, he replied, "Um, actually there are a lot of people I really do look up to kinda, because I'm short." I could not help but indulge Kevin and myself in a laugh. I was surprised when Kevin also described his "darker" side that he keeps to himself because "I don't want people in the world to feel bad because I feel bad." Kevin chooses to share private aspects of himself on *some* public platforms, like his Facebook profile—but not all. Interestingly, Kevin feels comfortable showing both his "lighthearted" and "emotional" sides on social media, and says that his social media profiles represent him "to a T." Kevin chooses to present his cheerful self, but preserve his darker self simultaneously—it appears that he wishes to protect other's feelings, and their possible worries about his wellbeing.

Bethany, aged 16, shares her public self in a similar manner to Kevin, though she does not believe that her social media profiles are accurate representations of who she is. Bethany only puts "out there what I want people to see. I can't really show them all of me. My posts are usually fun and funny, because I don't… want to put like, emotional stuff out there." Bethany acknowledges her decision to always withhold her "emotional" side from others, whereas Kevin shares that he censors his "darker" emotions on social media just some of the time. Interestingly, both Kevin and Bethany presented to me as enthusiastic, positive individuals, yet revealed to me through our conversation that they also have "darker" sides. Bethany is worried that "people will portray me different" than how she wishes to be perceived, should she share her true emotions. As Schlenker (2012) observes, people want others to see themselves in a positive light, or in ways that confirm how they see themselves, which leads people to present themselves in ways that give self-verifying feedback. When young people like Kevin say that their social media profiles are an accurate representation of the self, it is evident that social media is a very public way for their friends to confirm whether they are seeing them in the same way they see themselves.

As the methodology for the study presented in this book did not call for observations of young people in their daily life, for the purposes of this book, the distinctions between the private and public selves are apparent through the ways in which young people present themselves on the stage of social media. The remainder of this section will address what is shared and not shared by young people on their social media profiles. It is important to note that not all young people have social media accounts or profiles, and some of the reasons for this will also be addressed.

People experience connectivity online and through social media, which "offers new possibilities for experimenting with identity" (Turkle, 2011,

p. 152). Social media have become new stages on which people can perform different aspects of the self. It is therefore worth noting that in each interview, I asked young people who are social media users to share with me how well they believe their social media profiles represent themselves. Kevin shared that his social media profiles represent him very well, highlighting both "lighthearted" and "darker" parts of himself. Relatedly, 15-year-old Selah says that her social media profiles represent her as who she "truly" is and she is "not pretending to be anything I'm not, like some people." Selah alludes to how some people are superficial and do not show their true self or personality to others. Sachi, aged 17, believes his social media profiles are "a pretty good representation" of who he is, "how I'm feeling that day, or like… just who I am. I think it is …almost there. I'd say 80 percent. Not all the way, 'cause you're never who you are online, as they say."

Sachi's statement highlights a growing concern among young people and adults alike: while social media connects us all together, it is possible to experiment with different identities, whether that is through choosing to represent some aspects of oneself but not others, or pretending to be someone else entirely. This concern is not unfounded, and is supported by research by Gardner and Davis (2013), James (2014), and Turkle (1995, 2011), which suggests that people are hiding behind their screens, taking advantage of the anonymity of the Internet and pretending to be different versions of themselves, or different people altogether. This concern has been present since *The New Yorker* featured a poignant social commentary on this issue with a cartoon depicting two dogs: one dog sitting in front of a desktop computer, saying to a second dog, "On the Internet, nobody knows you're a dog" (Steiner, 1993). However, others disagree, arguing the "real and the virtual are mutually constituted" (Valentine & Holloway, 2002, p. 302), and young people present themselves to the world online in ways they would offline. In this study, no participants discussed pretending to be people other than themselves online, but still acknowledge the importance of how one presents oneself to others—and the effort they put into thinking about how they present themselves to others in the digital space.

Young people are aware that others form opinions of them based on how they present themselves, primarily through their appearance in photographs that are shared online. Joelle, aged 15, shares that her profile and page on "Tumblr shows more of me than my Instagram" because "I don't like the camera on my phone, so I don't really use it. I just barely post anything... I spend a lot of time with my cousin, so most of the time I'm just re-posting pictures that she posts." Joelle cares about the quality of the photos she posts to her social media accounts, and the image of herself that is created through these photos, so she re-posts the photos of higher quality that her cousin has already posted online. Joelle is an example of a young person who seeks to put their best self forward online. There are also people like Imani, aged 14, who comments on friends' selfies to say, "you're pretty," and thereby validates friends' posts. If Imani and Joelle were connected on social media, Joelle might appreciate a comment from Imani about how beautiful she looks in her high-quality photos.

Young people are concerned with their image, and some young people go to great lengths to control their image online, curating the content thoughtfully to manage what others see. While many young people starting in a new school view that transitional experience in and of itself as an opportunity to present a new self, and a new identity to new classmates, in today's digital world, that transition also includes reinventing oneself on social media. For instance, Tanesha, aged 16, recreated her Facebook profile to improve her image when she transitioned from elementary school to middle school, because her previous account had "a lot of bad pictures of me. And I was like, going to a new school, I gotta start over." Tanesha's decision to develop a new Facebook profile to reflect her new status in a new school emphasizes one way to curate the content of one's profile to manage one's image (Rui & Stefanone, 2013). Tanesha chose to keep her past self private, and display this new, more mature self to her new classmates.

In contrast, some young people, like Kaitlyn, aged 16, are more concerned about privacy—keeping private information safe—and less concerned about their online image. Young people with this concern for privacy do not share much personal information or pictures on their social media profiles aside from their name. Kaitlyn, in particular, does not "like the whole idea that someone can just look at your profile and get your information." Young people and adults often experience this concern, and every social media platform has different settings and policies for privacy, blocking, etc. (Davies & Eynon, 2013). danah boyd (2014) notes that young people find it difficult to keep up with ever-changing privacy settings on various sites, such as Facebook, making online content potentially less secure, or not as private as they think it is. But, sometimes privacy settings give an illusion of information safety (Gardner & Davis, 2013). For example, Snapchat is an app that allows users to send self-destructing pictures and videos to other users. Some users turn to Snapchat to send risky images to others (such as nude photos or sexts), but the recipient may take a screenshot or use a second device to capture the image, so the image has not really been destroyed. Similarly, even content that was posted online with the intent on leaving it there can be downloaded and saved by others without consent (Davis & Weinstein, 2017). Kaitlyn, and others, demonstrate reasonable concern about what is shared on a social media profile, leading to Kaitlyn's decision to limit the personal information and photos that she shares online. This sort of concern may lead Kaitlyn and her like-minded peers to share more about themselves with others in ways that are not digitally mediated, and to keep more aspects of the self private and hidden from others.

Others are concerned about the impact of present posts on one's future self. For example, 14-year-old Imani chooses to share some aspects of her life, but not others, on social media. Imani is wary of what others might think of her based on what she posts on her social media profile, including people outside of her normal social circles—especially future employers. Imani shows concern for her future employability, and does not like to post things "that are gonna affect me in the future." Imani knows that "people search through, say... their Facebook before they even go for the interview" and cautions against posting pictures of "doing drugs or drinking" because employers "just don't want that for their work environment." Imani, at 14 years old, already understands the idea of the digital afterlife: "I don't do it, but anything stupid, I wouldn't post it on social media because I know it doesn't go away forever." If Imani were to do anything that she would regret if it was posted online, this aspect of herself is kept private, and off social media. Similarly, Jackie, aged 16, says that her parents tell her to think about what would happen if her "grandfather saw" what she posted online, alluding to judgment from family members on social media profile content.

There are other reasons for limiting the personal information that is shared online: for example, young people like Joseph, aged 16, would rather have people get to know him in person than online, and does not share many things about himself on his social media accounts. He does not think his social media profiles represent him well, and explains that if someone wants to get to know him, they should "talk to me... people that see my Facebook would be like, 'oh, he's quiet, he doesn't do much.' But people that know me in like, the outside of technology, they'd be like, 'oh, he's creative. He's funny.'" Joseph highlights what many young people have difficulty articulating: while social media profiles can display pieces of one self, one's likes, interests, and friends, there is often more to each person than what exists on a social media profile. Joseph seeks a deeper connection with others that extends beyond the posts, photos, and Likes we share with our social media networks.

It is also clear that young people may also decide that they do not wish to share *any* aspect of themselves on social media at all, and actively choose to not have social media profiles. In some cases, this is a result of parental influence upon attitudes about social media. Kenai, aged 14, mentions that people are "surprised" to learn that he does not have accounts on "Instagram, Facebook, Twitter, and MySpace." Kenai believes social media is a "waste of time" and he would "much rather talk to someone in person and interact, instead of like, spending so much time on social media." Joseph, mentioned above, would agree. For Kenai, "over time, I've kind of gotten a bad impression of [social media], even though it's probably not that bad. My mom has been telling me, 'don't use Twitter!'" Kenai has received many negative messages about social media from his mother, which have shaped his beliefs about social media use. Concerned parents tend to warn their adolescent children about some of the negative consequences of sharing oneself on social media. Madeline, aged 17, says that on her social media profiles, she tries "to put a good representation" of herself, because "anyone can see it... when I first got [social media accounts], my parents told me 'if there was a billboard of you, would you want all the stuff you posted on there on that billboard?' So I try to keep true to that." Kenai's mother explicitly told him *not* to use social media, and he personally finds it to be a "waste of time," while Madeline's parents cautioned her to not share too much personal information, perhaps harboring similar fears as Kaitlyn. Kenai and Madeline have both experienced some form of parental control that influences what they share on social media, and the values they assign to social media.

Analogously, Jackie's parents—especially her mother, who advised her against posting anything online that she would be embarrassed by or ashamed of if her grandfather saw—seem to have some influence on Jackie's social media activity. Jackie revealed that she is "not allowed to get Facebook," but on Instagram and Twitter, she is "only allowed to Follow people I know," thereby keeping her personal information less accessible to others online. This level of protection may be preventing Jackie from connecting with others whom she might not have met through her existing social circles. Jackie's parents evidently have rules and guidelines regarding Jackie's approach to social media, as many parents of adolescents do, for the sake of their children's privacy and protection.

Parents often regulate their children's media use (Ito et al., 2010; Tapscott, 1998). A national survey of parents of young people ages 13 to 17 in the United States found that 60 percent of parents have ever checked their child's social media profiles, while 39 percent of parents have used parental controls to block, filter, or monitor the online activities of their adolescent children (Pew Research Center, 2016). Moreover, 16 percent of parents surveyed use parental controls to restrict their child's use of his or her cell phone (Pew Research Center, 2016). From this information and the personal anecdotes of Jackie and other participants in this study, we can infer that parental control may be stifling young people's ability to learn about current events, political issues, and different viewpoints, which may impact young people's means of connecting to others, especially through online platforms.

Maisie, aged 14, has had multiple social media accounts, but removed herself from Instagram for reasons of her own choosing—not her parents'. Maisie reflected on her own social media use, and that of her peers. She shared with me that she frequently notices the carefully curated nature of social media profiles, as "a lot of people are trying to photograph their life in a way that makes them look really good. And like… tells a cool story about them." Maisie notices what scholars have observed (Goffman, 1959; Paulhus & Trapnell, 2008; Schlenker, 2012)—that everyone is doing their best to present themselves to the world in the best possible light:

> I am friends with these kinds of people who have Instagram, and they spend a whole event just trying to get the right picture to post. And like, trying to get the right pose that looks naturally cool, but they're really making a huge effort to look that way. So it was just like, a lot of faking who you are. And I noticed I was starting to do that. Like… focusing on just getting the right picture, and then leaving somewhere. And not caring about having that actual experience… what they were using it for was not really anything positive, it was just kind of, like narcissistic, and trying to show off to people.

Scholars agree that social media are often curated as a "highlight reel" of the most positive moments of one's daily life (Steers, Wickham, & Acitelli, 2014). With individuals wishing to present a self that is "polished and glorified" (Schlenker, 2012, p. 543), recent trends demonstrate pressure to be perfect online (Davis & Weinstein, 2017; Gardner & Davis, 2013). Forty percent of social media users between the ages of 13 and 17 years old report feeling pressure to post only content that makes them look good to others, and content that will be popular as measured by the number of comments and Likes (Lenhart, 2015). Maisie has discovered the negative effects of this pressure, and that she herself is susceptible to it, and not able to enjoy each moment as much as she ought to be. Maisie indicated that there is indeed a struggle in choosing which personal aspects to share with social media networks, and how others will judge those aspects. Those who expend the energy to take the perfect photo to high-light that they were at a concert may want to illustrate that they are outgo-ing and enjoy music, and may not even realize that posting the "right picture" may be interpreted by others, like Maisie, as artificial. The nuances of people's perceptions of what is shared on social media are complicated, and often not thought about among this age group. Maisie was the only participant to vocalize this complexity of profile curation in this way, and decided to remove herself from the culture of "faking it" on social media by deleting her Instagram account. When Maisie decided to reactivate her Instagram account several months later, she acknowledged that editing and posting photos on the app is "fun," and she can still enjoy it while being consciously aware that Instagram is not a full representation of a person's life.

Individuals make judgments of themselves based on what they perceive others think of them (James, 2014). Indeed, as Maisie highlighted, young people vary what they share on social media based upon who from their social circles Follow them, and the judgments they might receive from others about the lives they lead. Participants like Elsie, aged 17, recognize a distinction between social media platforms, and therefore exercise vary-ing levels of discretion about the content that is shared, and who is allowed to Follow those profiles and posts. Elsie discerns her posts between Facebook and Tumblr. On Facebook, Elsie tends to be "more closed off" because she is Facebook friends with her rabbi and childhood nanny, and "can't talk about these things in front of them." Elsie's home, synagogue, and digital worlds have collided on Facebook, which influences the nature of her disclosures through social media (Gil-Lopez et al., 2018). Elsie does not feel comfortable divulging certain opinions and personal infor-mation—such as her relationship status—to these figures in her life, because they are close to her in a way that a parent is. Elsie eludes to a common struggle that individuals experience when presenting themselves to different audiences online: each audience expects a different image of Elsie (Rui & Stefanone, 2012).

Elsie goes online to communicate with friends—not share her feelings with the adults in her life. Teenagers, like Elsie, view space online as "private"—separate from the spaces that are controlled by parents and teachers (boyd, 2007a). While it may seem counter-intuitive, young people use social networking site profiles and comment areas as a private space with a public component (boyd, 2007a). On Tumblr, for example, Elsie would "re-blog stuff" that she "wouldn't want the rest of my family seeing," but she is content with publicly sharing certain interests as long as the post remains anonymous. Elsie asserts that, in her opinion, Facebook is "so much more public, and I'm much more surrounded by like, everyone in my life… whereas like, on Tumblr, it's like, well, there are a couple people from school or wherever who Follow me, but for the most part, it's just a bunch of random strangers." Elsie shared that her Tumblr page does not contain any identifying information—her given first name and surname are not listed. Elsie uses Tumblr to share with a few people from school and many strangers the things that she is not comfortable disclosing to her rabbi and childhood nanny, among other close relatives. Elsie is just one example of a young person who shares a public self and a private self on different platforms; other young people use different social media sites and platforms for different purposes and means of self-expression, which will continue to be explored in Section 3.3.

There are many different reasons for why young people wish to share some parts of themselves but not others. These preferences for presenting oneself exist because each young person has a different idea and goal of who they want to be in each social circle, including on social networking websites. Each person presents themselves according to their own values, or the values imparted on them by their families and communities, and wider society. We saw that parents, in particular, influence how young people view certain stages on which they present themselves, particularly on social media platforms. But young people are able to present and express themselves in many different ways, according to what is available to them, and what others expect of them.

In contemporary society, young people are often presenting themselves in digitally mediated ways, which afford young people the opportunity to share different aspects of themselves to different audiences (Turkle, 2011). The distinction between the private and public self is most significant when young people consider what to share on their social media profiles.

The private self is not always revealed, as demonstrated by Bethany's account of her keeping her sadness to herself. There is a pressure to be perfect—especially on social media. In this digital era, people want to control other's impressions of them by presenting and expressing themselves most favorably (Brown, 1998; Williams & Gilovich, 2008) in digital ways. Goffman (1959) argued that social life is a series of performances in which people project their identities to others, and in contemporary society, young people are often performing as the best versions of themselves: doing the activities, wearing the clothes, attending the concerts that will receive the most Likes on social media.

3.3   SELF-EXPRESSION

Expressing oneself is a tangible display of one's identity, and individuals are constantly aware of impression management: the expression that one gives, or what an individual intends to express, and the expression that one gives off, or how others interpret those actions (Goffman, 1959). In contemporary society, forms of self-expression vary, and may depend on their social contexts and motivations to try on new identities. Young people in this study express themselves through emotion (exhibited by the arts), experimenting with different physical appearances (such as hairstyles and dress), actions, and all the while using social media to develop and present themselves to others.

In particular, Robert, aged 16, likes to express himself through writing, especially through sharing quotes. Robert divulged, "On Snapchat, I write quotes and stuff like that. Like, if it's a certain type of quote that I see, I would screenshot it, memorize it, and then like, text it on Snapchat or something… 'When you're happy, you enjoy music, and then when you're sad, you understand the lyrics.'" Robert can relate to this quote because he has "a lot of songs on my phone that like, when I'm just like, in a good mood, I can listen to it, and I really don't understand what they're saying, but I enjoy the music. But then at certain times, you're feeling down and you're listening to sad songs, you can actually understand what that person's saying. Can feel their pain, also." Robert uses technology as a way to express and share himself with his social network on Snapchat. He also pinpoints music—which he listens to on his phone—as a way to discover his emotions. Similarly, Hannah, aged 16, likes to post

Selfies. And I like to post my favorite quotes …. My mom says that I post way too much about her… because people find her funny and I like to entertain people. I just like to do that so people get a sense of me, so they don't just see like a picture, and they're not like 'oh this girl is something.' And then if they read my posts and stuff, they'll be like, 'oh she's completely different.'

Selfies and status updates—whether they include quotes or not—are examples of identity exploration and expression in contemporary society (Davis & Weinstein, 2017).

Young people in this study referred to the concept of being "true to oneself" and represent themselves on their social media profiles according to how they characterize themselves and their values. Marcia's (1980) commitment stage of identity status theory is one in which adolescents adhere to their convictions and values. Values can be expressed to others as actions: Nadia, aged 16, values her involvement with her community, particularly related to her concerns about education and rights for people in her age group. These values translate into Nadia being a very active member of her community, specifically her citywide youth council. Nadia believes that it is incredibly important to be involved in one's community, because she is "very interested in these different issues that go along in our community and in the world in general." Nadia asserts that the topics that she and her fellow youth council members discuss are relevant outside of her immediate surroundings. It is important to Nadia to spread "the word to the world" because current events "affect everybody, at the end of the day." Beyond this youth council, Nadia spends some of her free time volunteering at her local library, and participating in rallies and events for the Black Lives Matter Movement. The youth council has even created Facebook pages for their campaigns as a means of getting other students involved. Sachi, Kenai, and Kaitlyn also like to express themselves through their actions. This exhibition of personal values connects to civic identity, which will be explored in depth in Chapter 4.

It is important to note that society and the communities of which one is a part can influence self-expression. In some cases, expressing oneself may serve a social and societal purpose, such as resisting stereotypes. Kali, aged 16, feels that it is her duty to live her life as a "rebuttal" to stereotypes about young women of color. Kali shared the stereotype that "we [women of color] are always angry, and that we always want to fight, and that we're so aggressive." Kali laughed and said, "That's not me at all!"

Instead of "getting online and writing a whole rebuttal," Kali says the biggest impact she can make to change people's misconceptions is to let her "life be one [a rebuttal]." By living her life and expressing herself as a "positive" and "considerate" and "optimistic" person, Kali believes that she can prove these stereotypes wrong. The first measure Kali alluded to taking to combat stereotypes was taking to the Internet as a platform for her voice to express herself, illustrating the pervasiveness of technology as a platform on which to share one's voice. In a similar vein, Martin discusses how he expresses himself as a young black male in America.

3.3.1   The Case of Martin

Martin expressed a widespread sentiment about police brutality toward black males, a sentiment felt throughout the United States during the time of this study, wherein nearly one-third of the participants identified as black Americans. Martin thoughtfully articulated complex thoughts and feelings about race, and what it means to express oneself in a way that combats stereotypes about peers with a shared identity. His case provides insight into the many factors that young people consider when they present themselves to others in contemporary society, especially the perceptions of others.

Martin first introduced his concern about how others perceive him based on his skin color in our first interview. Martin is cautious to express himself because he does not want to seem "better than anyone. We're supposed to be created equal." He enjoys creating characters that look like him on video games, such as "NBA, 2K. It's like a series. And you can create your own player. And... basketball, is seen as like, a black sport, but I think it feels kinda cool to create your own character and have them maybe like a likeness of you." Martin appreciates that people who look like him are represented in video games, but expressed a grave concern about the treatment of people like him in the physical world in our second interview several months later.

Martin talked a great deal about police brutality toward people of color in the United States. He shared some allusions to recent events of police brutality in Missouri and elsewhere in the United States. Martin "wasn't necessarily nervous. I don't know if it's because I live up in the North, you know... I mean, I had heard about it and obviously I was disappointed but I wasn't like, you know, I didn't want it... I didn't let it stop me, you know. I didn't want to pout about it. But it was difficult, because you had different teenagers dying every week." In the year prior to our interviews, there were several high-profile cases of police brutality against black Americans, including the shooting of 18-year-old Michael Brown in Ferguson, Missouri. Martin believed in his own relative safety, living in a "northern" more progressive state. The Midwestern and southern United States have a history of brutality toward people of color, even after the Civil Rights movement in the 1960s.

Martin went to what he referred to as a "gathering" in downtown Boston in the months leading up to our interviews, but did not want to get into any altercations there. The gathering that Martin alluded to was a rally for The Black Lives Matter movement, which, alongside the issue of police brutality against blacks, is very personal for him. Martin said he would still care very much if police brutality and inhumane treatment happened to people of another race, but he cares so much because it is *his* race that is most affected by police violence, and he feels "a connection, since those are your people." Martin identifies with others like him, and feels a stronger motivation to take action because "some people take matters into their own hands instead of maybe waiting it out," and while he normally "waits it out," he now finds that waiting will only delay progress on the issue. Martin decided it was time to do something, which led to his attendance of this "gathering" for the Black Lives Matter movement.

Martin had not always spoken out against police brutality, and cites two hindrances as his reasons for this: "I am underage, so … it isn't … I don't think, necessarily that what I would say would be that big. Um… I am African American, so…." Martin sees his age and his race as a black person as a barrier to his efficacy. He prefers to express himself

> through my actions, I'd say. I think… actions at times do speak louder than words… I may not look just like you, but I can still do the type of work you might do, maybe the same or even better. I know I'm like a big guy. You know, I should probably be [more] outspoken than most. But … I'm very humble and I try to … have my actions show who I am, what I am… what I stand for, stuff like that.

Martin reflected deeply on the way he represents others like him, and his actions to combat stereotypes:

> I'm kinda talking about like, you know like, the U.S. and like, um, African-American male stuff, like that…how we kinda get bad raps sometimes. What

I meant by like, speech and all that is like, you know, a lot of people...not necessarily a lot of people, but people that still have the traditional old ways... They don't really expect, you know, my type of people to really speak vocabulary words, rather than slur words together and make slang and stuff like that—dialect.

Martin highlighted that his manner of speaking "has a good impact. I feel more confident when I'm talking to anybody. You know, I don't feel nervous, or inferior, stuff like that. I feel more comfortable with my surroundings." Martin's story highlights what it is like to be a young black male in the United States today, and the consideration of his social contexts when presenting himself to others (Erikson, 1968; Goffman, 1959; Schlenker, 2012). His identity expression is cautious: he is careful about how he dresses and how he acts, so that others do not get the wrong idea about him. Martin, a young black male, highlights that in contemporary society—marked by technology use and, unfortunately, racial discrimination and violence—one must consider their race and voice. On some stages, this is simpler and results in fewer negative perceptions (i.e., selecting a black male character to represent himself on a video game) than others (i.e., using language that would make others perceive him as less intelligent).

3.4   TYPICAL TEENAGERS IN TODAY'S WORLD

Society expects certain things from young people in their teenage years. Society expects young people to utilize social media, which is a factor contributing to identity formation. Whether one chooses to keep parts of oneself private, or share some parts of the self in the public, each individual is deciding how to express and present oneself and with whom to share different aspects of the self. Sharing aspects of oneself with others is inevitable when people connect and interact with each other, on any kind of platform. In contemporary society, the pressure to be perfect on social media informs how young people consider what to share on the most public platforms. This form of expression on social media often leads young people to their identities as "typical teenagers"—an identity that some young people have for themselves, whereas some have that identity thrust upon them by others.

The young people in this study spend time hanging out with and texting their friends, and use technology in their everyday life. Kali, aged 16, confides that young people are "impressionable," and many typical conversations with her friends involve gossip. "You know, girls our age, we think about boys and stuff like that, but that's not our main focus, whereas in high school, that's all you'll hear in the hallways, is who's with who, and stuff like that," she says. Peter, aged 17, explains that he and his friends "like to play basketball, play video games, and you know the usual teenage stuff. Hang out... um... we went to a concert this summer. You know, just regular stuff." Naomi, aged 16, addresses the stereotype that teenagers are always on their phones: "I'm not a huge fan of texting. I do it, obviously: I'm a teenager, I text a lot." Gossiping, playing video games, and texting are all typical activities and ways of interacting that people in this age group engage in frequently. Young people sometimes view themselves via the same lens through which society sees them: as "typical" teenagers. When we hear that phrase, oftentimes we think about young people gossiping, using social media frequently, and being aloof in the world.

Unfortunately this characterization of young people as "typical teenagers" has sometimes prohibited them from engaging in society and in their communities in the ways that they would like to be involved. Veronica, herself a 15-year-old, judges others on their maturity, or her perception of it. She prefers to focus her time on "the people I know who are mature and won't stay in the mindset of a fifth grader and stuff like that, because at the same time I want friends that are impactful, not only to me but to society and to other people." During our hour-long interview, I noticed that Veronica seemed mature for her age to want to surround herself with "impactful" people—I later found this field note inappropriate, as I had made a judgment about Veronica's maturity based on her age, as many adults have. These judgments have "stifled" her and some of her classmates. Veronica is younger than most of her classmates, and "a lot of the time my friends will be doing something but I don't have the age for it yet." Her age precludes her from many opportunities that her classmates have, "like, jobs, for example, at stores, or I know there's one thing. Like working with kids and stuff like that. Even though I could do something, it's hard to find something for 15-year-olds because it's always like 16-year-olds." Laura has had similar setbacks. At 17 years old, Laura is not able to become an emergency medical technician (EMT), which is a necessary step in her pathway to her career goal of becoming a nurse. She said, "I think I'm gonna get my paramedic or EMT certification this summer... you have to be 18, so..." Kaitlyn, aged 16, says that even with some volunteer work, there is much she is excluded from until she is 18 years old:

"for volunteer work, I think I have to wait 'til 18 to do most of the stuff. I dunno, I think the whole just um… food pantries and stuff … that's good, but I want to do something more than that with my volunteer work, and my age prevents that."

This idea of the typical teenager can be helpful to some to situate young people in a stage of emotional development. Other times, this label can be harmful in that it dismisses young people in this age group, and perpetuates the perception that young people are apathetic about politics, and would rather spend time hanging out with friends, playing video games, or using social media, which will continue to be explored in future chapters. Many participants who discuss these activities—including Kali, Peter, and Naomi—would exemplify this aspect of the identity of an American young person. When young people are reduced to the stereotype of "typical teens," it dismisses the other parts of them—the parts that desire to be engaged, that show initiative, their other interests—and feeds into the stereotype even further. When young people don't see themselves beyond being "typical teens," it prevents them from looking outside the box to think about what else they could be doing beyond those activities that show their engagement in politics and the community. Young people are unique individuals with many diverse interests that go beyond texting, video games, and gossip: Maisie loves dance, Jane loves robotics, Peter enjoys teaching preschool children, and Nadia is an active member of the Youth Council of her city. Young people must be understood in this holistic way. This holistic understanding will help educators meet young people where they are to best design civic education curriculum—knowing young people's interests and communities can create opportunities for young people to be involved in ways that are meaningful and interesting to them.

3.5   Understanding Presentations of the Self in Contemporary Society

Young people are shaped by the digital world—the nature and multitude of the different stages on which young people can now present and perform their identities offers new opportunities to think about the self in new ways. Young people take aspects of their environment (Hasebrink & Paus-Hasebrink, 2007), relationships, and interactions with others to construct their identities (Côté & Levine, 2002; Flanagan, 2013), and can experiment with their self-presentation through technology (Gardner & Davis, 2013). Martin demonstrates this and how he shares pieces of his identity through his decisions about presenting himself in the online gaming community.

In a society characterized by widespread technology use, technology now informs the process of identity development through the presentation of the self. Young people now have a broader audience with whom to share themselves, and the nature of social media prompts young people to curate their social media profiles according to each audience. Some young people choose to present themselves to others on social media, and on specific social media sites, whereas others choose not to. Media and current culture "celebrates personal disclosure," and many young people express themselves on social media with selfies and status updates (Loader, 2007, p. 2). The private self is not always revealed to others, as illustrated by Kevin, who shares his "darker side" with a few others, but tries to keep it to himself so as not to upset anyone. Other young people wrestle with this tension of what to share and with whom. As young people pave their way into various social circles, they want to be seen in the best possible light (Brown, 1998; Williams & Gilovich, 2008).

Young people experience a tension when deciding between what to keep private and what to present to others, which may affect relations with the community. In the community and civic setting, young people must consider what others in the community will think of them and the opinions that they share, and whether they will be heard based on their identity. This is particularly difficult for young people, because adults may look at young people and make a quick judgment that young people are "too young" to have a concern about a specific issue. The burden then falls on young people to prove others wrong about these perceptions, putting them in a position to possibly struggle even further when deciding what to keep private and what to share with others. Presentation of the self has become digitally mediated, which has implications for considering how young people present their civic identities as well. Goffman (1959) argued that social life is a series of performances in which people project their identities to an audience of others. How one sees oneself fitting into and contributing to a group or larger society impacts how one presents the self to that group, and, consequently, the version of self that the group expects the person to be (Schlenker, 2012). Young people's values and belief systems are informed by these interactions and experiences with others. Chapter 4 will present the findings for the factors and contexts that shape young people's civic identity in today's world, and Chapter 5 will present how civic identity is experienced by young people in contemporary society.

REFERENCES

boyd, d. (2007a). Socializing Digitally. *Vodafone Receiver Magazine*, 18.

boyd, d. (2007b). Why Youth (Heart) Social Network Sites: The Role of Networked Publics in Teenage Social Life. In D. Buckingham (Ed.), *Youth, Identity, and Digital Media* (The John D. and Catherine T. MacArthur Foundation Series on Digital Media and Learning ed., pp. 119–142). Cambridge, MA: The MIT Press.

boyd, d. (2014). *It's Complicated: The Social Lives of Networked Teens.* New Haven, CT: Yale University Press.

Brown, J. D. (1998). *The Self.* New York: McGraw-Hill.

Côté, J. E., & Levine, C. G. (2002). *Identity Formation, Agency, and Culture: A Social Psychological Synthesis.* Mahwah, NJ: Lawrence Erlbaum Associates.

Davies, C., & Eynon, R. (2013). *Teenagers and Technology.* London: Routledge.

Davis, K., & Weinstein, E. (2017). Identity Development in the Digital Age: An Eriksonian Perspective. In M. F. Wright (Ed.), *Identity, Sexuality, and Relationships Among Emerging Adults in the Digital Age* (pp. 1–17). Hershey, PA: IGI Global.

Erikson, E. H. (1968). *Identity: Youth and Crisis.* New York: W.W. Norton & Company.

Flanagan, C. (2013). *Teenage Citizens: The Political Theories of the Young.* Cambridge, MA: Harvard University Press.

Gardner, H., & Davis, K. (2013). *The App Generation: How Today's Youth Navigate Identity, Intimacy, and Imagination in a Digital World.* New Haven, CT: Yale University Press.

Gil-Lopez, T., Shen, C., Benefield, G. A., Palomares, N. A., Kosinski, M., & Stillwell, D. (2018). One Size Fits All: Context Collapse, Self-Presentation Strategies and Language Styles on Facebook. *Journal of Computer-Mediated Communication, 23*(3), 127–145.

Goffman, E. (1959). *The Presentation of Self in Everyday Life.* Garden City, NY: Doubleday Anchor Books.

Goffman, E. (1978). The Presentation of Self to Others. In J. G. Manis & B. N. Meltzer (Eds.), *Symbolic Interaction: A Reader in Social Psychology* (3rd ed., pp. 234–244). London: Allyn and Bacon.

Hasebrink, U., & Paus-Hasebrink, I. (2007). Young People's Identity Construction and Media Use: Democratic Participation in Germany and Austria. In P. Dahlgren (Ed.), *Young Citizens and New Media: Learning for Democratic Participation* (pp. 81–101). New York, NY: Routledge.

Ito, M., Baumer, S., Bittani, M., boyd, d., Cody, R., Herr-Stephenson, B., et al. (2010). *Hanging Out, Messing Around, and Geeking Out: Kids Living and Learning with New Media.* Cambridge, MA: The MIT Press.

James, C. (2014). *Disconnected: Youth, New Media, and the Ethics Gap.* Cambridge, MA: The MIT Press.

Lenhart, A. (2015). *Teens, Technology and Friendships: Video Games, Social Media and Mobile Phones Play an Integral Role in How Teens Meet and Interact with Friends.* Pew Research Center.

Loader, B. D. (2007). Young Citizens in the Digital Age: Disaffected or Displaced? In B. D. Loader (Ed.), *Young Citizens in the Digital Age: Political Engagement, Young People and New Media* (pp. 1–17). London: Routledge.

Luyckx, K., Gandhi, A., Bijttebier, P., & Claes, L. (2015, March 29). Non-Suicidal Self-Injury in High School Students: Associations with Identity Processes and Statuses. *Journal of Adolescence, 41*, 76–85.

Marcia, J. (1980). Identity in Adolescence. In J. Adelson (Ed.), *Handbook of Adolescent Psychology* (pp. 109–137). New York: Wiley & Sons.

Paulhus, D. L., & Trapnell, P. D. (2008). Self-Presentation of Personality: An Agency-Communion Framework. In O. John, R. Robins, & L. Pervin (Eds.), *Handbook of Personality Psychology* (3rd ed., pp. 492–517). New York: Guilford Press.

Pew Research Center. (2016). *Parents, Teens and Digital Monitoring: Parents Monitor Their Teen's Digital Behavior in a Number of Ways, but Using Technical Means Like Parental Controls Is Less Common.* Pew Research Center.

Rui, J., & Stefanone, M. A. (2012). Strategic Self-Presentation Online: A Cross-Cultural Study. *Computers in Human Behavior, 29*, 110–118.

Rui, J., & Stefanone, M. A. (2013). Strategic Image Management Online. *Information, Communication & Society, 16*(8), 1286–1305.

Schlenker, B. (1986). Self-Identification: Toward an Integration of the Private and Public Self. In *Public Self and Private Self* (pp. 21–62). New York, NY: Springer.

Schlenker, B. (2012). Self-Presentation. In M. R. Leary & J. P. Tangney (Eds.), *Handbook of Self and Identity* (2nd ed., pp. 542–570). New York: Guilford Press.

Steers, M.-L. N., Wickham, R. E., & Acitelli, L. K. (2014). Seeing Everyone Else's Highlight Reels: How Facebook Usage Is Linked to Depressive Symptoms. *Journal of Social and Clinical Psychology, 33*(8), 701–731.

Steiner, P. (1993). On the Internet, Nobody Knows You're a Dog. *The New Yorker, 69*(20), p. 61.

Tapscott, D. (1998). *Growing Up Digital.* New York: McGraw-Hill.

Turkle, S. (1995). *Life on the Screen: Identity in the Age of the Internet.* New York, NY: Simon & Schuster.

Turkle, S. (2011). *Alone Together: Why We Expect More from Technology and Less from Each Other.* New York, NY: Basic Books.

Valentine, G., & Holloway, S. L. (2002). Cyberkids? Exploring Children's Identities and Social Networks in On-line and Off-line Worlds. *Annals of the Association of American Geographers, 92*(2), 302–319.

Williams, E. F., & Gilovich, T. (2008). Do People Really Believe They Are Above Average? *Journal of Experimental Social Psychology, 44*, 1121–1128.

CHAPTER 4

Civic Identity

Chapter 3 concluded that in contemporary society, young people have a broader audience to which they present themselves, and a diversity of stages from which to present these aspects of the self. Data from this study reveals that young people experience tension when deciding between which aspects of themselves to share with others and which to keep private, especially concerning political views. Elsie chose to keep her political views hidden from her social media accounts so that her nanny and rabbi would not see, and Martin is conscious to present himself as articulate so that the American public, who often perceives young black males as less capable, takes him and his views seriously. Conceptualizations of the self and one's values, and decisions about sharing these parts of the self with the world, can shed light on the understanding of individuals' positions within communities and societies, and how individuals can engage in them as citizens and community members, presenting themselves as group members, but also abiding by the expectations of others in the group. This process underlies the formation of civic identity. In this chapter I unpack the concept of civic identity and how its two components are understood and experienced by young people in contemporary society and what lived citizenship (Hall & Williamson, 1999) looks like for these young people.

While this study focuses on young people aged 14 through 17, it is important to recognize that children come to develop the ideas of citizenship, participation, and social organization before they have received

© The Author(s) 2020
J. K. Viola, *Young People's Civic Identity in the Digital Age*,
Palgrave Studies in Young People and Politics,
https://doi.org/10.1007/978-3-030-37405-1_4

formal schooling (Dias & Menezes, 2014), and reach the life stage that has been investigated in the present study. It is important to note this because as individuals mature, they have varying levels of understanding of what it means to be a citizen and a member of a community; the level of political understanding increases with age (Dias & Menezes, 2014). Gillman and Sofer (1978) found that maturity has more influence than individual factors (i.e., sex, social class, and intelligence) on young people's understanding of politics and political thought.

Bennett (2008) notes, "the entire question of civic engagement is confounded by how one chooses to define citizenship itself" (p. 8). To better understand how young people conceptualize their own civic identity and civic engagement, this chapter details the conceptualizations of citizenship as experienced and understood by young people. As noted in the literature review in Chapter 2, in this study, the notion of civic identity has been modified from Knefelkamp (2008) and Youniss and Yates (1997). Civic identity is a concept comprised of two parts:

1. a broader sense of how an individual develops and situates oneself and one's beliefs within a broader group of people,
   - and -
2. how that individual engages with others in the social, political, and economic structures within their society.

This chapter will be presented in two sections, each which illustrates a component of the civic identity definition, as experienced and expressed by the young people in this study. Section 4.1 will illustrate young people's conceptualizations of citizenship, which is the mechanism through which we can understand how young people situate themselves within society and the world around them. As one's understanding of citizenship "can provide the meaning for political action" (Loader, 2007, p. 5), this section will lead into Section 4.2, which will reveal how young people conceptualize civic engagement. With the context of citizenship and civic engagement for civic identity, Chapter 5 will later address the ways in which young people are engaging in the political world.

4.1   What Does It Mean to Be a Citizen?

Jones and Gaventa (2002) note that there is still more to learn about how individuals understand themselves as citizens, and Gillman and Sofer (1978) explain that political thought develops over time. There has been a lack of research in this area as it pertains to young people between the ages of 14 and 17 in the contemporary era. Understanding what young people mean by citizenship, and how they think about it, is an important component of civic identity and how young people might express that identity to others, both within and outside of their communities. How each person understands citizenship will impact how they perceive their ability to engage civically and effectively (Dias & Menezes, 2014), making citizenship an important concept to investigate prior to delving into how young people understand and experience civic engagement in today's political world, which can then inform civic education curriculum. This section will illustrate the ways in which young people define and experience citizenship.

While citizenship has been investigated in adults, the most recent study relevant to the population investigated in the study presented in this book is the Lister, Smith, Middleton, and Cox (2003) study on young people aged 16 through 23 years old. The patterns of citizenship conceptualizations that emerged from the study presented in this book reflect the five models of citizenship described by Lister et al. (2003). These principles of citizenship can be identified by people as young children, who further develop these principles in adolescence, when young people think more critically about civic and political participation, the right to vote, and community service (Dias & Menezes, 2014). The extent to which young people identified themselves as citizens in Lister et al.'s (2003) study mostly reflected social status developments: had they employment and paid tax, had they been involved in their communities or undertaken voluntary work; or had they voted? (p. 242). Similarly, the participants in the study presented in this book reflected on their own personal status and experiences in the community and in the United States when contemplating what citizenship meant to them, and deciding whether they felt like a citizen.

As the sections that follow will illustrate, technology plays a smaller role in young people's conceptualizations of citizenship than one might expect, given the ubiquitous use of technology in daily life. Young people did not relate their definitions of citizenship to extend to their practices and behavior online, which would fall under the concept of digital citizenship

(Hargittai, 2002; Lenhart et al., 2011; Seale & Dutton, 2012), but rather referred to citizenship as community or nation membership. As young people utilize social media as a primary source of information about current events, they were informed about the immigration debate and the anti-immigration sentiment that was disseminated through Twitter, especially through the Tweets made by then-presidential candidate Donald Trump. There has been an ongoing trend toward a personalization of politics (Mesch & Coleman, 2007), which the young people of this study exemplify. Being surrounded by this rhetoric prompted young people to consider citizenship in these very personal ways, related to their own family's history and the stories of their friends' immigration issues. As this is contemporary rhetoric that still exists in the United States and in other democracies, particularly in Europe, the five themes of citizenship that emerged from the data in this study could be experienced in other democracies in contemporary society.

The results presented here demonstrate that the conceptualization process of "citizenship" among young people is fluid (Lister et al., 2003, 2005), and the experiences that lead to these conceptualizations are digitally mediated. Young people understand citizenship in ways similar to the participants of Lister et al.'s (2003, 2005) work, but experience citizenship in different ways. For some, citizenship is the (1) emotional sense of belonging within a community. For others, citizenship has a (2) legal meaning, attached to various rights and privileges. Sometimes, (3) these emotional and legal meanings become intertwined. For others still, citizenship is a factor of one's (4) age and (5) active involvement in the community. Young people in this study understood citizenship as a function of one or more of these themes. The five sections that follow will present five themes of citizenship, as the 14–17 year old participants in this study understand and experience it in contemporary society.

4.1.1   *Citizenship as an Emotional Sense of Belonging*

The first theme of citizenship that participants in this study recognize is a sense of belonging and emotional connection that one feels as a member of a community. Many participants understood themselves as citizens through the theme of a sense of belonging, often referring to citizenship as being "part of" something: everyone is a citizen. This understanding of a sense of belonging has been observed in previous understandings of community membership throughout the 1960s through 1980s (Buss & Portnoy, 1967; McMillan & Chavis, 1986).

When I asked Imani, aged 14, about her understanding of citizenship, she seemed unsure of her answer, seeking confirmation that she had given the right definition for citizenship: "part of something?" Addie, aged 14, says citizenship is when "you're a part of a place." Analogously, Laura, aged 17, explains that citizenship is "being part of a larger community" even without "having a real factor in things." This feeling of belonging extends to all citizens, even if the legal rights and privileges are limited, as they often are for the young people in this study, as they are not yet old enough to vote. Aidan, aged 15, relates Laura's idea to the importance of being "recognized" and "included" by members of the community, and Zelda, aged 14, agrees. Being recognized and included also means understanding that "what you do does impact others," as Kali, aged 16, says. These young people situate themselves in a community around a physical place like a neighborhood or school, but this emotional sense of belonging to a community extends to people and areas that exist beyond these closer circles.

Martin, aged 15, likens citizenship to "community," as his aforementioned peers do, but Habibah, aged 16, explains that citizenship extends to a "bigger kind of community." For Habibah, this citizenship and community membership encompasses all of humanity, "Because… you're part of a community with people you've never even met before all around the world, just because they share something in similar, which is citizenship." Habibah explains that people all around the world are citizens, even if they are citizens of different places. Habibah compares the feeling of being a citizen to a common ground upon which people all around the world can stand. Citizens feel a sense of emotional connection to each other, and as Keegan, aged 18, says, being able to feel "the pain of the community" demonstrates citizenship—and kinship—within that community. Similarly, Robert, aged 16, says that citizenship goes beyond community "to represent" that community to others on the outside of that community. This idea translates into patriotism, expressed by Nora, aged 15, as she views citizenship as having "pride in [one's] country." Extending an emotional connection to people around the world demonstrates that a sense of belonging and feeling of being understood does not always have to be restricted to a physical place.

Kaitlyn, aged 16, believes that people are citizens wherever their "home is." This belief that citizenship is a sense of belonging to a group *and* a place is central to how Selah and Gwen, both aged 15, expand this definition of feeling a "part of" something. Selah was born in the United States, giving her legal status of citizenship that will be discussed in the next section, but she is also "from Bangladesh." Selah quietly stated that she feels like a citizen because "I've lived here for a very long time, and I just feel like I belong." Selah visited Bangladesh once at age seven, and spent a year there to learn the language. It is interesting that Selah says she is *from* Bangladesh, even though she is a United States citizen and has lived in the United States for all of her life. Young people today have multiple cultural identities, and "first and second generation immigrants may have less difficulty in identifying with both their countries of birth and those of cultural heritage" (Loader, 2007, p. 6). Similarly, Joelle, also aged 15, asserts, "If you have lived here long enough, you don't exactly have to be born here. If you live here and you can adapt to your surroundings, I think that's basically a citizen." Joelle said that her parents are immigrants to the United States, and have applied for United States citizenship. Her personal family situation has influenced her understanding of what it means to be a citizen—or, what it *should* mean to be a citizen. Young people feel this way because they have spent enough time in their communities and in school that they feel a strong connection and sense of belonging where they are currently living. Young people have been accepted by their community, and feel the government should accept them as well. At the time of data collection and at the time of writing still, young people are surrounded by anti-immigration rhetoric on social media—particularly through Tweets by Donald Trump and his supporters (Osler & Starkey, 2018). This anti-immigrant sentiment seems to have deepened these young people's sense that they have an emotional connection and sense of belonging to the United States, even if they are immigrants themselves or have an immigrant background.

4.1.2   *Citizenship as a Legal Status*

As Joelle alluded, some young people understand citizenship through its legal meaning. Nadia, aged 16, defines citizenship as "to be a part of something, legally," and Stephen, aged 14, says that citizenship means "being able to say that you live in a country or place legally." This legal meaning is attached to various rights and privileges, including commonly recognized "civic duties" such as voting and jury duty. In the United States, the model of citizenship as a legal status can be traced back to the fight to abolish slavery (Ansley, 2005), particularly after the landmark Dred Scot decision by the Supreme Court acknowledged that legally, blacks could not be United States citizens (*Dred Scott v. John F.A. Sandford*, 1856). While much has changed in the United States in the last 170 years, the concept of citizenship as a legal status has not, as evidenced by participants in this study.

Most participants who comprehend citizenship as a legal concept begin with the understanding that Camille, aged 15, has: a group of people who "live under the same government." Sean, aged 15, elaborates that this includes "understanding the U.S. politics system. And knowing what an actual citizen, like... the rules of being a citizen are." Madeline, aged 17, says it is important for citizens to "know the basic principles of what the community believes." Both Sean and Madeline allude to knowing the rules of the social contract (Lister et al., 2003).

Participants understand the government's role in determining who is a citizen, particularly because of their knowledge about the law in the United States Code that dictates a person born in the United States or to United States citizen parents are automatically granted United States citizenship (8 U.S.C. §1401). Bethany, aged 14, explained that she asked her parents when she was "little, and they told me that I was born here so I am a citizen." Hannah, aged 16, understands citizenship in the same way, and identifies as "a citizen of the United States because I was born here. And I feel like if you're a citizen it's somewhere you've known for your whole life." Participants commonly related their citizenship to their country of birth or long-term residency, which has been found in other studies as well (Lister et al., 2003, 2005).

Kevin, aged 15, Maisie, aged 14, and Peter, aged 17, relate their understanding of citizenship as a legal status to the wider societal and political debate about the status of immigration in the United States. Kevin understands citizenship as "where you were born, that's where you've been raised, that's where you should be. And... sometimes, it doesn't always dictate that's where you should be. Because I know a lot of immigrants move here because that's not where they want to be. I feel like citizenship really just shows where you're from." Kevin had been deeply affected by the information he consumed on social media and in traditional news media regarding Donald Trump's position on immigration. Kevin shares that Donald Trump "put a new meaning to citizenship" because Donald Trump takes immigration "very seriously, like building a wall on the Mexican border, not allowing Muslims into the country. He uses all of that to try to stop immigration, which he will try to do [as president]." At the time of our interview, in spring 2016, Donald Trump had not yet been elected President of the United States. At the time of writing, Donald Trump and his government twice attempted to ban travelers from Muslim-majority countries from entering the United States, and the contentious political and public debate surrounding a border wall with Mexico remains ongoing. Kevin also shared that his understanding of citizenship was "really shaped" by his United States History class. Kevin marveled at the fact that "a lot of people, back in the 1800s and 1900s, if you were born here, then yeah, you're a U.S. citizen, but back in the day, like women and um, African Americans, did not have a lot of rights. So that showed that … citizenship is having the rights in a country." Kevin, at age 15, demonstrates a nuanced and thoughtful understanding of the legal meaning and implications of citizenship within the United States, reflecting on the history of the citizenship and immigration debate and relating it to the contemporary debate on the issue.

Maisie, aged 14, further illustrated the nuances of the immigration debate in public discourse, particularly around the exclusivity of citizenship. "If you're born here, that's automatic citizenship, but that's not the only way to get citizenship. You can move here from another country… I don't like the process, but you can become a citizen. I think the idea of citizenship is practical, but also kind of exclusive." Maisie notes that keeping track of who is in the country legally is "practical" for the government to know so that they can "help them and do what they need you to do for them. But pride and exclusion comes with that, because then… you take the label of 'citizen' and people put all kinds of meanings into it that target other people who aren't citizens, and all of this controversy." Maisie acknowledges that citizenship based on legal status is "exclusive"—it literally excludes many people who have been in the country their entire lives, even if they were brought to the country as infants. It is also exclusive in the sense that is it an elite club—United States citizenship is highly sought-after and coveted by many immigrants. Scholars also note the exclusivity of citizenship, and often describe it as a "prize worth having" (Frazer, 2008, p. 285). Peter, aged 17, illustrates the great lengths through which some of his friends' families have gone through in order to gain this prize. Peter's friends' "parents came here… they had to do a long process to become an American citizen. And it's not just being involved, but like… it's a lot of hard work to be an American citizen." Peter alludes to the citizenship test, and the process of becoming a citizen that Maisie decidedly labeled as "exclusive."

4.1.3 Citizenship as a Legal Right to Belong

Several participants view citizenship through a combination of the emotional and legal meanings described in the previous two sections. For Veronica, aged 15, citizenship means "to fit in." While Veronica began to describe citizenship with this sense of belonging stance, she continued, "a lot of the time you're not actually a citizen until you actually get your citizenship. Which has to do with fitting in, in a way." Veronica explains that one is "a member of society if you fit into the expectations, which at the same time could be a citizen. People have to fit into certain rules; there is a way that people are expected to act, and at the same time, there are certain things that you can go around to find loopholes in where you can be yourself and do certain things that you want to do, too." Veronica's understanding of citizenship combines this legal sense of citizenship through the social contract with the importance of feeling like one "fits in" emotionally.

This sense of belonging, and feeling of emotional connection to a place, extends beyond feeling concerned that you fit the norms and expectations of the society and community. Tanesha, aged 16, stresses, "if you identify with a place and you feel like it's your home," then one is a citizen. Tanesha shared that her Advanced Placement U.S. History class has shaped this view of citizenship. She is "a citizen of... many things, depend[ing] on what group I'm talking about. People take it in different... tenses. Some people say they're not a citizen, but they could be, technically. But they say they're not because they have more pride in their actual homeland country, rather than America." At first, I thought Tanesha understood citizenship as pride in one's country. She continued, "If you identify with a place and you feel like it's your home, and that you have every right to be there, it should be citizenship. Not because you were born in a country or naturalized." In Tanesha's mind, citizenship is for anyone who feels a sense of belonging to a particular place, but also as a "right" to be there— "it is a mental thing, not a property thing." Despite this view, Tanesha said that she has never had an experience in which she felt like a citizen.

As Osler and Starkey (2006) note, citizenship goes beyond legal status: it is also a "sense of belonging" (p. 441). Gwen, aged 18, explains that "where your heart belongs" and "if you have the papers to show it" dictates where you are a citizen. Gwen's heart is "where I was born, so I consider myself a Cameroonian citizen...because I lived in Cameroon for eight years, and it's not easy to let that go, even if I was still a kid. I still remember the roads to my house, it's just like the experiences that you faced, and they shape where you feel like you're a citizen." Gwen alludes to the documentation necessary to prove one's legal citizenship, but focuses on the emotional component of citizenship by discussing that her heart is still in her childhood home country of Cameroon. Gwen is able to recall vivid images of Cameroon, making Gwen a Cameroonian citizen by Tanesha's definition of citizenship.

While Gwen feels she is still a citizen of Cameroon, even though she has been raised in the United States, Sawyer, aged 15, describes the opposite of this sentiment. For him, citizenship extends beyond being born in a place, and extends to "living and being raised here." There is a difference between being *born* in the United Sates and being *raised* in the United States. The experiences of growing up in a country and adopting the way of life and understanding are emotional investments, and go beyond the legal conditions of citizenship. The tension between these emotional and legal concepts of citizenship can be best illustrated by the personal experiences of 16-year-old Bibiana. When I first asked Bibiana what citizenship means to her, she said, "Nothing." After a moment, Bibiana clarified,

> Well... not really nothing. But ... because I was born in the D.R. [Dominican Republic], I know that I wasn't born a citizen here [in the United States]. So... I guess it doesn't really mean anything to me because I came here at a really young age. I've... grown up in America. But at the same time, I'm not considered a citizen. I guess it's more of like a legal thing. Like a paperwork thing. That's why I feel like it doesn't really mean anything because it's just paperwork.

Loader (2007) states, "citizenship rights and obligations are less dependent upon membership of a particular territorial and legal society" (p. 6), but overall there is a blurry line between the emotional sense of belonging and the legal status that evokes citizenship. Bibiana, aged 16, exemplifies this tension. Loader (2007) implies that sense of belonging is more important, but Bibiana highlights the importance of the legality to have any "real say" in things. While Bibiana is not a legal citizen, she does *feel* like one, even though she does not have any of the rights and privileges—Loader's (2007) "obligations." Bibiana highlights the complexity of growing up as an immigrant in the United States. She has spent the majority of her life in the United States, attending school and participating in her community, as her United States citizen peers have done. Reconciling how she can be "Americanized" because she has lived in the United States for all of her life and still not be a citizen is complex, and joins the elements of not being *born* in the United States with the significance of *growing up* in the United States. It frustrates Bibiana that she does not have the same rights and privileges of her peers, who, she claims, may not even know as much about politics or American society as she does. For Bibiana, the emphasis on legality, of lawful citizenship, is important. The word "citizen" triggers the idea of "paperwork." Yet, when she describes what it means to be an active citizen, citizenship does not reflect legality. Rather, it refers to a person who is "involved in a lot of things … in regards to what's happening around your neighborhood." Bibiana very clearly feels a sense of belonging in her community, and alludes to her ability to contribute and give back. Bibiana believes that an active citizen can be anyone, regardless of legal status—presumably because she wishes for herself that she had the same rights and privileges as her American-born peers.

At the time of these interviews, and even still at the time of writing, immigration policy in the United States pervades public discourse. During the 2016 presidential election campaign, Joseph, a 16-year-old Hispanic male, reminded his Hispanic friend that this friend would get deported if Donald Trump were to win the election and follow through on campaign promises, which were communicated through Donald Trump's Tweets and televised debate responses. Joseph shared a story about this friend (who he then referred to as his "associate" by means of distancing himself from his friend's support of Donald Trump). Joseph asked his friend why he supported Trump, and his friend replied, "Because [Trump] is gonna send all the Spanish people out." Joseph reminded his friend, "That includes you." Joseph was surprised that his friend did not believe that the policy would affect his own immigrant family, perhaps not making the distinction between being *born* in the United States and *growing up* in the United States, as Bibiana had. Joseph's understanding of citizenship as a combined emotional and legal status made him, like Kevin, more aware of the implications of the current immigration debate on his and his friends' daily lives as young people.

4.1.4   Citizenship as Defined by Age

Sometimes, citizenship can be understood as limited to people of a certain age. The participants in this study were very much dependent on others for their financial security, but their experience of citizenship as it relates to their age was not solely based on financial and economic factors, as it was for the participants in the Lister et al. (2003) study. Rather, the young people in this study wrestled with age as a factor that could potentially limit their role as citizens because they are not yet considered adults by the law and society. Kevin, aged 15, puts it simply: "I'm still a minor, I'm not an active citizen yet."

Young people have this perception of citizenship as restricted by age because they have grown up in a democratic society that withholds certain rights and privileges until individuals reach age 18. The age of 18 is the point in life when most democratic cultures accept young people as "adults" and grant them full legal rights for political participation (Finlay, Wray-Lake, & Flanagan, 2010; Stepick, Stepick, & Labissiere, 2008). Young people also understand the level of responsibility that comes along with some of these rights. Jillian, aged 15, shares that citizenship applies to people of a "certain level" of society: "if you're a political leader, you have a bigger job to do than a fifteen year old." Jillian discloses examples of responsibilities that come with adulthood: "legally drink, drive, have kids. There's more pressure on adults, and older teenagers—young adults. Because you can still make mistakes and not have it affect you so much when you're [younger]. But once you get to like, 16 and 17... 19 ... you're talking about college, voting, drinking, all of that stuff that could affect your life." Relatedly, Imani alludes to the responsibilities that individuals also have with their digital presence, because underage drinking is illegal, Imani cautions against teenagers posting pictures of "doing drugs or drinking."

Jillian explains that responsibility for being a citizen is a duty that comes with adulthood. Paying taxes is a responsibility that many participants called to mind. Joseph, aged 16, perceives citizenship in a similar manner to Jillian, and thinks of citizenship as "paying taxes, basically. So like, for grown-ups. Not teenagers like me....But people that pay taxes and buy houses. Because buying a house would mean less people in the streets, basically. And that's basically ... a working citizen." Joseph illustrates citizenship that only "adults" can take part in, because adults have the financial privilege and means to do so. Joseph suggests his lower socioeconomic status when he discusses how purchasing houses would get people out of living "in the streets," adding another layer of complexity to this definition of citizenship. Perhaps Joseph does not believe that people from his neighborhood will be citizens because of the economic hardships they face, as he alluded. Joseph is not wrong in his perception that economic security contributes to citizenship, as prior research demonstrates higher levels of engagement among those of higher socioeconomic standing (Verba, Schlozman, & Brady, 1995).

Naomi, aged 16, takes issue with these aforementioned ideas that citizenship is restricted to adults, and says, "I don't think that just because I am not 18 doesn't mean I'm not a citizen." I asked Naomi to elaborate about what it means be a citizen as a young person. For Naomi, "It means taking responsibility for yourself and how you treat your community and the people around you... in your town, and who you live with, and the town itself and making sure you're upholding what you should be doing, not doing bad things." Rather than citizenship being defined by age, citizenship is defined by responsibility—for some, like Joseph, that means paying taxes. For others, like Naomi, that means being socially responsible and being aware of how your actions may impact others. This final element of citizenship that Naomi discussed—the responsibility for one's actions—introduces the final theme of citizenship: being actively involved in one's community.

4.1.5 Citizenship as Active Involvement in the Community

Ava, aged 16, asserts, "I don't think age has anything to do with [citizenship]. Because you see such young people making an impact, and I think that's most people's goals, is to make an impact in some way." Ava stresses that young people are citizens by making an impact, by being involved in their communities. Thirteen other participants in this study viewed citizenship as an element of active involvement in community and society, similar to the constructive social participation model described by Lister et al. (2003).

It is worth noting that the participants who understand citizenship to mean active involvement in the community are young people who experienced education or afterschool programming that is strongly focused on community involvement. Some of these participants attended a private, Catholic high school, whose mission statement and curriculum emphasizes the importance of serving others. Previous research points to religious commitments as contributors to civic participation (Livingstone, Couldry, & Markham, 2007). Other participants were recruited from an after school academic and athletic program, which focuses on character development and volunteerism in addition to academic and athletic success. One student participates in the United States' largest student-run organization focused on civic engagement and community involvement. These young people have likely been influenced by the rhetoric of their educational and social environment, and understand the meaning of citizenship as it relates to their own experiences.

In particular, Jaden, Damon, and Jane, all aged 14, described citizenship as "helping." Aileen and Carly, aged 15, shared that "involvement" was key to citizenship. Mira, aged 15, also explained that part of citizenship is "helping the country thrive." Part of contributing to a "thriving" country is "wanting to participate," as Jackie, aged 16, says. This intrinsic motivation can drive young people to "keep our environment better for not only for us, but for others," according to Grace, aged 16. Sachi, aged 17, describes several ways in which young people can improve the environment, and "make a difference" in the community. He shares, "cleaning the park will help your community because you're making the park nicer to go and visit. Or, you're... helping a candidate campaign for city council or something. So... you go door-knocking."

Young people also recognized that key to participation and involvement is awareness of what is "going on" in the community, as Carol, aged 17, puts it. Kenai, aged 14, says that although he does not pay attention to current affairs often, he believes citizens "pay attention to what's happening around you. Citizenship is not always being there a certain amount of time, it can just be paying attention or caring about the community or what's around you." Sachi introduces the idea of canvassing for local political candidates as a way to be involved and demonstrate one's care for the community and its future, and Elsie, also aged 17, concurs, and considers a citizen as someone who is "concerned about legal issues, political issues." This awareness can lead to young people "voicing [our] opinions, and thinking there's something that can change," Carol says. Allie, aged 15, expressed this element of voice, who believes "you can be part of something, but if you don't say what you feel or speak your voice, I don't think you're a citizen." For Allie, using one's voice is a crucial aspect of citizenship, a concept that will be addressed in Chapter 5. Section 4.2 will outline civic engagement, and what it means to be an active citizen. The young people in this study understand and experience civic engagement in many different ways, which are often informed by how they conceptualize citizenship.

4.2 WHAT DOES IT MEAN TO BE CIVICALLY ENGAGED?

The second component of civic identity refers to an individual's manner of engaging in their community or society. The findings presented in this section provide a deeper understanding of how young people conceptualize civic engagement in their own lives, which will contribute to a better understanding of young people's civic identity in practice. To prompt participants to think about civic engagement, I asked them what civic engagement meant to them. Despite the longstanding tradition of education for democratic citizenship in the United States, it was not unusual for the group of young people in this study to have not formally heard the term "civic engagement" prior to my interview with them, but it was also not difficult for them to describe the meaning of civic engagement in their own terms. Bibiana, aged 16, told me she had never heard the word "civic," but she deduced that civic engagement includes community involvement, and also believes civic engagement involves "knowing what's going on in the world, or in your area." Similarly, Naomi, also 16 years old, agreed: "Community service, I think... and then like... paying attention to what's going on, really. You don't have to be in depthly [sic] aware of everything that's happening in your town, but having a general knowledge of what's going on and what the issues are and how you could help."

The role of a citizen in a democratic society is to engage politically (Loader, 2007), but young people in this study demonstrate that civic engagement goes beyond, and in tandem with, political participation. For young people today, civic engagement largely includes community service, or volunteerism, which other studies have demonstrated can promote civic development in adolescence and lead to political participation later in life (Hart & Kirshner, 2009). Volunteering as a young person correlates with turning out to vote as an adult, as does young people's involvement in nonpolitical organizations—such as religious institutions, extracurricular clubs, and after school sports (McFarland & Thomas, 2006; Smith, 1999; Youniss & Yates, 1997). Involvement in these activities enables young people to develop civic skills, such as giving speeches or organizing meetings that they can apply to political causes later on (Verba et al., 1995). Moreover, what is often considered to be traditional ways of engaging in politics may not be relevant to young people. They are engaged, but in the ways that are accessible to them, and the ways that matter to them. Young people understand civic engagement at both a general level and a personal level, and as a function of the ways in which they understand citizenship. Young people offer examples of the general level of civic engagement as improving the community, interacting with others, and participating in the community democratically and politically.

The citizenship themes presented in Section 4.1 inform the illustrations that will come throughout Section 4.2. Young people who view citizenship as an emotional sense of belonging tend to think of civic engagement as improving the community or interacting with others. It is their sense of belonging that they feel within their community that makes them feel like they matter, and therefore want to give back to their immediate communities. Those with a view of citizenship as a legal status tend to think of civic engagement as democratic participation, which includes voting, petitioning, and canvassing for candidates for public office. Young people who believe that citizenship involves certain rights and privileges may feel more of a duty to exercise those rights and privileges by engaging in democratic participation. For those who understand citizenship as a combination of a sense of belonging and legal status view civic engagement as interacting with others and sharing one's voice and opinion. Those who think citizenship is age-defined tend to view civic engagement as improving the community through volunteerism, which includes community improvement activities that can be done at any and all ages. Finally, those who perceive citizenship as active involvement are inclined to think of civic engagement as a way to improve the community, and interact with others. This is a very active way of showing civic engagement.

The following sections present examples of the participants' own civic engagement activities, using the themes that outline how young people understand civic engagement: improving the community, interacting with others, and participating in the community democratically. In each of these understandings and experiences of civic engagement, technology has been used as a tool (Bennett, 2008; Livingstone et al., 2007; Montgomery, 2008). In contemporary society, we should now expect young people to organize their engagement activities around issues they truly care about (Earl & Schussman, 2008), and these acts of engagement vary (Kahne, Middaugh, & Allen, 2014).

4.2.1   Improving the Community

An overwhelming majority of participants—29 out of 46 participants—understood the general meaning of civic engagement to include some manner of improving the community. This theme is the foundation of Raynes-Goldie and Walker's (2008) definition of civic engagement, presented in Chapters 1 and 2. Young people are concerned with benefiting others and the common good of the community, which is consistent with civic identity development among young people (McLeod, 2000).

Veronica, aged 15, believes "community is what builds your citizenship." The following section illustrates that although young people commonly understood civic engagement to mean community improvement, the ways in which young people view and experience community improvement varies considerably, from participation in fundraising events, to actions to protect the environment, to volunteering their time for community service. What often draws young people into improving their community is the social connection that comes with it, especially participating in these activities with friends.

Participation in Fundraising Events
Young people view fundraising as a means of improving their communities. Fundraising appeals to young people because it is a way to share support for a cause, or raise awareness about a particular issue. Fundraising campaigns are popular within American high schools, and often support foundations or charities related to medical research for specific diseases. Events such as Relay for Life, a fundraiser for the American Cancer Society, draw in classmates and community members to raise funds throughout the year. Nora, aged 15, donates to the Jimmy Fund, which raises money to support cancer care and research at the Dana-Farber Cancer Institute in Boston, Massachusetts, and Bibiana, aged 16, has participated in the Walk for Diabetes. Ava, aged 16, participates in local fundraisers for breast cancer research. Ava presents herself to others as an altruistic person, and cites that her personal community instilled in her the desire to help others. Ava says, "all people from [town] support… like if someone has breast cancer who is going through treatment, then they'll help them, they'll help other people." Similarly, Zelda, aged 14, saw a friend post on Facebook that her mother had beaten breast cancer. Zelda was "inspired" by that social media post to participate in a walk with her friends to raise awareness for breast cancer. Scholars have noted that civic engagement that is personally

relevant is more motivating (Serriere, 2014), which may explain why Ava and Zelda have been motivated to participate in these fundraising events.

While Ava and Zelda have had personal experiences that led them to support breast cancer research, others learn about fundraising events through other people, or through social media. Jane, aged 14, participated in the ALS Ice Bucket Challenge in the summer of 2014. The ALS Ice Bucket Challenge was a fundraising campaign that involved the filming of individuals pouring a bucket of ice water over their head, either by another person or on their own, and sharing the video on social media platforms to promote awareness of the disease amyotrophic lateral sclerosis (ALS).[1] Participants were encouraged to make a donation to the ALS Association and nominate several other family members and friends to complete the challenge. Jane completed this challenge after discovering it on Instagram. The fundraising campaign went viral on social media, particularly on Instagram and Facebook—even celebrities were filmed pouring buckets of ice water on their heads before nominating other famous friends to complete the challenge. Part of what made this fundraiser so effective was its social nature: participants enjoyed being nominated to complete the challenge and encourage their other friends to become involved.[2]

Social networking sites continue to use this viral fundraising strategy. Carly, aged 16, notes "on Facebook I usually Like the cancer fundraisers or the walk, and you can volunteer." Not only do Facebook and other social networking websites spread awareness of fundraising events, but today, Facebook also makes it possible to link one's personal profile to a nonprofit or personal cause, and raise money for that cause (Facebook, 2018). As Facebook notifies friend networks about one's birthday, it is becoming increasingly popular for people to use their birthday as a campaign to raise awareness and funds for a specific cause that they care about. It is as simple as clicking the "donate your birthday" link to create a Facebook fundraiser for any cause or charity (Veith, 2017). Friends who see the post can choose to donate, and can even Share the fundraising page to their own profile to expand the awareness for the fundraiser to

[1] This campaign reinvigorated the research community studying ALS, and led to the discovery of a new gene tied to the disease (Rogers, 2016).
[2] In summer 2018, a campaign based on the Ice Bucket Challenge model was launched by the United Nations to encourage people to pledge to reduce the waste and environmental harm caused by single use plastic (Chow, 2018).

their own social network, and encourage their social network to donate to their friend's cause. Young people who wish to present themselves to others as charitable can choose to post these fundraisers to their Facebook profile, and advertise to others that they have contributed to fundraisers through Facebook. Evidently, social media impacted how young people think about and become involved in this sub-theme of civic engagement.

Environmental Protection
In an era in which climate change is a dominant social issue, young people also recognize that improving their community can include activities and actions that preserve and protect the natural environment. Kali, aged 16, participates in street cleaning in her neighborhood every year. She works with others to "clean up and pick up trash and do recycling and plant flowers in beds and stuff like that. And that is in itself, humbling, you know, taking care of your own environment." Similarly, Addie, aged 14, collects trash and makes sure she recycles. Young people can be motivated to engage in community service projects if their friends are participating, too (Flanagan, 2013). Zelda, aged 14, participates in an annual event to pick up rubbish along the Charles River, an activity that Zelda finds enjoyable because it is something that she can do with her friends. This experience illustrates what Goffman (1959, 1978) and Schlenker (2012) described in their theories of identity: one presents the self in the way they wish to be perceived by others. Zelda demonstrates to her friends that she values her local environment, and presents herself as such. In turn, her friends wish to be seen in the same light, and participate in these cleanup days. The schools and after school programs from which participants in this study were recruited promote the community cleanup initiatives that Kali, Addie, and Zelda mentioned.

While choosing lifestyles and activities that promote waste reduction and keep the immediate environment free from litter, environmental protection on a larger scale includes talking about environmental issues with others. Mira, aged 15, attends climate rallies[3] because she believes it is important to "stand up for the fight that I want climate change to stop"

[3] This type of civic engagement has existed as long ago as the early nineteenth century (Wordsworth, 1835), and the participants of this study discussed this more than two years before Greta Thunberg's school strike for climate, which has gained millions of supporters and strikers—including young people and adults—worldwide since autumn 2018 (Singh, Oliver, Siddique, & Zhou, 2019).

and that her participation in these rallies will improve her community. Kali, Addie, Zelda, and Mira all demonstrate that youth care about issues of public concern, like civil rights and environmental concerns (Mesch & Coleman, 2007). Within this theme of environmental protection, technology did not play a role in how young people in this study were conceiving of this idea or participating in this form of civic engagement.

Volunteerism

Young people also believe it is important to serve their community by giving their time to individuals, or to more specific communities. In most cases, young people learn about volunteer opportunities through their school, and various clubs and organizations in which they are involved, especially those organizations that are oriented toward community service. Some community service is geared toward young people's immediate community. For example, Jillian, aged 15, enjoys volunteering at her dance studio and walking dogs in her neighborhood, and Camille, also aged 15, helps the elderly in her neighborhood. In the winter, especially, Camille will "shovel snow because the elderly can't do it for themselves."

More broadly, young people seek opportunities to help those in their larger cities or towns. Selah, aged 15, volunteers at homeless shelters. Through her school, she is an active member of "Club Four, in which you volunteer at homeless shelters. You are able to volunteer or you can make the meal plan and there's a lot of different people at the homeless shelter, and talking to them really just brings a new perspective into me." Selah highlights the positive effect that her contribution to the homeless shelter has on her: the feeling of connecting to others. Carol, aged 17, shared that she was a part of a program that challenged students to devise a way to improve the community. Her group recognized that in their neighborhood, there are "a lot of abandoned buildings," and they thought, "we can use those abandoned buildings, make them for people to get tutored and stuff like that." In her community, "there's a lot of kids on the streets. So we need to find a way to get them off the streets." Carol and her peers believed that spending the time to devise this proposal to repurpose the abandoned buildings for education and tutoring would be a way to meet their goal and improve the community overall. As the experiences of the participants suggest, volunteerism often takes place in a face-to-face environment. As such, technology did not mediate this sub-theme of civic engagement in the same way it had with participation in fundraising events.

4.2.2   Interacting with Others

A smaller number of participants viewed civic engagement as something that could be done through interaction with others, namely, sharing opinions and experiences. For many young people, these sorts of interactions can occur at any point in the day, often through technology and social media. Grace, aged 16, believes that sharing experiences with others and learning from other's experiences is a way of improving the community: "Even the way we... post something on Facebook or Instagram, it's kind of a way of showing my life or my experience with others. Maybe others saw your post... they will know what you thought and maybe your thought will convert their opinion about these things." Grace acknowledges that people post different things on social media—photos, stories, news articles—and that social media can be a way for people to learn about others and their beliefs through these different Shared posts. Laura, aged 17, agrees, "publicly posting" her opinion on social media is a way for her to be civically engaged, and a way for her to present herself to others by sharing her political views with others.

Allie, aged 16, believes that voicing your opinions can improve the community: "you have to be able to say what you think, and not be silent." Veronica, aged 15, would agree. She believes it is important to "give input" and interact with others to improve the community by sharing ideas. Camille, aged 15, believes that it's possible to share your opinion "through people, or through social media, I guess. By spreading the message, others will see it." As Camille alludes, taking concerns to social media can range from posting political thoughts, to sharing news articles about current political and social issues, to "cyberprotesting," which reflects the concerns of young citizens (Loader, 2007, p. 10).

In addition to sharing political news articles online, Elsie, aged 17, participates in the Junior State of America, the largest student-run organization in the United States. Through this organization, Elsie finds it possible to "have discourse with people. It's very important to me to find people who have different views than me and try to discuss things with them." The Junior State of America brings secondary school students together at conventions throughout the academic year to discuss salient current events and political issues. During the school year, individual school chapters of the organization provide students with the opportunity to learn and engage in parliamentary style debate to prepare them for discussions at these larger conventions. Elsie has been a part of this program throughout her secondary school years, and has found that it connects her to people who hold different views from hers, and empowers her to learn from others by discussing political and social issues.

4.2.3   Political Participation

The final way in which young people understand civic engagement is political participation, particularly through voting and protesting. For participants who define civic engagement in this way, many of them acknowledged the limitations of their age on their ability to become civically engaged in this manner. Imani, aged 14, believes that young people's "priorities are different" because "most of my friends can't vote and neither can I. But maybe if I was able to, then I would be more involved in it because I'd want to know who I'm voting for and why I'm voting for them if I agree with what they are saying." Imani suggests that she will follow politics more and become civically engaged by voting when she gets closer to voting age. Kevin, aged 15, agrees, and does not participate in politics yet because "I still have a lot of things to learn, I still have a lot of things to try to do before I can really like, affect other people."

Stephen, aged 14, has wanted to participate politically, but shared that he is not able to "do any of that stuff, considering most of those you have to be like, over 18 to do… But it feels good to be able to get my own point of view out there. As a kid, I just have to let all the adults make the choices for me, instead of my own views getting out there." Stephen struggles to find his voice and share his voice with others, and believes that he must let adults make decisions for him. Stephen says that theoretically, for his voice to be heard, he would "need supporters and people who understand my view to be behind me." In contemporary society, the supporters that Stephen alludes to could be Followers on social media, friends from school, family members, and teachers.

Stephen yearns for his voice to "count," and longs for the day that he can vote. Sometimes, the closest young people come to voting before they reach age 18 is by discussing elections with adults in their lives who are able to vote, and consider young people's views when they decide who to vote for. Bethany, aged 14, helped her mother, who is not fluent in English, make an informed decision about voting in an election. Bethany shared that she completed her high school "Civics course last year, so, I had to do research; I understood what was being taught to me, so I told my mom … because she had to vote, she wanted to vote, and she had no idea. So, told her the standings of each candidate and I kind of helped like, told her what they were gonna do. So then she could make a decision." Civics courses do indeed enhance civic knowledge (Niemi & Junn, 1998), and Bethany used this knowledge to help educate her mother about the candidates that she could choose to vote for. Hannah, aged 16, and Mira, aged 15, also discussed influencing their parents to vote in a certain way that would reflect their own views. These young people's actions also confirm results by Mesch and Coleman (2007), who have found that young people have tried to influence the voting behavior of others as a means of exercising their own voice.

Yet, while Stephen felt disempowered, Maisie, aged 14, had the opportunity to participate in her town's participatory budget vote, wherein "anybody over the age of twelve can vote to decide what the budget this year is going to be focused on." Maisie discussed several options that the city budget could be allocated towards, including "making more bike lanes, or improving stuff in the youth centers." Kenai, also 14 years old, participated in a similar initiative at his school. He described it as, "a ballot that they give out in schools, it's like a green ballot, and you get to vote what… where you want a million dollars to go. Like what projects you'd want it to go to. I forgot what it's called. But you can vote for like, outside wireless connections, more green space, stuff like that." Maisie's vote impacted her town, and Kenai's vote impacted his school.

Participation in formal democratic institutions through procedures, such as voting, has been criticized for not yielding the increased sense of self-efficacy that young people need in order to become civically engaged in the future (Loader, 2007). Age restrictions are codified in laws, making voting limited to individuals over age 18 (Camino & Zeldin, 2002), yet there are other ways in which young people can participate democratically without voting, such as protesting. Jaden, aged 14, asserts, "if you don't like something, protest, take a stand." That is exactly what Sachi, aged 17, has done since childhood. Sachi describes his personal value that it is important to stand up for one's beliefs. When Sachi was six or seven years old, he participated in rallies and protests with his parents to try to keep his elementary school from closing: "We'd go and camp in the square at night just to show that we wanted it open. All the rallies and like, people coming together… I think that showed a lot of strength." As a result, he says he is the type of person who will fight for what he believes in. Sachi's interest in politics began through participating in these types of rallies, and his upbringing. His mother is a political science teacher, and Sachi explains she "helped me guide my path." As Sachi described his own actions, he believes that actions to show civic engagement include going to a protest, helping strangers, and being a "good Samaritan." Sachi himself considered himself to be civically engaged when he was younger and had more time, but now he tries to get involved in church and his after school sports program.

Young Activists at Work: The Case of School Walkouts
Sachi's childhood protest experience in a neighboring town to Boston preluded a contemporary protest in Boston. The city faced a proposed cut to the school district's budget, and the young people affected by this policy harbored complex thoughts regarding the most appropriate course of action to protest the budget cuts. Robert, aged 16, understood the budget cuts as "they're trying to take, I don't even remember how much, but it was like millions out of the school budget to give it to private schools to fund them." In protest of the budget cuts, Robert shares:

> A lot of schools will have walkouts. So you have a certain time to just get up, get out of school, go meet at Faneuil Hall or something. And … a lot of people don't go to that. It shows, 'Oh, you really don't care about your education or anything or your future… Or even like, your siblings'. 'Cause like, if they cut your siblings'… if they take money out of our budget, your siblings won't have like, a better education or anything like that.

Robert discusses how presenting oneself and one's opinions in this matter is important to him: he has participated in every walkout. He said, "It was really interesting. It was mind-blowing to see that many young teenagers just being out there and speaking their mind. And showing they actually care about their education and the future of their family members and everything else." Robert refers to his peers who choose to keep their opinion on the school budget cuts private and do not act on them. He believes that it reflects positively on himself to demonstrate that he values his education and his future by participating in the protest.

Jaden, aged 14, agreed that the walkout was an important way to make his voice heard: "if you don't like something, like, for example, the fund for schools were gonna go down. And people didn't like that. So, we did a walkout… just like, taking a stand." Gwen, aged 18, shared that the initiative for the walkouts "was all over Twitter and Facebook and everywhere, everyone had to Share it and you had to walk out of the school in order to protest the budget cuts. So I guess that inspired me, and everybody else who all walked out of school. And we went to City Hall and we made posters, and stuff. And we protested." Young people of Boston used social media to organize, and exerted their collective agency to pool knowledge, skills, and resources together to effect change (Bandura, 2008)—or at least gain some visibility.

Habibah, aged 16, discussed the effect of young people gathering together for this type of action. She says, "Usually children get overlooked" and that young people's voices "don't really weigh a lot." Habibah reflected on the walkouts and said that the media reports demonstrated that adults "were really moved by the amount of people" who participated. Habibah revealed a sense of despair when she notes,

> The thing is, sure you can be moved by the amount of people, but I feel like they're still gonna do what they wanna do. Like, they could say, 'oh yeah, we were moved,' and there was a huge amount of people, but I still feel like they're gonna do what they wanna do, so like, the reason why they will do what they wanna do is if somebody within their community speaks up. Like, 'oh you know, but the way, I feel like this is gonna not only affect the children but also affect us.' Like, that's the only time they will actually [do something about the] situation, not just like, change their minds.

Habibah seems to have wanted to experience a greater sense of efficacy after learning that adults were "moved" by how many students walked out of their schools to protest the budget cuts. But Habibah still believes that the adults will only make a change if other adults will be affected. This is not the sort of positive reinforcement that might encourage Habibah—and her peers—to participate in civic action again in the future.

Several participants criticized the walkouts as a method of protest, and decided not to participate. Surprisingly, Sachi, aged 17, has "tried to stay out of" the walkouts, because he believes that there should not be budget cuts in the first place: budget cuts are just a symptom of a larger problem of "what's happening in the school system." While Sachi believed that a different approach would change education in his school district, Tanesha, aged 16, chose not to participate in the walkouts because she believes that the manner in which her peers approached the budget cut issue by walking out was the wrong way to go about a protest. Tanesha suggested that a better method of protesting school budget cuts "would be to sit in. Because by you walking out, you're showing you *don't* care about budget cuts in your education. So it's just like, a lot of people don't know exactly the way to protest. I think they're just trying things out and seeing what works, because at the moment, it's not working." Tanesha is concerned that her younger peers "don't listen" and are "stubborn, harder to make listen." While Tanesha views those younger than her as "stubborn," she does acknowledge the positive action, that her peers are "trying things out and seeing what works," and hopes they will continue to find effective ways to take civic action. These young people exemplify that individuals use whatever tools are available to them in order to undertake their chosen civic action (Gibson & Cantijoch, 2013)—in the case of the school walk-outs, this was a Facebook event to spread the word about this protest.

4.3   Understanding Civic Identity in Contemporary Society

This chapter has provided a basis for a new understanding of young people's civic identity through the ways in which young people in this study understand citizenship and civic engagement. How young people think of themselves as citizens and how they present themselves to others as active citizens through civic engagement is influenced by how others perceive them (Schlenker, 2012). For example, when young people feel their citizenship is restricted by their age, young people reveal their frustration for society's perception of them as incapable or unwilling to engage. Laura expressed her disappointment that she is not able to participate in certain volunteer activities, and Naomi revealed that citizenship ought to be less about age and more about a sense of responsibility. The five themes of citizenship that emerged from this study are not mutually exclusive: it is possible for young people to draw on the different themes simultaneously as they reflect on their understanding of what citizenship means to them.

In the 15 years since Lister et al.'s (2003, 2005) research was first published, there have been many technological developments that could influence how young people see themselves fitting into the world around them, and how young people view themselves as citizens. However, despite these developments, technology itself does not seem to *directly* affect young people's understandings of citizenship. Rather, technology informs and mediates the experiences that young people have related to citizenship and civic engagement. While technology has informed how people engage with news and learn about issues of public concern, such as the immigration debate, technology itself does not seem to impact young people's direct viewpoints on what it means to be a citizen.

Furthermore, despite the existence of technology in their everyday lives, technology does not play as large a role in young people's understanding and experiences of citizenship as I expected from the outset of this study. This might be because civics curriculum in the United States is not only lacking in quantity, but it also does not address the ways that young people can be civically engaged by harnessing technological tools. During the data collection phase of this study, I interacted with several officials in a large school district's Office of Data and Accountability, the office responsible for approving or rejecting research proposals within the school district. I received a voicemail from one of the officials in this office that stated "civic education is not a priority for [school district]." This spokesperson for the school district made it clear that civic education is low on the priority list for this district, especially. If this is the case in this district from which one third of participants were recruited for this study, it is possible to assume that Social Studies curriculum in this district and elsewhere is lacking in civics education and also lacking in an update to how civic education could include technologically enhanced activities for civic engagement. Young people have discovered tools for civic engagement on their own (i.e., finding out about the school walkout on Facebook, posting on Instagram about Black Lives Matter).

This study enhances the findings on citizenship put forth by Lister et al. (2003, 2005), and contributes the discovery that young people conceptualize civic engagement much in the same way as scholars do, with civic activities that include service-oriented endeavors, political participation, and "activism activities in which youth engage to improve their worlds" (Weinstein, 2014, p. 212). In most cases, young people's understandings of citizenship were informed by experiences in their own lives, such as the immigration debate that pervades public discourse. This issue of public concern may have shaped young people's views on citizenship, and the acquisition of news information online may have shaped young people's awareness of this public debate. The findings presented in this chapter illustrate that understandings and experiences of citizenship and civic engagement must be viewed together as civic identity. A new framework for civic identity will be presented in Chapter 6.

As the findings in this chapter demonstrate, young people think about citizenship in more nuanced ways compared to the participants in Lister et al.'s (2003, 2005) research, and there is more emotion, conviction, and personal voice involved in shaping these understandings, because of the personalization of politics (Mesch & Coleman, 2007). While Lister et al.'s (2003) findings focused on the ages at which young people grasp the understanding of each of the citizenship models, in this study, age is relevant only as a parameter by which young people assess their eligibility for citizenship and its rights and responsibilities. In their current life stage, some young people question whether they are citizens because they have not reached the age at which they have the power or responsibility to make decisions and have their voices heard.

This chapter illustrated a preview of how the Internet and social media are involved in civic engagement, and how social media informs young people about different ways in which they can become more involved in their community, whether that is participating in a fundraiser for ALS research, or learning about a school walkout. The Internet and social media are not the *prominent* means through which young people are developing their understandings of citizenship and engaging civically, but they are still contributors. The *reciprocity hypothesis* of technology's relationship to civic engagement that was described in Chapter 2 has appeared through the findings of this study presented in this chapter. Civic engagement activities that are digitally mediated tend to mirror the activities that young people are taking part in without technology (Nam, 2012; Vissers & Stolle, 2014), such as participating in fundraising events, interacting with others, and engaging in protests. Importantly, the themes that emerged from the data illustrate that young people view civic engagement in the more traditional sense of the term, through improving the community, interacting with others, and participating politically. The digitally mediated aspects of daily life that play into civic engagement lie primarily in fundraising events like the ALS Ice Bucket Challenge and political protests like the school walkout. Young people became aware of these events through social media, and without social media, might have heard of these events through word of mouth.

As noted in Section 4.2, young people believe that paying attention to current events is a form of civic engagement. I had expected technology to influence participants' ideas and experiences of civic engagement because young people are constrained by their parents and schools, and technology may give young people an outlet or platform from which to share their voice, as scholars have suggested (Jennings & Zeitner, 2003; Mossberger, Tolbert, & McNeal, 2008; Schlozman, Verba, & Brady, 2010). However, that has been the case for just a few of the participants in this study. Only a few young people mention technology as a way to express their voice, which will be more deeply discussed in Chapter 5. Chapter 5 will highlight specific examples of how young people are participating in civic life in contemporary society, highlighting the changing means through which young people are discussing current events, and how social and institutional structures impact their sense of efficacy.

REFERENCES

Ansley, F. (2005). Constructing Citizenship Without a Licence: The Struggle of Undocumented Immigrants in the USA for Livelihoods and Recognition. In N. Kabeer (Ed.), *Inclusive Citizenship: Meanings and Expressions* (pp. 199–215). London: Zed Books.

Bandura, A. (2008). An Agentic Perspective on Positive Psychology. *Positive Psychology, 1*, 167–196.

Bennett, W. L. (2008). Changing Citizenship in the Digital Age. In W. L. Bennett (Ed.), *Civic Life Online: Learning How Digital Media Can Engage Youth* (pp. 1–24). Cambridge, MA: The MIT Press.

Buss, A., & Portnoy, N. (1967). Pain Tolerance and Group Identification. *Journal of Personality and Social Psychology, 6*, 106–108.

Camino, L., & Zeldin, S. (2002). From Periphery to Center: Pathways for Youth Civic Engagement in the Day-to-Day Life of Communities. *Applied Developmental Science, 6*(4), 213–220.

Chow, L. (2018, May 30). *UN's #beatplasticpollution tag is the New Ice Bucket Challenge*. Retrieved June 05, 2018, from EcoWatch: https://www.ecowatch.com/beat-plastic-pollution-2573622594.html.

Dias, T. S., & Menezes, I. (2014, June 2). Children and Adolescents as Political Actors: Collective Visions of Politics and Citizenship. *Journal of Moral Education, 43*(3), 250–268.

Earl, J., & Schussman, A. (2008). Contesting Cultural Control: Youth Culture and Online Petitioning. In W. L. Bennett (Ed.), *Civic Life Online: Learning How Digital Media Can Engage Youth* (pp. 71–95). Cambridge, MA: The MIT Press.

Facebook. (2018). *Fundraisers and Donations*. Retrieved March 12, 2018, from Facebook https://www.facebook.com/help/1409509059114623

Finlay, A., Wray-Lake, L., & Flanagan, C. (2010). Civic Engagement During the Transition to Adulthood: Developmental Opportunities and Social Policies at a Critical Juncture. In L. Sherrod, J. Torney-Purta, & C. Flanagan (Eds.), *Handbook of Research on Civic Engagement in Youth* (pp. 277–305). Hoboken, NJ: John Wiley & Sons.

Flanagan, C. A. (2013). *Teenage Citizens: The Political Theories of the Young.* Cambridge, MA: Harvard University Press.

Frazer, E. (2008). Key Perspectives, Traditions, and Disciplines: Overview. In J. Arthur, I. Davies, & C. Hahn (Eds.), *The SAGE Handbook of Education for Citizenship and Democracy* (pp. 281–291). London: SAGE.

Gibson, R., & Cantijoch, M. (2013). Conceptualizing and Measuring Participation in the Age of the Internet: Is Online Political Engagement Really Different to Offline? *Journal of Politics, 75*(3), 701–716.

Gillman, S., & Sofer, E. G. (1978). Children, Adolescents, and Politics: A Selective Review. *Cambridge Journal of Education, 8*(2–3), 78–97.

Goffman, E. (1959). *The Presentation of Self in Everyday Life.* Garden City, NY: Doubleday Anchor Books.

Goffman, E. (1978). The Presentation of Self to Others. In J. G. Manis & B. N. Meltzer (Eds.), *Symbolic Interaction: A Reader in Social Psychology* (3rd ed., pp. 234–244). London: Allyn and Bacon.

Hall, T., & Williamson, H. (1999). *Citizenship and Community.* Leicester: Youth Work Press.

Hargittai, E. (2002). Second-level Digital Divide: Differences in People's Online Skills. *First Monday, 7*(4).

Hart, D., & Kirshner, B. (2009). Civic Participation and Development Among Urban Adolescents. In J. Youniss & P. Levine (Eds.), *Engaging Young People in Civic Life* (pp. 102–120). Nashville, TN: Vanderbilt University Press.

Jennings, M., & Zeitner, V. (2003). Internet Use and Civic Engagement: A Longitudinal Analysis. *Public Opinion Quarterly, 67,* 311–334.

Jones, E., & Gaventa, J. (2002). *Concepts of Citizenship: A Review.* Brighton: Institute for Development Studies.

Kahne, J., Middaugh, E., & Allen, D. (2014). *Youth, New Media, and the Rise of Participatory Politics.* The University of Chicago Press.

Knefelkamp, L. L. (2008). Civic Identity: Locating Self in Community. *Diversity & Democracy: Civic Learning for Shared Futures, 11*(2), 1–3.

Lenhart, A., Madden, M., Smith, A., Purcell, K., Zickuhr, K., & Rainie, L. (2011). *Teens, Kindness and Cruelty on Social Network Sites: How American Teens Navigate the New World of Digital Citizenship.* Washington, DC: Pew Research Center Internet & American Life Project.

Lister, R., Smith, N., Middleton, S., & Cox, L. (2003). Empirical Perspectives on Theoretical and Political Debate. *Citizenship Studies, 7,* 235–253.

Lister, R., Smith, N., Middleton, S., & Cox, L. (2005). Young People Talking About Citizenship in Britain. In N. Kabeer (Ed.), *Inclusive Citizenship: Meanings and Expressions* (pp. 114–131). New York: Zed Books.

Livingstone, S., Couldry, N., & Markham, T. (2007). Youthful Steps Towards Civic Participation: Does the Internet Help? In B. D. Loader (Ed.), *Young Citizens in the Digital Age: Political Engagement, Young People and New Media* (pp. 21–34). London: Routledge.

Loader, B. D. (2007). Young Citizens in the Digital Age: Disaffected or Displaced? In B. D. Loader (Ed.), *Young Citizens in the Digital Age: Political Engagement, Young People and New Media* (pp. 1–17). London: Routledge.

McFarland, D., & Thomas, R. (2006). Bowling Young: How Youth Voluntary Associations Influence Adult Political Participation. *American Sociological Review, 71*(3), 401–425.

McLeod, J. M. (2000). Media and Civic Socialization of Youth. *Journal of Adolescent Health, 27*(2), 45–51.

McMillan, D., & Chavis, D. (1986). Sense of Community: A Definition and Theory. *Journal of Community Psychology, 14*(1), 6–23.

Mesch, G. S., & Coleman, S. (2007). New Media and New Voters: Young People, the Internet and the 2005 UK Election Campaign. In B. D. Loader (Ed.), *Young Citizens in the Digital Age: Political Engagement, Young People and New Media* (pp. 35–47). London: Routledge.

Mossberger, K., Tolbert, C. J., & McNeal, R. S. (2008). *Digital Citizenship: The Internet, Society and Participation.* Cambridge, MA: MIT Press.

Nam, T. (2012). Dual Effects of the Internet on Political Activism: Reinforcing and Mobilizing. *Government Information Quarterly, 29*(S1), S90–S97.

Niemi, R. G., & Junn, J. (1998). *Civic Education: What Makes Students Learn.* New Haven, CT: Yale University Press.

Osler, A., & Starkey, H. (2006). Education for Democratic Citizenship: A Review of Research, Policy and Practice 1995–2005. *Research Papers in Education, 21*(4), 433–466.

Osler, A., & Starkey, H. (2018). Extending the Theory and Practice of Education for Cosmopolitan Citizenship. *Educational Review, 70*(1), 31–40.

Raynes-Goldie, K., & Walker, L. (2008). Our Space: Online Civic Engagement Tools for Youth. In W. L. Bennett (Ed.), *Civic Life Online: Learning How Digital Media Can Engage Youth* (pp. 161–188). Cambridge, MA: The MIT Press.

Rogers, K. (2016). The 'Ice Bucket Challenge' Helped Scientists Discover a New Gene Tied to A.L.S. *The New York Times.* Retrieved from https://www.nytimes.com/2016/07/28/health/the-ice-bucket-challenge-helped-scientists-discover-a-new-gene-tied-to-als.html.

Schlenker, B. (2012). Self-Presentation. In M. R. Leary & J. P. Tangney (Eds.), *Handbook of Self and Identity* (2nd ed., pp. 542–570). New York: Guilford Press.

Schlozman, K., Verba, S., & Brady, H. (2010). Weapon of the Strong: Participatory Inequality and the Internet. *Perspectives on Politics, 8*, 487–509.

Seale, J., & Dutton, W. (2012). Empowering the Digitally Excluded: Learning Initiatives for (In)visible Groups. *Research in Learning Technology, 20*(4).

Serriere, S. C. (2014). The Role of the Elementary Teacher in Fostering Civic Efficacy. *The Social Studies, 105*(1), 45–56.

Singh, M., Oliver, M., Siddique, H., & Zhou, N. (2019). Global Climate Strike: Greta Thunberg and School Students Lead Climate Crisis Protest – As It Happened. *The Guardian*. Retrieved from https://www.theguardian.com/environment/live/2019/sep/20/climate-strike-global-change-protest-sydney-melbourne-london-new-york-nyc-school-student-protest-greta-thunberg-rally-live-news-latest-updates.

Smith, E. (1999). The Effects of Investments in the Social Capital of Youth on Political and Civic Behavior in Young Adulthood: A Longitudinal Analysis. *Political Psychology, 20*(3), 553–580.

Stepick, A., Stepick, C., & Labissiere, C. (2008). South Florida's Immigrant Youth and Civic Engagement. *Applied Developmental Science, 12*(2), 57–65.

U.S. Code – Unannotated Title 8. Aliens and Nationality § 1401. Nationals and citizens of United States at birth.

Veith, E. (2017, May 11). You Can Now 'Donate Your Birthday' to Awesome Causes Using Facebook. Retrieved March 12, 2018, from Her Campus https://www.facebook.com/help/1409509059114623

Verba, S., Schlozman, K., & Brady, H. (1995). *Voice and Equality: Civic Voluntarism in American Politics*. Cambridge, MA: Harvard University Press.

Vissers, S., & Stolle, D. (2014). Spill-Over Effects Between Facebook and On/Offline Political Participation? Evidence from a Two-Wave Panel Study. *Journal of Information, Technology, and Politics, 11*(3), 259–275.

Weinstein, E. (2014). The Personal Is Political on Social Media: Online Civic Expression Patterns and Pathways Among Civically Engaged Youth. *The International Journal of Communication, 8*, 210–233.

Wordsworth, W. (1835). *A Guide Through the District of the Lakes in the North of England: With a Description of the Scenery, &c., for the Use of Tourists and Residents*. Kendal: Hudson and Nicholson.

Youniss, J., & Yates, M. (1997). *Community Service and Social Responsibility in Youth*. Chicago: University of Chicago Press.

CHAPTER 5

Engaging in the Political World

The findings presented in Chapters 3 and 4 revealed that how one sees oneself fitting into and contributing to a group or larger society impacts how one presents oneself to that group (Schlenker, 2012), which is normally by improving their communities. Chapter 4 described the relation between young people's conceptualizations of citizenship and their understandings of civic engagement, which informs a new framework of civic identity, to be introduced in Chapter 6. With the understanding of how young people grasp civic engagement, it is now possible to learn how young people are developing and using their civic identity and voices to engage in today's political world. Young people are making sense of the information that surrounds them in the form of current events from both traditional and new media sources, developing a sense of who they are politically and synthesizing this information as they decide to affiliate with a political party and develop their own political voice. This chapter will explore how young people are developing and sharing their political beliefs with others, and the importance of feeling that one's voice—an outward expression of civic identity—is heard.

5.1   BUILDING VOICE IN CONTEMPORARY SOCIETY

Voice is an expression of one's civic identity—it is a way of sharing one's opinions and beliefs from their position in a community and their actions of civic engagement. The data from this study reveal that voice is a tangible

© The Author(s) 2020
J. K. Viola, *Young People's Civic Identity in the Digital Age*,
Palgrave Studies in Young People and Politics,
https://doi.org/10.1007/978-3-030-37405-1_5

expression of one's civic identity and belief system. Young people can develop their voices through learning about information from the media and from others, and synthesizing that information to build their voice and, in turn, efficacy. Media exposure (Sotirovic & McLeod, 2001) and social modeling can build efficacy (Bandura, 2008), and successful experiences in sharing voice can lead to young people continuing these actions (Maddux & Gosselin, 2012). In the digital era, young people can look up to trusted adults in their lives as well as strangers they connect with digitally (Sotirovic & McLeod, 2001). People can model nearly anyone including strangers, because the ideas, belief systems, and lifestyles are frequently transmitted through social media. Parents and teachers are often the first models of civic engagement that young people see, and can model civic behavior and tell their children or students when they engage civically, for example when they vote or when they participate in a protest (Serriere, 2014). As civic engagement is a learned capacity (Dias & Menezes, 2014), young people require role models to demonstrate acts of civic engagement (Bandura, 2008; Kieffer, 1984).

Young people build voice by following current events, learning from trusted adults, and choosing a political party. Their interest in following current events and developing opinions on issues of public concern is affected by their news consumption habits at home and in their daily lives outside of the home. At the time of this study, such current events included the 2016 presidential election in the United States. Young people in this study choose to learn from adults, who have more developed political views, as a way for them to situate their own views within the political system of the United States. How young people see politics and political issues in the media, and how trusted adults discuss these issues, may influence how young people understand what is going on in the world around them, and their beliefs about the two political parties that dominate the United States' political system (McLeod, 2000). The following sections will illustrate how young people experience these factors as they build their voice and decide whether to share that voice with others.

5.1.1   Paying Attention to Current Events

Young people are developing their own civic identity and voice, and as they are doing so, they are interacting with information and people to understand current events and form their opinions of these issues of public concern. This section will illustrate how following current events contributes to building youth voice. Consuming news information is no longer considered a passive political activity (Krueger, 2002); rather, it is an active political activity (Katz & Rice, 2002), which underpins the extent to which people become politically informed (Pontes, Henn, & Griffiths, 2018). Research in Australia provides similar findings: young people demonstrate that paying attention to current events in digitally mediated ways is a more elaborate process of learning and synthesizing the issues, events, and actors involved (Collin, 2015). Young people are actively taking in the information about the world around them, and learning to make sense of it. As illustrated in Chapter 4, young people believe that paying attention to current events and being well informed about what is going on in the world around them is a facet of civic engagement. Paying attention to current events exposes young people to different viewpoints on prominent issues, and enables them to understand their own positions on these issues and develop their voice. Nevertheless, expectations of young people to keep up with current events are low (Livingstone, Couldry, & Markham, 2007), and these limited expectations of young people contribute to their overall sense of efficacy.

Nora, aged 15, is one of few participants who chooses not to pay attention to the news, and says that is because the news often saddens her: "[There are] a lot of bad things happening. And I don't really like to hear that stuff. I want to hear happy things…and the news doesn't really give out anything happy." Similarly, Mira, aged 15, personifies the stereotype that teenagers prefer to "look at the comics unless there is something interesting on the front page" of the newspaper. Despite these outliers, most participants expressed that they *do* follow current events, even though they realize that society does not expect them to do so at this stage in life. Maisie, aged 14, emphasizes that it is important for young people to be informed about current events, no matter how good or "bad" the events may seem.

Ava, aged 16, says that she learns most news "through my friends" who will be "texting 'Oh, did you see what just happened?'" Ava also shares that "Twitter is a big news thing, and I have one so I always check that for something" but she will occasionally learn something from her mother who "still gets a newspaper." Ava highlights how traditional and new media are used in her daily life to keep her informed of current events. Participants in this study followed current events in digitally mediated ways, from the traditional nightly news on television to the constant influx of current events information in the form of online newspapers and Twitter alerts. Participants were most interested in the current events that impact them—directly or indirectly—in their neighborhoods and school districts.

Often, young people tend to follow current events to which they are connected personally. When she thinks of current events, Bibiana, aged 16, considers what is happening in her own neighborhood. During our first interview, she recalled a recent time when she arrived home from school, and "the block near my apartment was barricaded and there was police and stuff. I guess some guy was trying to hold people captive there, and it was really dangerous. I feel like that's what I think of when I hear 'current events,' because you would see, 'Oh, there's been a shooting in [neighborhood],' which has a bunch of roses laid out for people who have died there." Bibiana's connection to her community, which she described as "like a family," gives her a strong sense of purpose to stay informed about the events that are happening around her and to talk about these events. Civic scholars have found that people engage with issues that are embedded in their everyday life (Ke & Starkey, 2014), and Bibiana's personal example of current events in her own community demonstrates the concerns of many young people in underserved areas throughout the United States. Participants from wealthier, more stable communities discussed fundraisers as examples of current events, illustrating the stark difference in issues at the forefront of young people's minds in different communities, a finding supported by Hart and Kirshner (2009).

Young people have many explanations for why they do or do not pay attention to current events: some participants do not pay attention to current events because they are not yet of voting age, and feel that politics is not relevant to them. Yet others understand that they are nearing voting age, so it would better serve them to pay attention to current events now to keep them as informed as possible before sharing their voices through votes in the future. Following current events may go hand in hand with sharing their voices on political and social issues— young people may hear about a current event, and wish to discuss it in more detail with others. The ways in which young people pay attention to current events varies, but is often motivated by what they see at home, and what is convenient for them within their daily lives. The next sections will outline the news consumption habits within participants' homes, as well as how young people are gathering news information in digitally mediated ways.

Picking Up News Consumption Habits at Home

It is common for young people to consume news information through traditional news media, like television news and newspapers, as well as through social media. These news consumption behaviors and interests start in the home and within family contexts, especially if parents or other relatives pay attention to the news. Hannah, aged 16, says that her mother "likes to watch Channel 7 really loudly" and that she comes from "a political family. My dad was in the Marines, and my uncle was in the Army, so when my uncle comes to visit, they'll have political debates." Allie, aged 15, will "look up things at home" after hearing her teacher or father talk about a current event. Allie shares that her teachers raise questions about topics in the news: "In Theology we're learning about Syria or what the land was... then [the teacher] brought up Syria today, and he was talking about that really briefly, but then I looked it up later and I thought it was kind of interesting and sad, what was going on." Hearing others—especially adults with whom young people have a trusting relationship—discuss current events often prompts young people to want to learn more, and conduct research online to discover more information to develop their own views about issues of public concern. Many participants watch television news to get their information, which increases their civic and political knowledge (McLeod, 2000), and, in turn, their confidence in sharing their voice and beliefs about these issues (Nasir & Kirshner, 2003).

As young people learn how to access news information from their family members and close adults in their lives, they also learn skills about interpreting news information. Addie, aged 14, learned from her mother about how to understand the news. Addie's mother told her "news always has a bias, so she said just 'listen to the facts.' So that's what I mostly try to do. But I don't usually listen to what the news reporter is saying. I watch the actual election to make my own opinions." Addie's comments, and her mother's lessons, have become particularly relevant at the time of writing, as the issue of "fake news" and the dissemination of disinformation came to light after the data collection process for this study, which was completed in advance of the 2016 presidential election. Addie tries to ignore the bias given by political analysts, and understands the election results by looking at the election returns herself. Discussions with family, teachers, peers, and others can mediate the bias embedded in mass communication and broaden young people's understanding of political and social issues (Shah, McLeod, & Lee, 2009). As Addie begins to think critically about the bias she sees on television, Tanesha will illustrate in the following section that young people may have these mediating experiences on websites such as Tumblr, where people are able to post their views and re-post others' content when they want to present their views to others. Evidently, the home is no longer the primary place for young people to learn habits of consuming news and become informed about political affairs and the nuances within social issues (McLeod & Shah, 2009) to build and voice their opinions on these issues. Twitter, Tumblr, and other social networking websites and online news sources have become central means through which young people are learning about the news and developing their news consumption habits.

Integrating News Consumption Habits into Daily Life

As expressed throughout this book, young people's lives are digitally mediated, and young people care most about the issues that are directly relevant to them. Sachi, aged 17, turns to "Snapchat, Twitter, Instagram, Facebook" to access information about what is going on in his community and the wider world, and asserts, "I don't really use anything else other than those, to just look at what's happening, or what's going on in my community." It is not surprising that young people, like Sachi, get their news information in digitally mediated ways that are relevant and convenient to them (Linton, 2015), such as through social media, which are a source of political information and a venue for political expression (Shah, Cho, Eveland Jr., & Kwak, 2005). People of all ages now use social media as a part of gathering information about current events (Dimitrova, Shehata, Strömbäck, & Nord, 2014; Gil de Zúñiga, Copeland, & Bimber, 2013; Holt, Shehata, Strömbäck, & Ljungberg, 2013; Pasek, More, & Romer, 2009; Towner, 2013). With 67 percent of Americans getting their news information from social media (Gottfried & Shearer, 2017), it is not surprising that growing evidence points to social media as a primary means of young people's access to political information (Sloam, Ehsan, & Henn, 2018).

Kaitlyn, aged 16, watches the news on television "in the morning, and then it's on my Twitter and Instagram, so I'll see stuff throughout the day." Social media enables people to stay informed at every moment of the day—information can be accessed from one's smart device with the swipe of a finger. Generally, participants often cited that they are "busy" and rarely have time to follow current events, but that technology has helped them stay informed throughout the day. Jillian, aged 15, is often busy with homework and dance class in the evenings and therefore does not use her smartphone at those times. But, "the next day I'll hear something, or I'll go onto my phone and it'll be blowing up with Twitter notifications, and people texting me [to ask] if I saw this, or if I saw that." For Jillian, it seems like her smartphone is her lifeline for learning about current events. Her friends will inform her via text message, or she will receive notifications on her phone from Twitter. All Jillian has to do is look at her phone and she will be up to date on the major headlines of the day.

Tanesha, aged 16, actively seeks information about politics and current events because she wants to learn how to "take it all in." Tanesha prefers to access her news information from print sources, not online, which is unique for this age group, but also relies on television and electronic news media such as CNN and Apple News "just for the political aspect" each morning. Throughout the day, she reflects and forms her opinion about what is going on, and then before she goes to bed, she looks at Tumblr to read others' opinions about the current events. Tanesha, in accordance with the view of civic engagement as interaction with others and making one's voice heard, believes that people should be exposed to more viewpoints so they can be "vocal," which "makes change." Tanesha values the opinions of others and integrates them into her own worldview by reading Tumblr pages related to current events. Kaitlyn and Tanesha demonstrate further examples of young people's unbroken connection to their digital devices throughout the day. A recent report from the Pew Research Center demonstrates that some youth even admit they are almost constantly using their digital devices (Lenhart et al., 2015); their technology and social media are the first thing they check in the morning, and the last thing they check before they go to sleep at night (Watkins, 2009).

Kenai, aged 14, does not follow current events every day, but uses an app on his phone called "Flipboard, which shows highlights on the news." While Kenai is not constantly connected to his social media, he acknowledges that social media has become integrated into politics much more as time goes on. When he thinks about contemporary elections, he thinks of "long speeches, huge crowds … people spamming on Twitter what they think." Kenai's statement highlights how social media has afforded many with a platform for their voices and opinions to be heard. The 2016 election cycle made one candidate infamous for using Twitter to insult others, which will be addressed later in this chapter. Sean, aged 15, also notes that social media is incorporated into political campaigns: "I think relating technology and politics is important to see the connection between how technology has impacted the way people hear about and talk about the election. It's easier to send one message to the entire public." Sean understands the influence of social media in disseminating information and amplifying voices, and shares how he knows politicians harness the power of social media to influence constituents during election campaigns.

All of the aforementioned accounts demonstrate that technology plays a role in how young people experience the world (boyd, 2009), and may offer new opportunities for young people to share their voices and participate in civic life. For Bibiana, social media has impacted her consumption of news about societal issues, and her career aspirations. For Bibiana, social media is a source of intrigue and information about what is going on in the world. Bibiana relates her civic engagement to how social media keeps her informed, a correlation that has also been identified by scholars (Shea & Green, 2007). Bibiana asserts, "I would be less involved if I didn't have social media" and highlights the power of "people from around the world saying something and coming together for a cause." She feels that "social media has shaped me to become more aware ... Not on like political issues, but more of like, societal issues." Bibiana's story represents several ways in which young people's civic experiences are digitally mediated: social media offers new opportunities for young people to contribute to a community, and as a way to learn about current events. Bibiana identified how exactly social media has made her more aware, and how it has changed her attitudes about following current events. Bibiana is now more interested in current events, and hopes to pursue a career in journalism.

Following the 2016 Presidential Election
The 2016 presidential election dominated public conversation during the time of this research, and now, at the time of writing, the 2020 presidential election is already making headlines. A majority of the young people in this study said they followed developments in the 2016 election campaign; very few young people are completely uninformed about current events or politics. One such participant is Laura, aged 17. She says politics and current events are "not relevant" to her, but when she turns "eighteen I probably will [pay attention to current events], just because... obviously it is relevant to me because I'm a United States citizen. But overall, I can't ... it doesn't seem that relevant for me to follow if I can't vote for anybody or I can't help figure out what they want to do about passing a certain law." Laura's age precludes her from following current events because she feels she cannot do anything—she is not yet eligible to vote.

Carly, aged 15, refutes adults' perception that young people do not want to pay attention to politics because it is difficult for young people to understand. She says, "Politics kind of confuses me, but that doesn't make me not want to watch it." Several participants mention that current events, especially the presidential election, are topics of discussion in Humanities and Social Studies classes at school, and in the home. Selah, aged 15, says, "I haven't watched much of the debates, but I always hear my homeroom teacher talking about it. And she's also a history teacher, so I definitely trust her." Selah's teacher is in a position of trust and power, which influences Selah's understanding of current events. Damon, aged 14, says that his Humanities class discusses the election, and "who is highest in the polls." Similarly, Ava, aged 16, says that she discusses current events in her Social Studies class. In other cases, the discussions about the election begin in the home. Kevin, aged 15, shares, "most of the time, it starts with me, and sometimes I'm with one of my uncles, watching the news, and something pops up about the presidential election, and he just starts talking about it...And we just get that conversation going, and other people join in."

Zelda, aged 14, enjoys watching the debates between the presidential candidates because she finds them "really funny and... really interesting." Zelda describes that she has gathered that there is so much "to learn about politics and government." Zelda was most able to recall what the candidates post on Twitter: "Donald Trump sometimes says what he'll do if he's the U.S. President. Or... insults Hillary Clinton." Zelda notes that after watching the debates, and reading what candidates post on their Twitter pages, the candidates highlight "the same things, but someone puts it better... they say it better. If Donald Trump says, 'I want to build the Mexican border over again,' Hillary Clinton will say, maybe say the same thing, but he'll make it sound more like... powerful." Zelda describes how each candidate appeals to certain voters through their rhetoric, and topics they bring to the forefront of political debate. "Donald Trump has one to three ideas that everyone seems to like. Like, ISIS and then the Mexican border. A lot of people think that should change. But Hillary Clinton, she has a lot of different ideas, but she's not making a really big effort to do every single one of them. She'll ... pick a couple... and then she'll emphasize how that will impact the U.S." Zelda considers how the candidates present themselves, and notes the use of social media in this election campaign. Several other participants used this time in our interview to critique how candidates have utilized their social media to connect with the public—particularly Donald Trump.

Naomi, aged 16, shares, "I don't like Donald Trump... he's a grown man and he's willing to stoop to social media to insult someone." Naomi notes the juvenile nature of this tactic, and highlights that she has "sixteen-year-old friends who do that, so to me the person who's supposed to be running my country and keeping me safe shouldn't be insulting someone on Twitter." Naomi asserts that some of her peers are more mature than the person running for President of the United States. Martin, aged 15, notes that while social media is a way for people—including presidential candidates—to express themselves, this freedom can have both positive and negative consequences. Publicly sharing beliefs can bring people closer together by facilitating communication and breaking barriers between public figures and everyday people, but it can also lead to individuals abusing that freedom and using social media to bully or insult others, as Naomi suggests Donald Trump has done. With freedom on social media, Martin claims, "You can't tell somebody not to do this or that.... They might send out a picture, throw some shade.... You know, they might say something about somebody else, like, subliminally. I think the freedom is a great thing, but ... after awhile you get power-hungry and you lose yourself in the power." Martin speaks to the way social media gives people a voice—but that voice might not always be sharing positive ideas. Sachi pointed this out as well, the fact that politicians and political candidates use social media as a tool to acquire votes, and "insults work." Other participants mentioned their view of the 2016 presidential candidates insulting each other as "immature" or "childish," but few participants went so far as to say, "it seems like it works for that candidate," as Sachi concluded.

Young people are well informed to consider the candidates for President, and have learned about the status of the election in digitally mediated ways. Kaitlyn, aged 16, shared concerns as "these people [presidential candidates] could be the future of our country. So ... since I'll be eighteen soon, I'm interested in knowing what their beliefs are and how they could help us." Her peers of age 16 do not believe they are close enough to voting that it is necessary to pay attention to the election, but, as young people grow closer to voting age, they become more likely to pay attention to current events, and the 2016 presidential election. In many cases, the 17-year-old participants in this study would become eligible to vote by the time the 2016 election occurred. Kaitlyn, Peter, Sachi, and Elsie all determined that it is important for them to be informed in the present, so that they know their views and understand which candidates and policies would best represent them and their voices when they are able to vote.

While some young people are close enough to the voting age that they choose to pay attention to the election coverage, others follow the election in order to learn more about the diversity of political beliefs within the United States, as a way of informing their own beliefs and views about the country. Aidan, aged 15, shared his surprise about "the amount of people that support [Trump]," which "kind of wakes you up and shows you how the different parts ... how like, different people are ... and it kinda makes you think...politically-wise, as a country, we're not really diverse at all." Aidan explains that there are so many people in the "Southern and Central" United States who support Donald Trump's promise to "build a wall between Mexico and the U.S." but "there's a lot of people on the coasts that just... don't. So there's politically like safe [areas] for a Republican country or Democratic country." Aidan has learned about the political diversity of the country, just by paying attention to the coverage of the 2016 presidential election. By following the presidential election, these young people have synthesized the opinions and beliefs of the candidates to help them establish their own position on the candidates and the issues of public concern. As the next section will illustrate, young people are learning more about the political beliefs around them, and developing their own, through discussions with trusted adults.

5.1.2   Learning from Trusted Adults

Young people talk about issues of public concern with adults as a way to inform their own political beliefs, as these political beliefs are often "derived from parents, teachers, the mass media, and observations in their own neighborhood," as Gillman and Sofer (1978, p. 82) noted in their research forty years ago. Teachers and family members were the most commonly cited people to whom young people look for information about current events and politics. Participants often mentioned family discussions about politics at the dinner table, in which the adults at the table would debate which candidate to vote for in the forthcoming election. Selah, aged 15, learns from others: "it's the people around me that have really affected that aspect about me, because usually, when they talk about it I have no idea what they would be talking about. They do educate me, and I think that's helpful." In particular, Selah prefers to talk to her teachers, because "they know more. They are more wiser [sic]." Young people lack confidence in their knowledge about how politics works (Henn & Foard, 2012), and the sentiment of being "just a kid" and not knowing much about politics was a common explanation among participants for why they most often prefer to talk to adults about politics. Previous research demonstrates that young people rely on support and advice from adults (Lenhart et al., 2011).

While Selah says that she learns most from her wise teachers, young people primarily talk to their parents to develop their own views. Nora, aged 15, shares that her mother and aunt discuss the 2016 presidential election, and she will "pay attention to what they're saying" to learn from them. Likewise, Sachi, aged 17, talks about politics with his parents because "they know more" than his peers, and Martin, aged 15, says that he enjoys learning from his mother, who is "wise." Interestingly, many participants, like Selah, Nora, and Martin, tend to listen to adults, rather than sharing their own voices and engaging in dialogue. Young people perceive the wisdom of their elders because these adults have already had the experience of voting and participating in elections before. Extensive research demonstrates this link between family and political identity (Hess & Torney-Purta, 2005). Imani, aged 14, talks to her mother about politics, and voting in particular. Her mother sometimes does not vote because she does not agree with everything that the candidates stand for. Imani's mother demonstrates that *not* voting is a way to exercise political voice as well, especially if it is difficult to agree with any candidate. Young people learn about voting as a way to participate, but they can also decide to not vote. Imani's mother has shared many of her beliefs with Imani, especially related to being a Democrat, and her opinions on Donald Trump. Imani's mother notes that Donald Trump says "a lot of ridiculous things" that would "apply" to her family, particularly because Donald Trump campaigned on anti-immigrant rhetoric (Osler & Starkey, 2018). Imani worried that should Donald Trump

> become president, and make sure all the immigrants go back from where the hell they came from, then that would apply to my family, because my family … most of them are immigrants. They came from Cape Verde. So that means we'd all go back to Cape Verde. And, say, if my family was Muslim, and… he has a lot of things to say about Muslims, but say if my family was Muslim, that would really like… upset my family and me.

Imani brings current events close to home: she understands how politics can affect specific groups of people, including her own family.

The immigration debate that continues to pervade public discourse has also influenced the political dialogue occurring between young people and their parents. Kenai, aged 14, says that his "view on immigration was originally that... it's okay for people to be free to immigrate. And my mom is really strong in that belief." Kenai explains that his and his mother's beliefs are "partly religious, because my mom thinks that everyone should be kind to each other. Honestly, the only thing I really see on media about immigration is frustration from people about it, especially Donald Trump." Kenai thinks critically about his own beliefs, acknowledges that they have been shaped by his family values, and connects these beliefs to the current headlines around immigration reform in the United States. Evidently, parents inform the values and belief systems of young people, but young people are not always able to separate their beliefs from their parents'. Jaden, also aged 14, reflected on his own beliefs and shares, "I just kinda go with what my parents say. If they say, 'Vote for Hillary,' I vote for Hillary." Jaden exemplifies that not all young people have taken ownership of their beliefs, and illustrates a potential negative effect that emerges from young people looking to adults as they form their own political beliefs. If young people only listen to their parents, then they are in danger of not being exposed to different ideas, or thinking critically about their own.

5.1.3   Choosing a Political Party Affiliation

Political identity is informed by how young people understand what it means to be a citizen and what it means to be civically engaged. Almond and Verba identified (1963) five key influences, including family, peers, voluntary organizations, schools, and the mass media, which serve as social contexts and sources of information and opportunities for political learning and behavior (McLeod & Shah, 2009). People's associations within their neighborhoods, schools, workplaces, and clubs define the political preferences to which the individual is exposed (Huckfeldt & Sprague, 1995). Of these, family and school experience has been found to have a strong influence over young people's civic identity development (Dassonneville, Quintelier, Hooghe, & Claes, 2012; Kisby & Sloam, 2014; Print, 2007; Quan-Haase & boyd, 2011). When young people have an understanding of what their beliefs are and how they align with the beliefs of others, they may choose to affiliate with a political party. Young people "test out" their political opinions on their families (Livingstone et al., 2007, p. 29), and, often, family members' political identity or affiliation would come to light in family conversations, as described in Section 5.1.2. The effect of family communication is indirect, "mediated through its influence on the extent to which adolescents engage in various forms of expression and exchange outside of the family, in classrooms, and within social networks" (Shah et al., 2009, p. 113).

Membership in a political party is a public presentation of one's belief system, and an expression of voice. When it comes to choosing a political party affiliation, young people may or may not identify with a particular political party or candidate. Few participants assert that they are members of a political party, but in many cases, political party affiliation stems from the family and community in which the young people have grown up. Some young people deliberately do not wish to affiliate themselves with a political party because they disagree with the two-party system in the United States, or they do not trust the political parties, or they feel the current status of the political parties are not aligned well-enough with their beliefs. This section will illustrate how young people are thinking about their own political party affiliation—or lack thereof.

Sachi, aged 17, sounded proud to reveal, "I'm a Democrat," and subsequently excited upon sharing his opinion about Democratic presidential candidate Bernie Sanders as "too radical," and his support of Hillary Clinton as the candidate for president. Correspondingly, Joseph, aged 16, relates his own beliefs and values to Bernie Sanders, who he feels would represent his own values in political office. Joseph finds it important that Bernie Sanders "said once that he would try to make college more available for people." Joseph, who was not eligible to vote in the 2016 presidential election, nevertheless has preferences for a presidential candidate based on his own desires as a low-income student pursuing higher education.

While young people relate their political preferences to their own beliefs and circumstances, others recognize the influence of their community on their own beliefs and political party affiliation. Addie, aged 14, describes that her political community is homogenous, leaning heavily toward the Democratic platform. Addie and her friends are "always just trashing on Donald Trump, mostly." Addie and her peers have witnessed Donald Trump's use of Twitter as a platform for his voice, and his insults to other candidates. The ways in which Addie has learned about Donald Trump and other candidates in the election have been digitally mediated, particularly on Twitter.

Addie shares that "everyone I'm friends with is Democrats, so it's not like I'm stepping on anyone's toes" and that her city "is like the most Democratic city ever." Addie shares that the political beliefs of those around her shape her beliefs. She has decided not to discuss politics with her best friend, a Republican, in order to preserve their friendship, a dilemma that will be discussed in Section 5.2.1. Sean, aged 15, who grew up in the same city as Addie, says that he is a "Democrat, probably. I've shaped my beliefs to align... I mean, everyone I know is a Democrat. And like everyone I grew up with." Sean says that he shaped his views to match the views of others in his community, and that the politically homogenous community shaped his views, illustrating a reciprocal effect. It is not surprising that Addie and Sean noticed this political composition in their city, as the geographic region of data collection, an urban area on the east coast of the United States, is known to be Democratic, as are other cities and pockets along the coast.

Tanesha, aged 16, expressed her concerns about what each of the two political parties in the United States represent, and therefore does not see herself in alignment "with any political party." This is in line with prior research, which indicates that young people are fed up with party politics and political polarization (Boulianne & Theocharis, 2018). Tanesha shares that when she is "of the age" to vote, she will not become a member of a political party. Tanesha has learned through her advanced United States history course that "sometimes parties' views like, slowly gradually change. I take A. P. US History, and I've seen that Democrats and Republicans, their viewpoints have somewhat kinda switched over the years back and forth." With this understanding in mind, Tanesha shares that most recently, she aligns "more with the Democrats than Republicans. And no I'm not the Democratic Party, but I do agree with their viewpoints at the moment, in this current stage." Tanesha sees herself on the political spectrum closer to the Democrats than the Republicans because "Democrats are more involved [and want a] government that's there to help. And personally, I think I need a government that's willing to help because some things won't be ...well, 'cause there are a lot of corrupt [people] about to give in within the Republican government." Tanesha comes from a community that benefits from social welfare programs, which is exemplified by her belief that it is important for the government to "help" people. Martin, aged 15, holds similar sentiments as Tanesha, and demonstrates his understanding of how political parties developed in the United States. Martin chooses to identify as an Independent, because "you learn what history has to say about what originally these parties stood for." Martin disapproves of the Democrats having been "pro-slavery at one time, and the Ku Klux Klan was sent by Republicans against the Democratic Party. And like, nowadays it's kinda switched."

Tanesha wrestles with where her beliefs fall on the political spectrum, and acknowledges that her beliefs align closer to Democrats, but several participants deliberately choose to not have a political party affiliation. Damon, aged 14, prefers to "separate myself from them and like, think about the possibilities, just be by myself." Damon also chooses not to identify himself with anyone on the current political stage because these figures "are only based on one thing." Damon suggests that the politicians he is aware of are focused on single issues, and do not appeal to his own interests. Equally, Robert, aged 16, says that he does not wish to affiliate with a political party because he is "not that political yet" and does not see himself voting for a "Democrat or a Republican each time. I'd rather like, switch it up. Like if one side has somebody who I see that can make a change, or something like that, I would vote for them instead of just voting for a Democrat every single time." Robert wishes to vote for the candidate who "presents themselves" the best, with interests and ideas that appeal to Robert, rather than always voting on party lines.

Most participants shared a view about their political party affiliations, and it is important to note that there were several who deliberately chose not to affiliate. Young people deliberately decide to not affiliate with political parties because they feel a personal disagreement with the issues and values that the parties each represent. These young people choose to express their voice by disagreeing with how the political parties evolve to change positions on certain issues over time, or not wishing to label their identity. Moreover, use of social media by public figures to promote their agenda and insult others has even turned off some young people, like Tanesha, from choosing to identify with a political party. A trend in the data demonstrated that for the few participants who have not had much thought about affiliating with a political party and how to discuss their beliefs, they tend to pay less attention to current events.

Political Identity Development: The Case of Elsie

Elsie, aged 17, is an outspoken critical thinker who is very interested in politics. Elsie developed her political ideas and beliefs throughout her upbringing by following current events, participating in the Junior State of America, and discussing political and social issues with her parents. Elsie provides a strong vignette to demonstrate the evolution of political identity throughout adolescence, as her first political memory is from when she was nine or ten years old, when she noticed an Obama pin on her friend's backpack. Elsie became truly interested in politics at age 11 or 12. At that point, Elsie recalls being a "Libertarian Republican because that was what my father was. I was one of the only conservatives in my grade." Today, Elsie describes her political views as "left-wing Libertarian" because she believes that "government involvement leads to it being bureaucratic and poorly-run." Elsie believes that gay marriage and abortion are two examples of issues that the government should not "be a part of." For Elsie, "the government shouldn't say who you can and cannot marry beyond like, protecting children from being sold into sex slavery. There's no reason for the government to be like, 'Well, you can't marry someone who's like this.' And you know, abortion should be a decision between a woman and her doctor, and the government shouldn't be involved." Key to the Libertarian philosophy is individual liberty, and Elsie's beliefs align with this attitude.

Elsie illustrates that political party affiliation is something that develops over time (Pickard, 2019). At first, Elsie was more "conservative," like her father. She agreed with everything he said, but in high school, she started "arguing with people" and began learning more about her own beliefs through such conversations. Elsie enjoys finding "grey areas to argue about" and genuinely wants to understand different viewpoints. She complained that when others ask her about her views, they do not share theirs. Elsie blames this on the fact that she goes "to a liberal school that doesn't really train people to have discourse." So, Elsie seizes any and every opportunity to "have discourse" with others and share her voice.

For someone who appreciates learning from the arguments with those with differing opinions, it frustrates Elsie that she is mostly surrounded by people who agree with her. For example, no one in Elsie's family is pro-life, so her pro-choice stance on abortion is not challenged. Elsie reflected on this issue and others. Certain events or issues "anger" her, and she feels "this is an issue in our community and we should do something about it. But I find a lot of the time that there aren't things I can do about the problem." Elsie specified that she is concerned about Islamophobia in her synagogue youth group: "It's one of those things when I feel like I should say something, but I don't know how to say something." Elsie does not seem afraid to speak her mind, yet feels stifled or tongue-tied when compelled to stand up to prejudice and injustice. Elsie's sense of efficacy is tied to her feeling that she could speak up—but she does not know what to say to make a difference.

Elsie acknowledged that environment forms individuals and identities, and "education informs a lot of your prejudices." It upsets her when she discovers that people from her community—from a similar educational and socioeconomic background—have "all these prejudices." She seems more understanding of prejudice from a community unlike her own. For Elsie, she is "a little less fazed by absurd things" that strangers might say in her interactions with them on social media. However, "if it's someone I know, and if it's someone, for example, I go to school with, and so they have the same educational background as me, I'm a little more, like… 'Okay, what's your problem? Because you should know better.'" For example, "you could be arguing online with someone who's stopped going to school in the eighth grade, is from the deep, deep South, and of course, you know, they have white supremacist views, they joined the KKK when they were 17 because that was their community." Elsie concedes, "That's what kept them going. So it's like, well, they need to get educated, but they're a lot less likely to listen to you, and … you know, it's just a very different experience where, like… if it's someone I know, it's someone who should know better." Elsie preaches that she wants to hear diverse perspectives, but the beliefs she expresses suggest she also may hold prejudices against talking to others with "radical" beliefs. The following section will describe how young people are expressing their political beliefs and learning from their peers.

5.2   SHARING ONE'S VOICE IN CONTEMPORARY SOCIETY

In shaping their views of the political world, and their own political beliefs, young people in this study often discuss political and social issues with trusted adults in their lives, and with their peers. Previous research indicates that young people's understanding of political issues develops through their social ties and discussions with others (Kahne, Middaugh, & Allen, 2014), which complement the influences of mass media discussed in Section 5.1 (McLeod & Shah, 2009). These conversations within one's closer social network enable people to "interpret media messages, and construct meaning about public affairs" (McLeod & Shah, 2009, p. 5). The degree to which young people feel their voices are heard depends on how others perceive them and their beliefs, and their personal investment in the issue being discussed. Influential factors include friends, the tensions within the formation of political beliefs, and their relationship with adults, which influences self-efficacy. This section will explore the dynamics that affect whether young people share their voices in contemporary society.

5.2.1   Maintaining Friendships

Key to exercising political voice is discussing issues of public concern with people in one's community. There are several factors that influence whether or not a young person chooses to discuss these issues with friends or peers. While there was an assumption that adolescence is a period of exploring ideologies and having thought-provoking political discussions with friends, this is not always the case (Gillman & Sofer, 1978), particularly because adolescents care very much about getting on with their peers. Conflict—or the perception of its existence—diminishes young people's engagement (Hodgin, 2016). For those young people who choose not to discuss issues of public concern, some have a fear of losing friendships over a difference in opinion or values, and therefore hesitate to disclose their political opinions.

Kaitlyn, aged 16, describes the tension she feels with a friend from whom her political beliefs differ: "I know [discussing politics] is just starting an argument...on her Facebook she'll Share all these things I disagree with, so I know if I say something, it's just going to cause issues. And I would rather... I care more about our friendship than about our political views, so I just keep it to myself." Kaitlyn believes it is especially important to "keep politics out of" social media, especially "because everyone has different beliefs. I don't voice it with my friends too often because I know... they have the right to believe what they want, and it would just cause arguments. But I'll talk about it with my family, definitely." Kaitlyn felt "acute disappointment" when she learned that her close friend and her friend's family supported Donald Trump. Addie, aged 14, notes that her community is politically homogenous, and she shares that her "best friend, she's a Republican" and when they talk they do not "go into depth about politics because we have different views of what's happening. So I wouldn't say anything really controversial." In fact, often, Addie will go so far as to "ask someone are they Democrat or Republican, before I want to talk about the elections and stuff." Kaitlyn and Addie note that people have different beliefs and affiliate with different political parties—but do not acknowledge the possible benefits of interacting with others whose beliefs are different from theirs. While young people are at a critical stage in development to process information from the media, formulate and express their own ideas and opinions, and understand others' points of view (McLeod, 2000), it seems that sometimes friendship is more important than understanding what that friend's beliefs are. Young people are hesitant to share their views for fear of disagreement or being taken seriously (Hodgin, 2016).

Furthermore, Jillian, aged 15, notes that she sometimes discusses news and current events with her friends, and the conversations go like this: "'Do you agree on what they said last night? Do you like it? Do you dislike it? What do you like about them?' and then most of the time, we'll agree … on what they're talking about." Jillian shares that sometimes, when she and her friends disagree, they decide to "stop talking about politics, because once you disagree, you can ruin friendships." Jillian referred to her mother's advice to "never talk about politics." It is troubling that Jillian was advised in this way, as discourse with others can be beneficial for perspective taking and developing one's own views (Hess & McAvoy, 2015). Kaitlyn, Addie, Jillian, and other young people are more drawn to others with similar interests and attitudes, as adolescents primarily view other people based on these factors (Coleman, 2011). In contrast, Maisie, aged 14, comments, "I think that everybody does have their own, like, political opinion and I don't think … I'm even knowledgeable enough to tell somebody that, (A) they're wrong, or (B) that I am right." When Maisie talks to others about politics, she states her "opinion but not in a threatening way." Maisie appears to have risen above the desire to please friends, and has come to an understanding of what it means to have a respectful discussion with someone who holds different political views.

While Kaitlyn and Jillian feared losing friendships, other participants felt uncomfortable admitting to their friends that they pay attention to current events and have an opinion about politics. Imani, aged 14, thinks her peers would frown upon her if she asked them if they watched the presidential debates: "If I was like, 'Guys, did you watch the debate?' they'd be like, 'Why the hell are you watching debates?'" Imani fears judgment from her peers, which echoes the judgment and expectations of society that young people do not pay attention to current events and voice their opinions. Similarly, Jackie, aged 16, does not Share news articles through social media because, "It's kind of cliché but I don't want to re-post or re-Tweet a news story because people will be like 'why is she doing that?' Other people see it as weird, so I don't really want to do that." Kevin, aged 15, would not talk to his friends about politics, because he perceives his friends as "very immature" and not capable of having productive discussions about political and social issues. Kevin indicates, "most of my friends just get very mad when somebody talks about a certain person. Like, if I start talking about Donald Trump, my friends will start screaming, 'Donald Trump sucks!' It's… just bad."

Kevin alludes to his own friends not being "mature" enough to have discussions about political and social issues, which was a common concern among participants. Young people choose not to share their political views because they fear judgment because their ideas and beliefs are not yet fully formed, and because society—and their peers—expect them to not voice their beliefs. For example, Ava, aged 16, describes the tension of not knowing what to believe: "It's hard to form an opinion, and at my age… I don't know which one's right, which one's wrong… because there are so many opinions." Ava feels like she "should do more research and form my own [opinions], not based on what other people's opinions are, because you don't know if it's right or wrong." Ava explains, "that's why on social media, when the person was Tweeting it, I don't know, like… what their opinion was, so I don't wanna re-Tweet what's wrong, or they just like put a twist to a bad thing and just made it sound better."

Tanesha, aged 16, talks to friends (but not family, because her family is "never home") who agree with her political opinions, and sometimes these conversations happen via Snapchat. Throughout the primary election season, which occurred over the course of our interviews, Tanesha explained to me that Snapchat had image filters that one could add to the photo to show the election results in real time. While Tanesha and Zelda, aged 14, have digitally mediated discussions with their friends about politics, Jackie, aged 16, prefers to have discussions in person, because it is easier to interpret the other person's tone: "It's harder to get your tone across through text message. So if we're hanging out, and if we see on social media if there's an article or something or a headline that says something about Donald Trump for example, we'll talk about what we think." Misinterpretation is more likely to occur when there is not a face-to-face interaction because the context in which one reads a text on social media may be different from the context in which the author made the post (Jones, 2012). Young people who have prior experience of text misinterpretation shy away from having these discussions through text or social media. Elsie, aged 17, also identifies the issue of misinterpretation within digitally mediated discussions, and therefore prefers to have conversations about current events in person. On the Internet, "it's hard to tell which people are serious, and which people are trolling. And um… I've found when it's with people you can sort of, understand moreso where they're coming from." Elsie tries to "stay out of stuff on Tumblr, because like, no matter what you say, you're probably wrong." More often than not, Elsie says, "Online, I'm always worried about what I say is going to get misinterpreted."

In contrast to Tanesha, Bibiana would find it more interesting to talk to people who had views differing from her own. Bibiana does not always talk to her friends about current events, because she feels like her peers are "kind of in the same boat" as she is, and do not offer "a different view on like, the surroundings." Bibiana feels that talking to "someone who's actively involved or who actually votes or likes to be involved in politics" is more useful, because they "would be actively involved in trying to get more information." Bibiana describes herself and her friends as those who "observe" things that are going on in the world around them, like "riots," through social media. Bibiana is more interested in talking to adults, who have more experience in the political world, than her peers. Like Bibiana, Elsie, aged 17, genuinely wants to learn about "the other side" and "understand where they're coming from." Bibiana and Elsie allude to the homogenous political communities that Addie and Sean mentioned in Section 5.1.3, and their experience highlights how they have difficulty shaping their opinions without the opportunity to talk to people of different perspectives. The young people in this study are most concerned with people and issues that are of immediate concern to them, their families, friends, and communities. Perhaps this is why young people like Bibiana and Elsie have not taken to social media to interact with others outside of their homogenous political communities—young people are more interested in the issues and people that are closer to home.

Ava previously alluded to social media as a database of opinions—but she does not know which is "right" or "wrong." It appears that Ava, like many of her peers, wants to avoid making a mistake by re-Tweeting something "wrong," and giving others the impression that she holds a certain belief, when in reality she is trying out different beliefs and identities, and discovering what her values are. This may be a function of the tension between one's private self versus their public self that Goffman (1959, 1978) and Schlenker (1986, 2012) described as discussed in Chapter 3: young people are not sure of what to disclose, or how to disclose it, or at what point in the thought process to disclose it. On some social media platforms, like Tumblr, young people can create or Follow blogs to explore their political beliefs without anyone knowing their name—there is less ownership of these fluid beliefs. Tumblr allows for this fluid identity experimentation and discovery, whereas some more rigid platforms, like Facebook, do not. Facebook requires a name or identifying feature for the profile page, thereby automatically attaching anything that is Shared to that person's name. Young people may be hesitant to disclose their political beliefs on their Facebook profiles for this reason, as everyone in their Facebook social circle would then know their beliefs. Elsie is an important example: she prefers "to keep political stuff off my Facebook. I like to be somewhat in control of who knows what about me and my views."

Young people are in a limbo state of transition: they are grappling with understanding their own political views, yet are reluctant to discuss them with friends for fear of losing friendships. This hesitance leads to how young people display their beliefs on social media pages, often keeping their views private, or within their family circles. Young people most often trust adults, but face issues of efficacy in that their voices are not always heard by the adults they look to as role models in their lives, as the next section will demonstrate.

5.2.2   Young People's Perceptions of Being Heard

While it is evident that many young people approach political conversations with their peers in trepidation, some young people believe that sharing their viewpoints is an essential factor of citizenship and belonging. Martin, aged 15, says that one can be a citizen by "having a say in things, voicing your opinion. You can have freedom of speech, but a time when I felt like a citizen... voicing [my] opinions." Yet, as this section will reveal, the dilemma is that many young people voice their opinions, but do not feel they are *heard*. This section will illustrate the experiences of nine participants who have felt that adults do not hear them when they voice their opinions.

Maisie, aged 14, described the desire for young people to be heard and taken seriously by adults. Maisie asserted that there are other ways to be civically engaged beyond voting, such as the citywide youth council in Maisie's city. Unfortunately, Maisie has been unsuccessful with the issues she has tried to change and for which she has tried to make her voice heard, resulting in a low sense of efficacy, and skepticism about adults who truly listen to the youth council, and whether her voice will ever be heard. Maisie notes, "the younger you are, the less respect you get for your opinions and engagement. There's always something keeping you from being respected, but I'll always have to be as confident as possible… like… 'I respect myself and I respect my opinion, and I'm saying it in a way that's confident, so you should respect it, too.'" Maisie is unsure of whether there will be a time in her life that she feels that her voice is heard: "I don't think it's a specific age, I don't think the day I turn eighteen it's gonna be like, 'You're an adult now.' I think even then, there will be other reasons to look down on me." This feeling of being looked down upon can be frustrating for anyone, of any age. Maisie continues, "Some people even still consider eighteen like, 'just a kid,' even when you're in your twenties or thirties, there's always an age difference, or like, something that's keeping you from being respected." For Maisie, this idea of always being younger sets a difficult challenge that seems impossible to overcome.

Sean, aged 15, expounds upon the issue of feeling like one's voice is not heard, especially when one is too young to vote: "I think there are some opportunities for people who can't vote to be able to let what they think be heard. And that's … partially enabled by technology, because people don't always know how old you are on technology." Sean highlights that technology can be a way around the age barrier in making one's voice heard, an idea that will be further addressed in Section 5.3. Sean also expresses that voting is a possible way to make one's voice heard, but does not always have its desired effect: "Once you're able to vote, that does enable you to vote for a candidate, but voting for a candidate … doesn't always mean that your specific voice is being heard." Sean details the complexity of the right to vote: a vote represents a medium through which one can express an opinion, but the person or issue one votes for may not win. Sean also speaks about the student council at his school, how it is meant to give students an opportunity to enact change in their school. However, he is frustrated that the student council "literally don't have much power. Like, we don't have any authority. I mean like… we take votes but … on the school policy we have no like, actual say… it's the administration's job, basically.... It's their job to run the school." This idea of authority is complex, and perceived by other participants in this study, such as Habibah, aged 16. She believes that adults "in authority, their voice gets heard more than the young people, because if they have authority, then they have the power, so their voice weighs more than just a regular high school student that doesn't really have that much power or authority." Habibah feels that if her voice were to be heard, she would need to be endorsed by someone "powerful," like the President—someone who would entice others to listen to her.

As Maisie, Sean, and Habibah expressed their frustration that their voices remain unheard at school or by the city government, another arena in which young people's voices are not always heard is the home. Martin, aged 15, likes to talk with his mother about current events because she is "wise," but acknowledges that in those conversations, "it's more... um... her talking, rather than me talking." Similarly, Jaden, aged 14, has parents who "don't ask" what he is thinking. And, in the case of Kenai, aged 14, his family boldly excludes him from these discussions. Kenai explains that his family will "want to know my opinion and if they don't like my opinion it'd be really obvious that they don't like it. And if they do like it, they just say 'stay out of that until you're like, eighteen or something like that, or you can vote.'" In the past, parental attitudes toward politics have been, "not in front of the children!" (Gillman & Sofer, 1978, p. 82). Some parents, like Kenai's, have told young people to stay out of political conversations, keeping young people from the space and time to grapple with their beliefs, and reconcile them with beliefs of people they know and trust. But, when families and trusted adults shut down the voices of young people in the home, it becomes more difficult for young people to feel confident that their voices will be heard elsewhere (Shah et al., 2009).

Kenai revealed his family dynamic, which plays a part in his low sense of efficacy. He is interested in politics but, as described above, he does not often have the opportunity to discuss the views that he is forming, despite his desires to have these discussions. He wants "to be involved in the conversation, because I think ... from like, the younger side to the older side, it's good to give them my opinion of things. And just to get my voice across." When his family will not talk to him about politics, Kenai turns to Google to research the topics he wants to discuss. Kenai is excited to vote in the future, because he will finally have the freedom to express his own beliefs. Interestingly, he thinks his family "would allow me to vote, but they would... try to sway my opinion to theirs ... before they would let me [vote]. That's one of the things that can happen. Or they would... just let me vote and not be too strict on it. Now that I'm of age, I should have the right, or like, the responsibility to do so myself." When young people do have the opportunity to talk with parents and other adults, some young people, like Robert, aged 16, view the adults as having an "advantage" in the conversation. This "advantage" comes from being older and perceivably more knowledgeable about the issues. When Robert talks about current events with his father, "he can say things that I don't understand, and I'll just like, sit back. I'm like, 'Okay, you got it.'" Robert defers to his father for knowledge about current events.

The findings presented here raise an important issue: if young people are discouraged from talking to adults they trust about their opinions as they formulate them because they are seen by adults as "too young" to have opinions, how can young people shape their ideas and be prepared to work with others in the future to resolve complex issues? Some young people turn to technology, as Sean alluded, and as Kenai does with his Google research. However, young people are often so disempowered that they do not develop or even share their views by posting their own views on social media. Dahlgren and Olsson (2007) note that one must feel empowered and that civic engagement must be meaningful. However, what has become clear through findings presented here is that young people often feel too disempowered to become civically engaged, even through digital means like social media.

5.2.3   Using Everyday Tools for Political Voice: Young People in the Black Lives Matter Movement

It is important to address the factors that influence why young people feel limited in their ability to express themselves as citizens. This problem might be partly due to the fact that they are perceived as too young. Young people seem to be stuck in this perception of being "too young" for years, as the definition of what it means to be a young person becomes blurred. Galland (2007) notes that this is a result of the individualized status of reaching "adulthood," as people prolong their years in formal education, delay marriage, and hold short-term employment at the start of their working lives, all factors in the normative dimension of age (James, 2014). Changing societal norms are keeping young people in this "youth" status for much longer, which has the potential to greatly harm their sense of self-efficacy: because if "adulthood" means achieving certain milestones in education, relationships, and employment that society uses to mark adult-hood, young people will achieve this status, and the respect it demands, at different ages. The voting age in the United States is 18—legal adulthood—but if young people are perceived as adults much later, young people might not feel fully heard by other adults when they *do* reach voting age.

Among participants, there was a strong feeling of restriction and a sense that teenagers are not full citizens, which stems from the fact that the young people in this study are not yet 18 and eligible to vote. Some young people feel that teenagers are not full citizens because they genuinely believe that a citizen is someone who is able to vote, an adult as defined by the law, and someone who has authority over others. This perception of power structures, particularly in schools, where participants allude to adults having control, comes into play by yielding a lower sense of self-efficacy.

Kenai believes "I can't really do much, politically. Like I can't really have that big of an impact on what's going on." After a moment, he mentioned the ballot initiative in his school, as discussed in Chapter 4, and shared that it was important to him to "participate" in "stuff like that." Robert agrees that it is important for young people to "participate" as Kenai says, because "for young people, like my age to be like, pushing… putting themselves out there to like, show that we actually care about what's going on, it means a lot. So like, I guess that can start some type of change." Because people assume that young people will not be engaged, actually having young people engaged seems to make a big impact. Jillian says "even some adults, they're like 'They're just a kid, they can't do any-thing, they're just a kid.' But kids actually have a lot of impact. Because they know what they want to grow up in. Sometimes being a citizen means that you're too young, can't do it … the adults are the only ones who can do that." Kenai and Jillian put out a call for young people to become engaged and share their voices in order to make a change, but still feel frustrated that their impact as citizens is often relatively low.

Indeed, young people in this study expressed their frustration with feeling unheard, and illustrated examples of how they can attempt to make their voices heard without having to contend with adults. As Sean expressed, one can use technology and social media because in many cases, one does not need to reveal age online. Buckingham (2013) notes, "the Internet provides *some* [emphasis original] children with the opportunity for their voices to be heard, in ways that transcend hitherto insurmount-able barriers of geographical distance or social difference" (p. 81). Scholars also note that the Internet provides a "route to pursue already existing civic interests" (Livingstone et al., 2007, p. 26). A lower sense of self-efficacy and a feeling that teenagers are not full citizens has been overcome by some young people who use social media as a platform to make their voices heard. Technology is "transforming and connecting [young people] to one another, providing them with a new sense of political self" (Katz, 1997, p. 173). This has become especially true as young people become involved in the Black Lives Matter movement in the United States.

Participants who became involved in the Black Lives Matter movement spoke about their racial identity during our interviews. When racial identity was revealed, participants delved into the personal nature of race, and how this racial identity manifests itself in their daily lives. Tanesha, aged 16, and a black female, demonstrated her racial identity when she says she feels a connection to former President Barack Obama because he "was the first African-American President, and … I'm really big on social issues, especially when it comes to gender discrimination and race discrimination." Tanesha herself has "become involved in those movements." Bandura (2008) notes that when people find role models that are similar to them, they have an increase in efficacy when they see that other person doing something they want to do. Tanesha has done just this after noting the causes championed by Barack Obama. Tanesha shares that her personal identity affects the issues that she cares about and wants to become involved in. Related to this issue of racial discrimination is the ongoing Black Lives Matter movement.

The Black Lives Matter movement began in 2013 as a response to the acquittal of the man on neighborhood watch who fatally shot 17-year-old Trayvon Martin, a young black man. The movement is "an ideological and political intervention in a world where Black lives are systematically and intentionally targeted for demise" (Black Lives Matter, 2018). Black Lives Matter has developed through the leadership of its organizers Alicia Garza, Patrisse Cullors, and Opal Tometi, and in the years since the movement began, there have been countless incidents that have resulted in deaths, and in collective action. In 2014, 18-year-old Michael Brown was shot and killed by a police officer in Ferguson, Missouri (BBC News, 2014), a further incident of racial profiling and brutality against blacks, which subsequently led to violence and unrest in Ferguson (BBC News, 2015), which participant Martin discussed in his interviews. The movement has grown through the use of social media, and the hashtag #BlackLivesMatter, which seeks to amplify how anti-Black racism pervades the United States (Black Lives Matter, 2018). Young people have not only caught on to this movement, but they have become involved with it through social media.

Addie, aged 14, reflected on her level of engagement and activism following the news of excessive force against blacks in the United States. In her former school, "a public school, there were only five black kids out of like three hundred kids." Addie was one of these five students. She notes, "There is a lot of racism going on" in the United States, "especially with Donald Trump." Addie's efficacy to resolve this social issue has wavered:

> Well, at times, with the shootings and everything, I don't really get inspired to do something... Actually, no. When I had Instagram, I would always post stuff about that. Because I know how I have a lot of Followers so I thought I should say something ... to speak my mind, you know. And I would do that. That was the most I'd do, because ... I'm only a kid, I really can't do as much stuff, I don't think.

Addie's sense that her age—being "only a kid"—precluded her from taking action led her to take a step toward making her voice heard on social media. Addie also sees her posts as a way for others to learn about other opinions. Addie wants others to know "what's happening. And also, if someone heard this story but from a different point of view, and from my point of view of how it's wrong, that could help and making them change their... idea of what was happening." While Addie does not know how many people read or see her posts—what Levine (2008) has established as the "audience problem"—she is confident that at least some of her social network will be exposed to her views, and will learn from them. Most commonly, friends are the intended audience for such posts, but not all young people realize that their friends may not always see—or pay attention to—what they post (boyd, 2009).

As indicated in Section 5.1, information about current events is easily accessed through social media. Nadia, aged 16, recognizes the ease with which people can access information through social media, and therefore claims that social media is the best way to get the word out about any issue because "people are always on their phones. So it's like, if you constantly keep seeing it, it's like, 'oh, maybe I should check it out.'" While Addie uses the Internet to share her views on Black Lives Matter, Veronica, aged 15, consumes news about the movement through social media. Veronica says that social media informed her about what was happening to black teens, and the Black Lives Matter movement: "I wouldn't have known about Sandra Bland if it weren't for Facebook. Same thing about Trayvon Martin. If it wasn't for Facebook I wouldn't have known about it unless someone else had come up to me and told me, because I'm not really a big TV person, I don't really watch anything. That's how I find my information."

Social media has become a platform for activists of all ages to spread awareness about the police brutality affecting black communities throughout the United States, and to share voices and suggest civic actions. Addie took to Instagram to share her own beliefs about and reactions to current events. Young people across the United States learned about marches and vigils through social media, including Martin, who discussed this in Chapter 3. Veronica recognized how important social media has been for the movement—perhaps most importantly, Addie recognized social media as a way for young people to be heard.

5.3   ENGAGING IN THE POLITICAL WORLD IN CONTEMPORARY SOCIETY

Young people's sense of their position in society as "too young" to participate contributes to their understanding of how they might engage in the political world. While young people feel that society does not expect them to pay attention to current events, they follow current events anyway, and pursue discussions with trusted adults to learn more, and develop and articulate their own views. Young people may not be rebelling against society on purpose, but they are certainly demonstrating that their generation is far more capable and interested than adults surmise, as a growing body of research suggests (Pontes et al., 2018).

Young people interact with and contribute to the world around them by following current events through social media, which aids young people in developing their political beliefs. Young people are also becoming aware of current events and shaping their beliefs by interacting with others, primarily with people who are close to them, such as teachers and parents, but shy away from discussing these issues with their peers. Young people prefer to discuss these issues in person, rather than online, because of the fear of being misinterpreted through text message or another online platform. Young people feel this way primarily because they prioritize preserving their friendships, and seek to avoid confrontation with friends who may have differing political views. In the region where data was collected, most participants felt their political communities were homogenous, and therefore these young people did not have access to a diversity of perspectives. Notably, the participants who were recruited from a Catholic high school—which draws students from suburban and rural towns surrounding the urban area of fieldwork—voiced more concerns about losing friendships as a result of political disagreement. It seems that the political diversity within this high school is greater than that experienced by the participants who attend public schools in the liberal, urban setting. While previous studies have demonstrated that people can expand their social circles by meeting people online who they might not have met face-to-face (Holloway & Valentine, 2003), the young people in this study did not seek out online interaction to explore political issues with others they did not know. While young people did wish to have political conversations, it is clear that they prefer to keep these conversations within the family.

How young people understand citizenship impacts their sense of self-efficacy (Dias & Menezes, 2014). The findings presented in this chapter indicate that key to active citizenship is exercising one's voice. Maisie, aged 14, shares frustration that young people are completely "overlooked" from the political process because at their age, "Kids aren't expected to know about these things, so they're never taught about them. And then it's an endless loop, because if you don't teach them, then you can't expect them to know it, but if you expect them to know it, then you're never gonna teach them." Maisie wants teachers to explain how taxes work, how voting works, and how to register to vote, "things you're not expected to know, but at the same time, you're expected to figure it out by yourself, unless your family teaches you." Maisie argues that if young people are taught more in school about democratic society and how to participate, then "people would grow up to be more active citizens and more responsible citizens. Then you could have real conversations with kids about their opinions on stuff, and educate them further and like, hear what they have to say. Because I think a lot of kids have good ideas but they just don't really have a voice in anything."

Young people might have the motivation to share their voices, but they do not always have the confidence or support of those around them. Young people are in a catch-22, and at a crossroads in their development as citizens and social actors. They are not yet adults who are eligible to vote (Finlay, Wray-Lake, & Flanagan, 2010; Stepick, Stepick, & Labissiere, 2008), but they do have their own beliefs and opinions (Erikson, 1968; Sherrod, Torney-Purta, & Flanagan, 2010), and understanding of how they wish to develop and express those beliefs and opinions. If young people are exposed to diversity, they seem to not want to embrace it, but the individuals from the homogenous political community crave diversity. Young people prefer to talk to older adults because they are not confident in their own knowledge about current events and politics; but they talk to these adults even though they feel adults do not listen to them, that their voices are not heard. Young people feel disenfranchised but do not discuss politics with their peers, for fear they will lose friendships. Very few young people are sharing their voices and opinions online or on social media, because many young people do not want to share what they feel are under-developed views, and do not want to know whether their friends have different views. Young people who are not listened to at home are unsure of their digital audience: some post their views on social media with the hope that some of their Followers will read them, while others are convinced that no one will read them. Young people have been stifled in their attempts to express their views, but they need the space and understanding from others to develop those views. Findings from this study expose young people's development of civic identity and voice in today's world as a nuanced function of their experiences in contemporary society, and yield a framework of civic identity that will be presented in Chapter 6.

These tensions and restrictions of voice result in an overwhelmingly low sense of self-efficacy among young people. What has been helpful to some young people is the use of social media as a means of making their voices heard, even when they avoid directly discussing their political beliefs with peers, and feel that adults do not take them and their beliefs seriously. The future implications for young people turning to social media to amplify their voices will be addressed in the next chapter, which highlights the lessons to be learned from the #NeverAgain movement that emerged in February 2018 and the civic skills of those involved, a new framework of civic identity, and recommendations for the future of civic education.

REFERENCES

Almond, G., & Verba, S. (1963). *The Civic Culture: Political Attitudes and Democracy in Five Nations.* Princeton: Princeton University Press.
Bandura, A. (2008). An Agentic Perspective on Positive Psychology. In S. Lopez (Ed.), *Positive Psychology: Expecting the Best in People.* New York: Praeger.
BBC News. (2014, November 25). *Ferguson Protests: What We Know About Michael Brown's Last Minutes.* Retrieved April 5, 2018, from BBC News: US & Canada http://www.bbc.co.uk/news/world-us-canada-28841715

BBC News. (2015, August 10). *Ferguson Unrest: From Shooting to Nationwide Protests*. Retrieved April 5, 2018, from BBC News: US & Canada http://www.bbc.co.uk/news/world-us-canada-30193354

Black Lives Matter. (2018). *Herstory*. Retrieved March 27, 2018, from Black Lives Matter https://blacklivesmatter.com/about/herstory/

Boulianne, S., & Theocharis, Y. (2018). Young People, Digital Media, and Engagement: A Meta-Analysis of Research. *Social Science Computer Review*, 1–17.

boyd, d. (2009, April 18). Living and Learning with Social Media. *Symposium for Teaching and Learning with Technology*. State College, PA: Penn State.

Buckingham, D. (2013). *Beyond Technology: Children's Learning in the Age of Digital Culture*. Cambridge: John Wiley & Sons.

Coleman, J. C. (2011). *The Nature of Adolescence* (4th ed.). London, England: Routledge.

Collin, P. (2015). *Young Citizens and Political Participation in a Digital Society: Addressing the Democratic Disconnect*. Basingstoke: Palgrave Macmillan.

Dahlgren, P., & Olsson, T. (2007). Young Activists, Political Horizons and the Internet: Adapting the Net to One's Purposes. In B. D. Loader (Ed.), *Young Citizens in the Digital Age: Political Engagement, Young People and New Media* (pp. 68–81). London: Routledge.

Dassonneville, R., Quintelier, E., Hooghe, M., & Claes, E. (2012). The Relation Between Civic Education and Political Attitudes and Behavior: A Two-year Panel Study Among Belgian Late Adolescents. *Applied Developmental Science, 16*(3), 140–150.

Dias, T. S., & Menezes, I. (2014, June 2). Children and Adolescents as Political Actors: Collective Visions of Politics and Citizenship. *Journal of Moral Education*, 250–268.

Dimitrova, D., Shehata, A., Strömbäck, J., & Nord, L. (2014). The Effects of Digital Media on Political Knowledge and Participation in Election Campaigns: Evidence from Panel Data. *Communication Research, 41*(1), 95–118.

Erikson, E. H. (1968). *Identity: Youth and Crisis*. New York: W.W. Norton & Company.

Finlay, A., Wray-Lake, L., & Flanagan, C. (2010). Civic Engagement During the Transition to Adulthood: Developmental Opportunities and Social Policies at a Critical Juncture. In L. Sherrod, J. Torney-Purta, & C. Flanagan (Eds.), *Handbook of Research on Civic Engagement in Youth* (pp. 277–206). Hoboken, NJ: John Wiley & Sons.

Galland, O. (2007). *Boundless Youth: Stories in the Transition to Adulthood* (T. Matthews & P. Hamilton, Trans.). Oxford: The Bardwell Press.

Gil de Zúñiga, H., Copeland, L., & Bimber, B. (2013). Political Consumerism: Civic Engagement and the Social Media Connection. *New Media & Society, 16*(3), 488–506.

Gillman, S., & Sofer, E. G. (1978). Children, Adolescents, and Politics: A Selective Review. *Cambridge Journal of Education, 8*(2–3), 78–97.

Goffman, E. (1959). *The Presentation of Self in Everyday Life*. Garden City, NY: Doubleday Anchor Books.

Goffman, E. (1978). The Presentation of Self to Others. In J. G. Manis & B. N. Meltzer (Eds.), *Symbolic Interaction: A Reader in Social Psychology* (3rd ed., pp. 234–244). London: Allyn and Bacon.

Gottfried, J., & Shearer, E. (2017). *News Use Across Social Media Platforms 2017*. Pew Research Center.

Hart, D., & Kirshner, B. (2009). Civic Participation and Development Among Urban Adolescents. In J. Youniss & P. Levine (Eds.), *Engaging Young People in Civic Life* (pp. 102–120). Nashville, TN: Vanderbilt University Press.

Henn, M., & Foard, N. (2012). Back on the Agenda and Off the Curriculum? Citizenship Education and Young People's Political Engagement. *Teaching Citizenship, 32*, 32–35.

Hess, D., & McAvoy, P. (2015). *The Political Classroom: Evidence and Ethics in Democratic Education*. New York: Routledge.

Hess, R. D., & Torney-Purta, J. V. (2005). *The Development of Political Attitudes in Children*. London: Transaction Publishers.

Hodgin, E. (2016, June 27). Educating Youth for Online Civic and Political Dialogue: A Conceptual Framework for the Digital Age. *Journal of Digital and Media Literacy*.

Holloway, S. L., & Valentine, G. (2003). *Cyberkids: Children in the Information Age*. London: RoutledgeFalmer.

Holt, K., Shehata, A., Strömbäck, J., & Ljungberg, E. (2013). Age and the Effects of News Media Attention and Social Media Use on Political Interest and Participation: Do Social Media Function as Leveller? *European Journal of Communication, 28*(1), 19–34.

Huckfeldt, R., & Sprague, J. (1995). *Citizens, Politics, and Social Communication: Information and Influence in an Election Campaign*. New York: Cambridge University Press.

James, C. (2014). *Disconnected: Youth, New Media, and the Ethics Gap*. Cambridge, MA: The MIT Press.

Jones, J. (2012). Social Media and Persuasion: Crowdsourcing Arguments on Digital Networks. In H. S. Al-Deen & J. A. Hendricks (Eds.), *Social Media: Usage and Impact* (pp. 23–38). Plymouth, England: Lexington Books.

Kahne, J., Middaugh, E., & Allen, D. (2014). *Youth, New Media, and the Rise of Participatory Politics*. Chicago: The University of Chicago Press.

Katz, J. (1997). *Virtuous Reality: How America Surrendered Discussion of Moral Values to Opportunists, Nitwits, and Blockheads Like William Bennett*. New York: Random House.

Katz, J. E., & Rice, R. E. (2002). Syntopia: Access, Civic Involvement, and Social Interaction on the Net. In B. Wellman & C. Haythornthwaite (Eds.), *The Internet in Everyday Life* (pp. 114–138). Oxford: Blackwell Publishing Ltd.

Ke, L., & Starkey, H. (2014). Active Citizens, Good Citizens, and Insouciant Bystanders: The Educational Implications of Chinese University Students' Civic Participation Via Social Networking. *London Review of Education, 12*(1), 50–62.

Kieffer, C. H. (1984). Citizen Empowerment: A Developmental Perspective. *Prevention in Human Services, 3*(2–3), 9–36.

Kisby, B., & Sloam, J. (2014). Promoting Youth Participation in Democracy: The Role of Higher Education. In A. Mycock & J. Tonge (Eds.), *Beyond the Youth Citizenship Commission: Young People and Politics*. London: Political Studies Association.

Krueger, B. (2002). Assessing the Potential of Internet Political Participation in the United States: A Resource Approach. *American Politics Research, 30,* 476–498.

Lenhart, A., Duggan, M., Perrin, A., Stepler, R., Rainie, L., & Parker, K. (2015). *Teens, Social Media & Technology Overview 2015*. Pew Research Center.

Lenhart, A., Madden, M., Smith, A., Purcell, K., Zickhur, K., & Rainie, L. (2011). *Teens, Kindness and Cruelty on Social Network Sites: How American Teens Navigate the New World of Digital Citizenship. Pew Internet & American Life Project*. Washington, DC: Pew Research Center.

Levine, P. (2008). A Public Voice for Youth: The Audience Problem in Digital Media and Civic Education. In W. L. Bennett (Ed.), *Civic Life Online: Learning How Digital Media Can Engage Youth* (pp. 119–138). Cambridge, MA: The MIT Press.

Linton, A. (2015). Politically Engaged and Alienated Youth: Reevaluating 2010 UK Student Protests. In E. Middaugh & B. Kirshner (Eds.), *#youthaction: Becoming Political in the Digital Age* (pp. 191–207). Charlotte, NC: Information Age Publishing, Inc.

Livingstone, S., Couldry, N., & Markham, T. (2007). Youthful Steps Towards Civic Participation: Does the Internet Help? In B. D. Loader (Ed.), *Young Citizens in the Digital Age: Political Engagement, Young People and New Media* (pp. 21–34). London: Routledge.

Maddux, J. E., & Gosselin, J. T. (2012). Self-Efficacy. In M. R. Leary & J. P. Tangney (Eds.), *Handbook of Self and Identity* (2nd ed., pp. 198–224). New York: Guilford Press.

McLeod, J. M. (2000). Media and Civic Socialization of Youth. *Journal of Adolescent Health* (pp. 45–51). Society for Adolescent Medicine.

McLeod, J. M., & Shah, D. V. (2009). Communication and Political Socialization: Challenges and Opportunities for Research. *Political Communication, 26*(1), 1–10.

Nasir, N. S., & Kirshner, B. (2003). The Cultural Construction of Moral and Civic Identities. *Applied Developmental Science, 7*, 138–147.

Osler, A., & Starkey, H. (2018). Extending the Theory and Practice of Education for Cosmopolitan Citizenship. *Educational Review, 70*(1), 31–40.

Pasek, J., More, E., & Romer, D. (2009). Realizing the Social Internet? Online Social Networking Meets Offline Civic Engagement. *Journal of Information Technology & Politics, 6*(3–4), 197–215.

Pickard, S. (2019). *Politics, Protest and Young People: Political Participation and Dissent in 21st Century Britain*. London: Palgrave Macmillan.

Pontes, A., Henn, M., & Griffiths, M. D. (2018). Towards a Conceptualization of Young People's Political Engagement: A Qualitative Focus Group Study. *Societies, 8*(1), 17.

Print, M. (2007). Citizenship Education and Youth Participation in Democracy. *British Journal of Educational Studies, 55*, 325–345.

Quan-Haase, A., & boyd, d. (2011). Teen Communities. In G. A. Barnett (Ed.), *Encyclopedia of Social Networks* (Vol. 1). Thousand Oaks, CA: SAGE.

Schlenker, B. (1986). Self-Identification: Toward an Integration of the Private and Public Self. In *Public Self and Private Self* (pp. 21–62). New York: Springer.

Schlenker, B. (2012). Self-Presentation. In M. R. Leary & J. P. Tangney (Eds.), *Handbook of Self and Identity* (2nd ed., pp. 542–570). New York: Guilford Press.

Serriere, S. C. (2014). The Role of the Elementary Teacher in Fostering Civic Efficacy. *The Social Studies, 105*(1), 45–56.

Shah, D. V., Cho, J., Eveland Jr., W. P., & Kwak, N. (2005). Information and Expression in a Digital Age: Modeling Internet Effects on Civic Participation. *Communication Research, 32*(5), 531–565.

Shah, D. V., McLeod, J. M., & Lee, N.-j. (2009). Communication Competence as a Foundation for Civic Competence: Processes of Socialization into Citizenship. *Political Communication, 26*(1), 102–117.

Shea, D. M., & Green, J. C. (Eds.). (2007). *Fountain of Youth: Strategies and Tactics for Mobilizing America's Young Voters*. New York: Rowman & Littlefield, Inc.

Sherrod, L., Torney-Purta, J., & Flanagan, C. (2010). *Handbook of Research on Civic Engagement in Youth*. Hoboken, NJ: John Wiley & Sons.

Sloam, J., Ehsan, R., & Henn, M. (2018). 'Youthquake': How and Why Young People Reshaped the Political Landscape in 2017. *Political Insight, 9*(1), 4–8.

Sotirovic, M., & McLeod, J. (2001). Values, Communication Behavior, and Political Participation. *Political Communication, 18*(3), 273–300.

Stepick, A., Stepick, C., & Labissiere, C. (2008). South Florida's Immigrant Youth and Civic Engagement. *Applied Developmental Science, 12*(2), 57–65.

Towner, T. (2013). All Political Participation is Socially Networked?: New Media and the 2012 Election. *Social Science Computer Review, 31*(5), 527–541.

Watkins, S. C. (2009). *The Young and the Digital: What the Migration to Social-Network Sites, Games, and Anytime, Anywhere Media Means for Our Future*. Boston, MA: Beacon Press.

CHAPTER 6

Conclusion: Youth Voice in Contemporary Society

Young people demonstrate the ability to analyze issues of public concern when they are provided with time to reflect and debate these issues, and, most importantly, when they "perceive that their opinions are valued and listened to" (Dias & Menezes, 2014, p. 264). The feeling of being unheard has been a longstanding issue and experience for young people, a finding that has been well documented in this study and in previous research (Kahne & Westheimer, 2003, 2006; Keating, Kerr, Benton, Mundy, & Lopes, 2010). If young people do not feel heard, they might be more inclined to keep their views and thoughts private, presenting a more censored self to the world than they might wish to. Yet, despite this trend in keeping views private, young people have found a motivation to share their voices. In this life stage, young people are growing closer to voting age, and continue to develop their opinions as they interact with news information and others' opinions about issues of public concern, often in digitally mediated ways. In contemporary society, some young people have taken to the Internet to make their voices heard where they otherwise might not have been heard in the past, but still are not always utilizing digital tools for this purpose in the ways we might expect.

Young people who are exposed to diversity of opinions do not seem to want to embrace it by learning from others around them through digital means or otherwise. For those young people who do wish to be exposed to the opinions of others, the majority of this group rarely interacts with others who hold views different from their own. Contemporary society

© The Author(s) 2020
J. K. Viola, *Young People's Civic Identity in the Digital Age*,
Palgrave Studies in Young People and Politics,
https://doi.org/10.1007/978-3-030-37405-1_6

affords digital means for exposure to diverse opinions, yet young people do not often take advantage of these opportunities, such as a liberal-leaning individual reading right-leaning Tumblr blogs, or Following right-wing leaders on social media platforms. Young people do not often enjoy discussing political topics with their peers for fear they will lose friendships, yet do not embrace the possibility of social media connections to people in their age group from other communities. Instead, young people prefer to learn from older adults in their lives because of these adults' previous experiences with voting or other forms of political participation. At the same time, however, young people are not sharing their own voices with these adults because they are not confident in their own knowledge about current events and politics and they feel that adults do not listen to them. Young people do turn to digital means to learn more about current events, such as following news outlets and politicians on social media, but even when they utilize social media to share their voices, they are uncertain of their audience and whether that audience is indeed listening (boyd, 2009; Levine, 2008). Adults and educators must encourage young people to explore and use these digital spaces, because the more encouragement they receive (i.e., through curriculum and opportunities to write political blogs in the classroom), the more likely they will be to feel their voices *could* be heard (Bandura, 2008). Drawing more young people to create content online to share their views might also draw young people online to read their peers' views, and have a sense that at least their peers may hear them.

The problem of young people feeling unheard is not new, but in contemporary society, young people have taken to social media as a way to both share their voices and learn about ways to participate (Jennings & Zeitner, 2003; Mossberger, Tolbert, & McNeal, 2008; Schlozman, Verba, & Brady, 2010). In this study, while few voiced their political opinions directly in conversations with friends, family, or through digital means, many young people participated in a walkout from their schools in spring 2016 to protest the budget cuts in their school district, as described in Chapter 4. These young people felt it was important for their voices to be heard. Being seen leaving school and physically joining the growing numbers at city hall created a great impact on these young people's peers and policymakers. Participation in this walkout galvanized many young people into future action. In this case, young people used social media platforms as a means of learning about and spreading the word about the walkout and organizing each other to participate for the greatest impact.

In a digital age, identity and civic identity must be conceptualized with the understanding that interactions and experiences are digitally mediated at varying degrees for each person. For example, those young people who consumed their news through social media were more likely to bear witness to the immigration debate, which in turn tied into their understanding of citizenship. Moreover, while there is potential for young people to discover volunteer opportunities through Facebook, Instagram, and Twitter, young people in this study who pursued volunteer work as a part of the *Actively Involvement* theme of citizenship did not experience volunteerism in a digitally mediated way, but rather learned about opportunities through their church or school groups.

Social media has informed the ways young people come to understand and think about civic engagement and the issues they care about, and has provided "some children with the opportunity for their voices to be heard" (Buckingham, 2013, p. 81). In the digital era, young people have the opportunity to speak out about current events and issues of public concern in which they have an interest or personal stake. At the time of data collection for this study, young people utilized social media to gain access to information about events outside of their local spheres, which has made them more aware of events happening in other states. At the forefront of young people's minds were police brutality incidents in Ferguson, Missouri and the subsequent creation of the Black Lives Matter movement. As Chapter 5 illustrated, several participants in this study felt evermore connected to the victims of police brutality, and subsequently chose to become more involved in the Black Lives Matter movement. Addie disclosed that as a young black woman, she had experienced racism in her schools, where white students are the majority. Understanding her social network and her large audience, Addie took to her social media accounts to post statements about the young black men who had been killed by police. Without posts like Addie's, and access to news alerts through social media, young people such as Veronica may not have learned about what was happening to black teens, and may not have become involved in the Black Lives Matter movement.

This chapter returns to the three research questions that framed this study, and explains how the findings from this study, presented in Chapters 3, 4, and 5, fit in with the existing body of literature on the civic habits and experiences of young people, and how these links can build a framework for understanding civic identity and inform a reformation of civic education. Section 6.1 will address the ways in which young people present themselves to others in this digital era, and will illustrate how young people present themselves in ways that society expects them to, and struggle to reconcile which aspects of the self to keep private and which to share with the public. Section 6.2 will address the mechanisms through which young people form their civic identity in contemporary society, and will describe the new framework of civic identity that emerged from this study. Section 6.2 will also address the means through which young people engage in the political world, and the factors that contribute to this engagement. Section 6.3 will return to the notions of efficacy and voice, and suggest changes might be made in the education system to foster a greater sense of efficacy among young people.

6.1   Youth in Contemporary Society

The first research question of this study asks, "*In what ways do young people, ages 14 through 17, present themselves to others in contemporary society?*" As Chapter 3 illustrated, young people take aspects of their environment (Hasebrink & Paus-Hasebrink, 2007), relationships, and interactions with others to construct their identities (Côté & Levine, 2002; Flanagan, 2013), and present themselves in digitally mediated ways (Gardner & Davis, 2013). Some young people in this study understand themselves as typical teenagers who enjoy spending time with friends and using technology and social media. However, while this idea of the typical teenager can sometimes help to situate young people in a life stage, at other times this label dismisses young people in this age group, and perpetuates the perception that young people are disengaged and apathetic about issues of public concern. This perception further limits young people in sharing their voice—as Maisie lamented in Chapter 5, young people feel disempowered when adults "overlook" them and do not view them as fully contributing members of society. As the participants in this study demonstrate, while they do enjoy the activities and lifestyles of "typical teenagers," many young people are interested in current events, and want to be engaged, despite feeling overlooked. A recent school shooting in Parkland, Florida brought out a group of empowered young people to begin a national social movement for stricter gun control laws in the United States. There are differences between the participants of this study and the young people in Parkland, Florida, primarily with regards to their civic education and use of social media to make their voices heard. This section will discuss the findings from this study alongside an emerging social movement that stemmed from a school shooting in Parkland, Florida on February 14, 2018. This section will illustrate the differences in how the young people in Boston and Cambridge are presenting themselves, and how the young people of Parkland are presenting themselves, and the implications of these presentations of the self for civic identity in contemporary society.

Several years have passed since the data collection phase of this study, and issues beyond the school budget cuts, Black Lives Matter movement, and immigration debate have surfaced. One such issue is that of gun reform, which has come to the fore in the wake of mass shootings in the United States. The #NeverAgain movement arose after a shooting at Marjory Stoneman Douglas High School in Parkland, Florida in which 17 people were killed by a shooter with a semi-automatic weapon. From this tragedy emerged grief, strength, and a social movement to eliminate gun violence, especially from schools. The young people of Marjory Stoneman Douglas High School took to the local and national news television networks and social media, and began a movement for gun control reform in the United States that has since spread nationwide (Alter, 2018). Survivors of the school shooting started a hashtag on social media, #NeverAgain, to illustrate that what happened at their high school should never happen again. This new movement has emerged through a collective voice of young people who are exhausted by the mass shootings that occur too regularly in the United States, especially in urban underserved communities. Young people in the United States are now gaining momentum on social media and organizing marches across the country, the largest of which was called the March for Our Lives and took place in Washington, D.C. in March 2018. The young people of Parkland know how to harness their collective voice so that the adults in power—politicians and lawmakers—will have no choice but to listen to them. Upon learning of the young people's actions and appearances on television, Parkland students' own United States Senator, Marco Rubio, publicly scolded them for being "infected with arrogance" (Lithwick, 2018). Senator Rubio illustrates a wider societal issue: young people's voices are being dulled and even ridiculed, despite young people's knowledge, personal experience, and desire to effect change.

What is most notable is that the #NeverAgain movement arose from the students of the high school themselves, who deliberately decided to exclude adults from the movement, except where necessary (i.e., renting a car to drive to march and rally locations). Young people own the movement.

One of the movement's leaders, Emma González, did not have a Twitter account at the time of the shooting at her school, but within days she and her colleagues took to social media, and within a week, had more Followers than the NRA[1] (Alter, 2018). This current movement at the national level illustrates what the young people of this study have been doing on their own, but without much traction, like Addie, who posts on Instagram about Black Lives Matter. While the participants in this study seem to be solo actors, other young people—trapped between childhood and adulthood—have created a movement after a specific incident devastated their community.

Returning to Goffman (1959, 1978) and Schlenker's (2012) social interaction theory, the social movement that emerged out of the tragic events in Parkland provides more insight into how young people are presenting themselves to others in the digital era, and how young people can be perceived in contemporary society. In the eyes of adults (the figures who are the leaders and gatekeepers in contemporary society), the young people of Parkland, with their ability to organize effectively and efficiently, and their motivation to make their voices heard and stand up to politicians like Marco Rubio, present themselves as young adults. They have demonstrated their civic knowledge and understanding of how to effectively engage civically, and reveal that they are mature and capable individuals. In contrast, the young people in this study tend to present themselves as young people who are still finding their place in the world, and have difficulty reconciling this life stage of discovery with the opinions that they have already made about the world and desire to share those opinions with others. It is understandable that the young people in this study are discovering who they are, but the Parkland teens have demonstrated that it is advantageous to demonstrate and present maturity and knowledge to others, so that their voices are heard. These presentations of the self illustrate the point of civic identity development that young people experience at this life stage. The young people of this study are still processing and coming to their own beliefs, are unsure of which parts of the self to keep private and which to share with others, and how to effectively share their voices and make their voices heard as citizens and community members. Young people are often presenting themselves in ways that society

---

[1] The NRA, as the National Rifle Association is commonly known, is the largest organization that advocates for gun ownership rights, with membership of approximately 4 million people (Steidley & Colen, 2017).

expects—but what young people are actually *doing* without many adults noticing demonstrates that the young people of this study are more engaged than society may have thought, which Section 6.2 will highlight in more detail.

6.2   Civic Identity in the Digital Age

As Chapters 4 and 5 elaborated, young people are experiencing tensions as they navigate their place in the world because society has expected little of them by way of civic engagement. Society has not expected young people to care about current events or to voice their opinions, and in some ways, the laws and regulations imposed by society make it difficult for young people to disprove these beliefs. Society has restricted young people's ability to participate based on their age, limited not only to voting, but also to community service activities, like volunteering. At 17 years old, Laura is not able to become an emergency medical technician (EMT), and at 16 years old, Kaitlyn is unable to volunteer at food pantries. While some young people feel the limitations their age has on their ability to be involved in formal community service and present themselves in ways that society expects (Schlenker, 2012), other young people have rejected society's expectations of them to be apathetic, and have found new, digitally mediated ways to become civically engaged to learn about current events and, in some cases, voice their opinions. The reciprocity hypothesis first mentioned in Chapter 2 applies to the participants in this study. Young people's civic experiences are digitally mediated: learning about immigration via social media affects their beliefs and experiences of citizenship. These experiences then influence the actions young people take for civic engagement, like participating in a school walkout or Black Lives Matter march.

Young people like Tanesha believe it is important to be vocal to make change, and that it is by being vocal that one can share values and opinions and learn those of others, to further shape one's own beliefs. Young people are forming their civic identity through their engagement with news information and through interactions with others: Tanesha reads Tumblr pages related to current events and integrates the opinions of others into her own worldview, and Elsie seeks out discussions with others who have opinions that differ from her own. While society evidently expects young people to not vocalize their opinions on issues of public concern, participants in this study presented themselves as civically engaged and demonstrated their concern related to the national immigration debate, particularly as they reflected on their conceptualizations of citizenship, which was discussed in Chapter 4. The primary area of worry for young people concerned Donald Trump's Tweets that reflected a growing anti-immigrant sentiment around the country.

Naomi shared her criticism of Donald Trump's insulting remarks on Twitter, and Martin and Sachi expressed concern that while social media can be used as a megaphone for one's voice, not all voices are sharing positive messages. This use of social media by public figures has made more young people aware of what each of the political parties represent, and the beliefs that each public figure stands for. As described in Chapter 5, young people in turn exhibit caution about sharing their own political beliefs on their social media profiles, for fear that someone might misinterpret their voice as it was presented through text. This is in contrast to Hess and McAvoy's (2015) finding that young people are most likely to communicate with each other about politics through social networking websites. Rather, most young people in this study show mixed interest in discussing their political beliefs with others. Those who are interested in learning from others do not often seek contact with others beyond their existing social network, despite the affordances of social media that would allow them to do so.

The young people who participated in this study shared their voices and opinions with me in the research context—but are often not comfortable enough to share their voices with the adults in their lives. For some young people, like Kenai, families do not respect or ask for the opinions of young people, an act that diminishes young people's sense of efficacy (Bandura, 2008). This challenge can be addressed when society has a better understanding of what shapes young people's civic identity, and how they are experiencing the world. Chapter 4 detailed thematic ways in which young people identify themselves as citizens, and understand what it means to be civically engaged. The contemporary struggles of presenting the self and sharing one's voice that young people face have led to a new framework of civic identity.

6.2.1   A New Framework of Civic Identity

The second research question that motivated this study asks, "*What are the mechanisms through which young people form their civic identity in this digital era, and how do young people understand citizenship and civic engagement?*" As Chapters 2 and 4 discussed, civic identity is informed by social interaction theory and the theories put forth by Youniss and Yates (1997) and Knefelkamp (2008). Social interaction theory posits that people view themselves through the role they play in public and how others react to those presentations of the self (Schlenker, 2012). People are considering who they would like to be, and who they feel they can be in a particular social context (Schlenker, 1985). Young people see themselves fitting into the world around them as measured by their presentations of the self. Like identity, civic identity is individually and socially constructed (Haste, 2004). Civic identity emerges from participation in informal and formal activities that develops a sense of agency and social responsibility (Youniss, McLellan, & Yates, 1997), as well as through engaging in conversations with others, to learn from different perspectives (Knefelkamp, 2008). As society changes, the means of engagement change. So, as society becomes more defined by digitally mediated interactions, so too will civic engagement be defined.

The findings from this study improve the understanding of both the individual, reflective component of civic identity, measured by the conceptualizations of citizenship, and the collective component of how that individual engages with others in the social, political, and economic structures within their society. A new framework of civic identity, informed by the digitally mediated experiences of young people ages 14 through 17, emerged from this study, and includes five themes of citizenship and three themes of civic engagement. These themes are not mutually exclusive: young people can understand citizenship and civic engagement in any single or combination of themes. The components work together to contextualize the civic experiences of young people, which can inform civic education curriculum.

Lister, Smith, Middleton, and Cox (2003, 2005) detailed five models of citizenship that emerged from a study investigating 16- to 23-year-olds nearly two decades ago. Today, young people are surrounded by information and opinions on social media, which then inform their own beliefs about what it means to be a citizen, what it means to be civically engaged, and issues of public concern. This framework of civic identity emerges from the experiences of young people and their sentiments about feeling caught in their life stage, wherein they need to develop their own views, but feel that no one will listen so therefore rarely express those views to others. This framework can help adults—parents, educators, and policymakers—to understand the civic experiences of young people, and revitalize civic education to best support young people in expressing their voices about issues of public concern. The framework is illustrated in Figure 6.1 below, and will be addressed in further detail in the sections that follow.

The First Component: Conceptualizations of Citizenship

The first component of civic identity involves conceptualizations of citizenship, the sense of how an individual develops and situates oneself and one's beliefs within a broader group of people. While citizenship has been an elusive concept (Ignatieff, 1995), conceptualizations most often include legal, social, and political components (Marshall & Bottomore, 1992; Osler & Starkey, 2006). The findings from this study reveal five

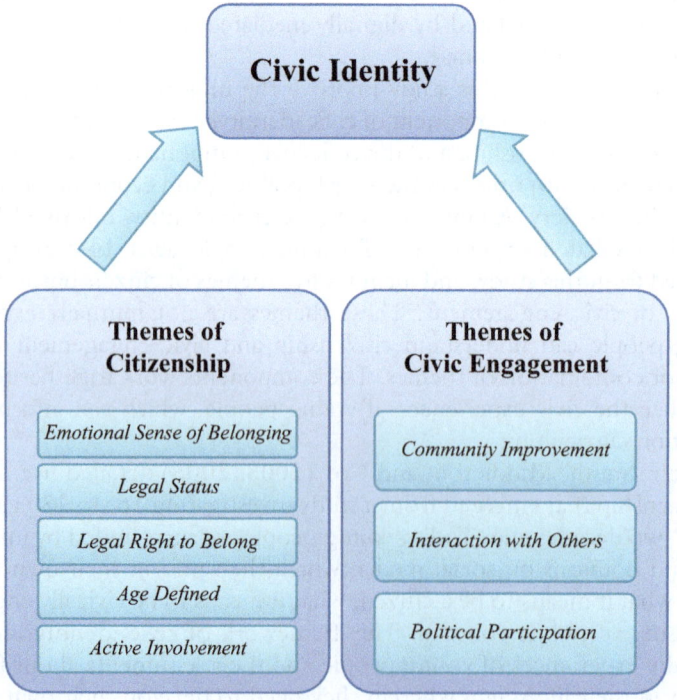

Fig. 6.1 Framework of civic identity. Civic identity is a function of two components: (1) conceptualizations of citizenship and (2) conceptualizations of civic engagement. Themes of citizenship and civic engagement emerged from the civic experiences of participants

themes of citizenship that emerged from the lived citizenship (Hall & Williamson, 1999) experiences of young people in this study:

1. *Emotional Sense of Belonging* – feeling like one belongs, and is a part of a community.
2. *Legal Status* – legally a member of the country, either by birth or naturalization; abiding by legal rights and responsibilities.
3. *Legal Right to Belong* – feeling like one belongs to a community, but also having legal rights and responsibilities.
4. *Age Defined* – being old enough, as defined by the law, to exercise the legal rights and responsibilities of citizenship, such as voting and participating in jury duty; being perceived as old enough to have opinions and share one's voice.
5. *Active Involvement* – actively contributing to the community.

Many of the same themes from the Lister et al. (2003) findings, which were presented previously in Chapter 2, apply today, but these themes are experienced in more nuanced and digitally mediated ways. Young people in this study recognize that citizenship is not universal, and has multiple meanings that are informed by individuals' personal experiences. Within the *Emotional Sense of Belonging* theme of citizenship, young people feel a part of something, and, to some extent, recognized and included. This *Emotional Sense of Belonging* theme of citizenship stands as its own theme as it represents the necessity of a sense of belonging within a community, a concept that has been well documented since the 1980s (Brint, 2001; McMillan & Chavis, 1986; Riger & Lavrakas, 1981). Interestingly, young people link this theme of citizenship to both a sense of support (Brint, 2001) and to a physical place of "home." Several participants in this study connected their understanding of citizenship to the contemporary immigration debate that permeates public discourse. For those young people who are immigrants, or children of immigrants, it was common to allude to their cultural identities and sense of belonging to their country of heritage. Young people were often informed about the immigration debate in digitally mediated ways, like Donald Trump's Tweets. The conditions under which the *Emotional Sense of Belonging* theme developed provide insight that not all young people feel that they belong, and that this idea of citizenship is not as universal as the young people of the Lister et al. (2003) study experienced.

The *Legal Status* theme reflects one of the most common ways that people define citizenship as the legal rights and responsibilities that belong to anyone born in the United States and anyone who has become a naturalized citizen. Primarily, young people recognize their citizenship as a birthright because they were born in the country, and identify rights and responsibilities such as voting and jury duty, which aligned with previous research in this area (Haste, 2005; Kennedy, Hahn, & Lee, 2008). Again, the immigration debate largely informed young people's views on this matter. Even for young people whose families have been in the United States for generations, like Peter, it was still understood that there are many obstacles to legal citizenship, giving citizenship the "exclusive" status that Maisie discussed. While the *Legal Status* theme addresses the rights and duties that Lister et al. (2003) describe, this theme also incorporates young people's understanding of the legal implications of being a citizen by birthright, being a citizen by naturalization, and not being a legal citizen at all. This theme is especially important to consider in contemporary society, as anti-immigrant sentiments exist not only in the United States, but in other nations as well (Osler & Starkey, 2018). With the understanding of the *Legal Status* theme of citizenship, it is possible to consider how public policy and public discourse may affect people's sense of citizenship, and responsibilities as a citizen. If individuals only see citizenship as the rights and responsibilities of engaging in society, those who are not citizens by birthright or naturalization may feel more excluded from the political process, and become disengaged—even though the young people of this study have demonstrated that civic engagement goes beyond political participation, which will be addressed in the next section.

Sometimes, tensions define citizenship for young people, particularly in the third theme, the *Legal Right to Belong*. The tension between meanings of citizenship including belonging, legality, duties, and contributions to the community has been well documented in other studies (Brubaker, 1992; Haste, 2004; Lister et al., 2003; Young, 1995), and rings true in the findings presented in this book. Bibiana highlighted the complexity of growing up as an immigrant in the United States and assimilating to American culture, but lacking the legal rights to fully participate in society. Bibiana explained that while she was not born in the United States, she is confident in her knowledge about current events and how the government works. Bibiana noted that if it were not for her interaction with the news through social media, she would be less knowledgeable about societal issues, and she would not be pursuing a career in journalism. Perhaps Bibiana will someday produce news content of her own that will be shared among young people in digitally mediated ways, just as she accessed the information that prompted her to take action on social issues, actions that she cannot take because she is not a United States citizen. The *Legal Right to Belong* theme of citizenship emphasizes that it is possible and common for people to view citizenship as a function of one or more of the themes of citizenship in this framework. The tensions that connect the sense of belonging and the coveted, legally recognized form of citizenship are more likely to be felt in contemporary society, with international migration becoming more common as globalization continues (Colby & Ortman, 2014). As immigration policy changes, it is important to maintain awareness about the sentiments that young people, like Bibiana, would feel as they contribute to American society but are not able to vote for candidates and issues that matter to them, such as supporting immigration.

Along those same lines, recent global migration trends mean that there are likely to be more young people who feel an attachment to their home country/country of origin before they feel like they belong in the country where they have settled and experience this *Legal Right to Belong*. For example, Gwen, from Cameroon, felt more of a connection and sense of belonging to Cameroon, and a legal status of citizenship there as well because it is her country of birth. In recent years, Europe has gained an influx of refugees from the Middle East and Africa (Goodman, Sirriyeh, & McMahon, 2017). As Europe welcomes these young people into society, we must take into consideration their experiences of coming to Europe, which may have been impacted by trauma, and how they may hold onto their civic identity from the place where they call home.

The theme of *Age Defined* citizenship relates to the *Legal Status* theme, in that this theme recognizes that there are certain legally imposed age restrictions on certain means of engaging in the rights and responsibilities of citizenship. Young people who do not view themselves and their peers as citizens tend to feel that their voices are not heard because they do not have the right to vote, and they are not yet 18 years old—an age that many young people and adults feel young people will be taken seriously. When individuals are restricted by age, they may feel disempowered and choose not to engage. In some cases, they choose not to engage because they do not feel ready for the responsibility. This sense of readiness for responsibility is important to address because this is a case where parents, educators, and other adults in young people's lives can scaffold young people with the skills they need to develop confidence in their voices and their abilities as citizens. Perhaps when young people develop this confidence, the *Age*

Defined theme of citizenship will no longer be experienced by young people, as young people will recognize their ability to have their voices heard and make an impact before they reach voting age.

Finally, the *Active Involvement* theme of citizenship reflects the desire of many young people to participate in their communities and to help in any way they can—as Damon and Jane desire—and engage in political participation and keep informed about current events. Young people who described citizenship in these ways often alluded to tangible activities of civic engagement: cleaning the park, canvassing for local political candidates, and sharing political opinions with others. Young people also recognized that sharing opinions and exchanging ideas in digitally mediated ways is a form of active involvement. While young people expressed their frustration and concern for feeling unheard or restricted in their engagement because of their age, this fifth theme of citizenship outlines the ways in which young people identified that they *can* be civically engaged without reaching age 18. The *Active Involvement* theme often includes what many people view as "good" citizenship: improving society, acting responsibly, solving social problems, and helping the community (Kennedy et al., 2008; Westheimer & Kahne, 2004). While good citizenship has become a normative concept (Ke & Starkey, 2014), the *Active Involvement* theme of citizenship illustrates that individuals are not always considering "good" or "bad" citizenship, but rather an *active* component that involves contributing to society. This final theme of citizenship leads to the three themes of civic engagement that compose the second component of this new framework of civic identity, to be addressed in the following section.

Lister et al. (2003) propose that "right to a voice" ought to be its own theme of citizenship. The findings from this study suggest that citizenship ought to include this concept of voice, especially because not all young people feel like citizens, but participants never explicitly addressed the right to a voice as a singular conceptualization of citizenship. Young people may feel restricted for all sorts of reasons, mainly with consideration of age and legal citizenship status under the law. These individuals may be less likely to be engaged in the political world and demonstrate apathy, but they might use that frustration as a motivation to become engaged, like Addie and Veronica, who took to social media to make their voices heard as a part of the Black Lives Matter movement. Despite the growing use of social media since 2007, it has had limited impact on how young people *think* about citizenship, but rather, has informed *how* young people are engaging civically. As the findings from this study show, feeling that one's voice is heard is essential to efficacy, but rather than this theme standing alone, it is *embedded* within each of the five themes presented here, and the three themes of civic engagement that the next section will describe.

The Second Component: Civic Engagement
Three themes of civic engagement contribute to the second component of the civic identity framework that emerged from this study, and build upon the definitions of civic engagement that were put forth in Chapters 2 and 4. Rheingold (2008) explicitly addresses civic engagement as digitally mediated, "participation in the public sphere through direct experience with online publishing, discourse, debate, co-creation of culture, and collective action" (p. 102). Raynes-Goldie and Walker's (2008) definition is broad and applicable to the first theme of civic engagement in this framework, as "any activity aimed at improving one's community" (p. 162). The findings from this study suggest that the definitions of civic engagement by Rheingold (2008) and Raynes-Goldie and Walker (2008) are too narrow, and therefore I argue that the definition of civic engagement include community improvement, interaction with others to develop and share beliefs, and political participation. These themes follow Bell's (2005) recommendation that the definition of civic engagement must include what is civic in the everyday lives of young people:

1. *Community Improvement* – activities to improve one's community vary considerably, and include the three most common means: participating in fundraising events, protecting the environment, and volunteering.
2. *Interaction with Others* – sharing opinions and experiences with other people, and learning from others' opinions and experiences in return.
3. *Political Participation* – formally engaging in democratic institutions through activities such as voting and protesting.

The three themes of civic engagement that emerged from the findings demonstrate that contrary to popular belief, young people are both thinking about civic engagement and engaging in civic activities. A great number of participants—29 out of 46 participants—understood civic engagement through the *Community Improvement* theme, which includes participating in fundraising events, protecting the environment, and vol-

unteering. This theme supports Raynes-Goldie and Walker's (2008) definition of civic engagement, and represents the civic experiences and beliefs
of a majority of young people, who view improving the community as a
key component of civic engagement (Kennedy et al., 2008). While many
participants *understood* civic engagement in the more traditional sense of
the term, in *practice* in contemporary society, many of these themes of
civic engagement are experienced in digitally mediated ways. For example,
within the *Community Improvement* theme lies fundraising events, which
are often advertised and participated in through social media, such as the
ALS Ice Bucket Challenge, as experienced by Jane. Understanding that
most young people view civic engagement in this way could encourage
educators to embed service learning opportunities within their curriculum
to encourage civic engagement through school (Annette, 2008; Camino
& Zeldin, 2002; Dudley & Gitelson, 2002).

The second theme of civic engagement as *Interaction with Others* is a
more nuanced theme that involves the sharing of opinions and experiences
with other people, particularly related to politics. This theme is based on
the notion that people must learn from each other to help form and share
their beliefs about issues of public concern. Young people are interacting
with others in myriad ways, from Following public figures on Twitter, to
participation in the Junior State of America, to posting opinions about
police brutality on Instagram. Diana Hess (2009) recognizes the importance of political discussions among young people, but in practice, very
few participants recognize civic engagement as it is defined in this theme,
and fewer still feel comfortable interacting with their peer groups about
issues of public concern. Just as the *Age Defined* theme of citizenship
related to young people's experiences of feeling unheard, so too does the
Interaction with Others theme. It is important to recognize that the individuals who understand civic engagement as *Interaction with Others* may
or may not seek out this type of interaction and dialogue on their own. For
young people to fully realize this theme of civic engagement, they may
need encouragement from their peers and the adults in their lives to
encourage this type of dialogue. Organizations like the Junior State of
America encourage civic engagement through parliamentary style debate
and volunteerism, a part of the *Community Improvement* theme, and
through formally engaging with institutions through the *Political
Participation* theme. The Junior State of America holds debate workshops
and conferences to foster the development of youth voice. Further

recommendations for empowering young people to have these kinds of conversations will follow later in Section 6.3.1.

Finally, young people understand civic engagement as *Political Participation*, particularly through traditional means like voting and protesting. This third theme highlights traditional ways that individuals can participate politically, such as voting, but also encompasses the activities that young people can do before reaching voting age, such as protesting. Many young people acknowledged the limitations of their age on their ability to become civically engaged in this manner, because they are not yet eligible to vote. Yet, despite this obvious legal restriction on their formal political participation, a few young people do not let this age barrier prevent them from influencing an election: several participants discussed their attempts to convince parents and teachers to vote for the candidate or issue that they supported, a trend that has been recognized in previous research (Mesch & Coleman, 2007). Moreover, some communities allow—and even encourage—young people to vote on community issues, like Maisie, aged 14, who participated in her town's budget vote, wherein anybody over the age of 12 is allowed to vote. With the understanding that young people conceptualize civic engagement as political participation, but often feel they are too young to participate and therefore their voices are unheard, parents and teachers can educate young people about the other means of political participation, and encourage young people to participate in the voting that they are eligible for. Political participation can include contacting elected officials to raise awareness about a concern, and, in the digital era, means of communicating with elected officials include interactions on social media and in other ways mediated by technology. Many participants of this study were involved in a citywide walkout of high schools as an effort to protest against budget cuts, which was organized through Facebook and other social media as a way for young people to alert others of the event, and to encourage participation from young people in schools across the city.

As there is no single agreed upon definition of civic engagement, it is important to identify the key elements of civic engagement that young people understand and experience in their everyday lives, and incorporate each of these themes into a wider understanding of civic engagement. With these three broad themes as a framework to understand civic engagement, individuals may evaluate the many ways that one could choose to engage, and choose which theme would be the most effective means to reach a certain end goal. The new framework of civic identity presented above provides insight into how young people see themselves fitting into today's society, and how they may contribute to it. The two components of civic identity, citizenship and civic engagement, work together to illustrate the reflective and participatory nature of civic identity. Both components are shaped by personal experiences, such as being born in or immigrating to the United States, and societal factors such as the immigration debate that spreads through social media and in peer-to-peer discussions. It is most important to recognize the personal nature of civic identity and that individuals' experiences shape how they view and experience civic identity. This framework is not designed to pigeonhole young people into specific categories of citizenship and civic engagement; rather, it presents the possibilities of views that young people may have, and can help adults gain an understanding of the types of personal experiences of young people that would inform their views and expressions of citizenship and civic engagement. Echoes of young people's concerns and feelings of being unheard ring throughout this framework, and further emphasize the need for increased opportunities for young people to develop their voices, and for adults to listen. This framework can be applied to future investigations into the civic experiences of young people, and to the development of civic education curriculum to address the needs of individuals at this life stage as they form their civic identity.

6.2.2   Digitally Mediated Civic Engagement: Opportunities for Youth Voice

The third research question of this study asks, "*What are the means through which young people engage in the political world, and what factors contribute to this engagement?*" The participants in this study experienced civic engagement through digital means, and social media affords opportunities for young people to engage with news information and other people outside of their normal social sphere, but their discussions of issues of public concern tend to occur mainly in the home. In the past, these sorts of discussions occurred in private spheres, like the home, but now, dialogue can be experienced through technology and can take place any time, anywhere (Hodgin, 2016). Contemporary society affords social media as modern soapboxes to give voice to those who have previously been excluded from the public sphere, and enable a greater distribution of ideas, collaboration, and collective action (Bennett, 2008; Erikson, 1968; James, 2014). Findings from this study demonstrate that there is little doubt that young people are being exposed to politics and issues of public concern online, and may have the inclination to participate through online means: social networks enable a lower cost to coordinate and communicate civic activities (Rheingold, 2008), such as learning about school walkouts and Black Lives Matter marches.

The Internet lends itself well to civic engagement, because the speed with which information can be gathered and transmitted has increased, and there is now a greater amount of accessible information and increased opportunities for interaction (Montgomery, 2008). Participants like Elsie and Tanesha are curious to learn others' opinions, and seek them out through conversations with peers in civic organizations like the Junior State of America, or reading others' reflections on current events on Tumblr. Social media impacts political expression worldwide: today, young people have the opportunity to interact with each other and with people in the public sphere through the type of civic engagement that Rheingold (2008) defines (Cohen, Kahne, Bowyer, Middaugh, & Rogowski, 2012). Over time, content creation and sharing has grown rapidly: social networking sites like Facebook, Twitter, and Tumblr have enabled young people to share and repost content (Ito et al., 2010), whether it is a photo from a weekend event, or a political statement originally posted by a public official (Bennett, 2008). Participation in new media technology can be empowering, and even ignite participation in the wider society (Hartmann, Carpentier, & Cammaerts, 2007; James, 2014), which the #NeverAgain movement and, more recently, the global School Strike for Climate, demonstrate.

Many participants in this study follow current events that are relevant and convenient to them (Linton, 2015). Scholars have observed young people utilizing technology for civic purposes to learn about the issues of public concern (Davies & Eynon, 2013) that matter to them. Kaitlyn watches the news on television before she goes to school, but checks Twitter and Instagram throughout the day. Kaitlyn prefers to stay informed about current events on a more regular basis, and Jillian relies on the text messages from her friends to alert her about top headlines of the day when she is otherwise too busy to seek out the information on her own. Young people develop the habits and attitudes relevant to civic life when they first encounter the world of current events and political issues at this age (Levine, 2008), but they are not always expected to follow current events (Livingstone, Couldry, & Markham, 2007). It is important to note that there are well-documented discrepancies in how young people perceive and discuss current events, and experience efficacy. Individuals from wealthier backgrounds and parents with higher levels of education tend to discuss current events at home, an early form of civic engagement (Flanagan, 2013). Kahne and Middaugh (2009) found that higher-income families experience greater numbers of civic opportunities, such as participating on a campaign, protesting, and sitting on a board. Furthermore, this population of individuals often experience more classroom-based civic opportunities. Such disparities in education contribute to inequalities in later civic and political participation (Gimpel & Pearson-Merkowitz, 2009).

Young people engage in the political world through digital means. Contemporary society and the expectations of young people are factors that have contributed to this civic engagement: while society expects young people to not follow current events or care about issues of public concern, society expects young people to use social media. Young people demonstrate that social media is one of the primary sources of news information, and a way for them to attempt to share their own voices. Even while participants in this study did not seem to view social media as a *formal* tool for civic engagement, many participants used social media for civic purposes. Jane used social media to engage in her community after discovering the ALS Ice Bucket Challenge on Instagram, while Addie and Veronica voiced their concerns about police brutality on their Instagram and Facebook pages. Young people of Boston used social media to organize a citywide school walkout to protest budget cuts to their schools. Jaden, Gwen, and Habibah all expressed their pride for taking a stand and making their generation more visible to public officials so that their voices would be heard. While civic engagement takes many different forms in the digital era (Jennings & Zeitner, 2003; Mossberger et al., 2008; Schlozman et al., 2010), civic education must be revitalized and improved in consideration of the contemporary experiences of young people, and their needs for building efficacy and voice in this digital age.

6.3   BUILDING EFFICACY FOR ENGAGEMENT IN THE POLITICAL WORLD: A CASE FOR CIVIC EDUCATION

Chapter 5 highlighted the significance of efficacy—the feeling that one's voice is heard—as a factor for civic engagement among young people. Experiences of the participants in this study build on previous findings that young people feel disempowered and unheard, even while they are civically engaged. Key to an engaged citizenry is the feeling that one has the knowledge, skills, and power to enact change, and such civic efficacy is a goal of schooling (National Council for the Social Studies, 2008). Youniss and Yates (1997) highlight the importance of this sense of efficacy and the feeling that one's voice is heard:

> If individuals did not believe their actions counted, they would not feel responsible to register new voters, boycott, strike, march, argue politics, or join movements. Adults do these things because they believe democratic society depends on people acting democratically. It is important that the behaviors that make up adult agency are not extraordinary and have incipient forms in the repertoire of youth. (p. 28)

Research in the United States demonstrates that young people's frustration with not being heard is widespread and longstanding (Kahne & Westheimer, 2003, 2006; Keating et al., 2010). A survey by the National Association of Secretaries of State demonstrated that two thirds of young people agreed, "our generation has an important voice, but no one seems to hear it" (Kahne & Westheimer, 2006, p. 289). Similarly, the Citizenship Education Longitudinal Study of young people and their civic practices in the United Kingdom concluded that there has been a steady increase in young people's civic participation, but a decreased level of efficacy (Keating et al., 2010). As they aged, the young people studied felt only moderately likely to feel that they, as individuals, could influence the political and social world (Keating et al., 2010).

Young people have been limited in their ability to become engaged in their communities, especially because of the daily segregation of young people from adults and the negative stereotypes that adults have of youth as apathetic (Camino & Zeldin, 2002). In Chapter 3, Martin discussed his identity as a young black male, and how he needed to adapt his behavior and appearance for his own safety, even to attend a Black Lives Matter rally. Martin alluded to how he adjusted his own voice and manner of speaking in favor of personal safety and positive perceptions from others, and, in doing so, his voice is stifled, limiting his efficacy, a trend that has been observed among black youth (Kahne & Middaugh, 2009). Because of stereotypes that affect all young people and young people of color especially, young people are often viewed as disengaged. It is well documented, however, that young people are engaged, but do not feel heard (Mesch &

Coleman, 2007). What makes one efficacious is having the civic skills necessary to participate, which includes collaboration, public speaking, protesting or petitioning for change (Kahne & Westheimer, 2003).

6.3.1   From Perspective Taking in the Classroom to Efficacy in the Community

Few young people have been able to amplify their voices to engage in the way the young people of Parkland have. This is because the participants in this study have not had the same level of civic education and have not had a single cause with which they identify. Moreover, the young people who participated in this study are not as well networked and supported by their parents, teachers, and community leaders. This discrepancy in efficacy is correlated with a lack of civic knowledge, which in turn can be attributed to the steady replacement of civic education funding with funding for STEM subjects (Keating et al., 2010). The quality or quantity of civic education experienced by the young people of Parkland served the #NeverAgain movement leaders well in providing them the educational foundation for civic engagement. Many of the participants in this study were not aware of "civic engagement" terminology, and generally have limited civic knowledge due to civic education being classified as "not a priority" for their school district (Boston Public Schools, Office of Data and Accountability, 2015). The Parkland youth had the educational resources and understanding of civics to have conversations with their peers in ways that the participants from Boston do not have. While the young people who participated in this study indicated their passion for and personal connection to issues like the Black Lives Matter movement, it is also possible that there was not an incident immediate or personal enough to the participants that would ignite a fire of activism, as the school shooting had done in Parkland. It is crucial that the current generation, and generations to follow, is educated about how their government works, and how to become engaged and active citizens.

The findings from this study and recent events in the #NeverAgain movement suggest that the reprioritization of civic education in schools is imperative for providing young people in contemporary society with the skills and tools they need to build their efficacy (Rousseau & Warren, 2018). There are inequalities in efficacy itself, but fostering civic efficacy from an early age can promote sustained efficacy, which is one means to help close the civic empowerment gap (Serriere, 2014). While there is no single point in maturation when individuals learn about politics or active citizenship (Dudley & Gitelson, 2002), civic education should start in elementary school: it is possible to encourage civic habits in young people from an early age (Ito et al., 2008). Civic habits include developing the ability to take perspectives of others, solve problems collectively, and participate in community service. All of these things can be done at all ages—in elementary school, for example, classroom meetings provide opportunities for discussions and collective problem solving. Young people of all ages should engage in personally meaningful civic activities in school, which can then inspire them to continue their actions later on in the community (Serriere, 2014).

Educators and policymakers must focus on reinvigorating civic education in schools because formal education is the only learning opportunity to which young people are "legally entitled" (Middaugh & Kirshner, 2015, p. 5). It is the right of all young people to be educated and equipped with the skills they need to engage in their society, and it is incumbent upon educators to scaffold young people's development of these civic skills. With this trend in decreasing levels of civic knowledge, and concern for civic education, scholars have called for an updated civics curriculum (Middaugh & Kirshner, 2015). Recommendations from the Center for Information and Research on Civic Learning and Engagement (CIRCLE) include student participation in some kind of democratic process, rather than listening to lectures on government (Korbey, 2017). A reinvigoration of civic education in schools can equip young people with knowledge and understanding about the political institutions—an understanding that would empower them to use their voices (Lagemann & Lewis, 2012). Programs and curriculum that promote understanding of social issues, sense of belonging, and agency can contribute to civic identity and efficacy (Kahne & Sporte, 2008; Shapiro & Brown, 2018; Youniss & Yates, 1997).

There is disagreement in public discourse about the role of the school in educating citizens. Should schools be devoid of politics and political discussion? Or should they be a place where students may safely engage in thoughtful and respectful discussions with other young people, some of whom have opposing views? Scholars recommend that young people have the opportunity to take the perspective of others by having discussions and debates about political and social issues with their classmates, because debate and dialogue are key to the development of one's civic identity. Respectfully engaging in conversations about controversial issues is therefore paramount to civic education (Kahne & Westheimer, 2006). Such discussions lead young people to report greater engagement in school, greater interest in politics, improved critical thinking skills, and higher civic knowledge and likelihood to participate in civic life later on (Gould, 2011). One way to reinvigorate civics curriculum is to include classroom discussions about current events and political issues, which benefits young people's social perspective taking skills and their awareness and understanding of issues of public concern.

Hess and McAvoy (2015) believe that schools should be a space for fostering perspective taking, and Hodgin (2016) agrees that core to civic participation are the skills to have discussions about political and social issues, which young people have often not had the opportunity to discuss in school (Vilchis, Scott, & Besaw, 2015). Diana Hess (2009) found that civil political discussions in a classroom setting enable better critical thinking, communication, and interpersonal skills, and the development of attitudes and knowledge for engaged citizenship. Engaging in the discussion of social issues and public problems with people whose views differ from one's own can foster political tolerance, which in turn can lead to better policy decisions in the future (Hess, 2009). Discussing these controversial topics will help young people develop their own voice and opinions and express them to others (McLeod & Shah, 2009).

Dias and Menezes (2014) call for experiential civic education through this type of dialogue, in which children are asked to solve a collective problem, and must "express their ideas ... cooperate, and negotiate" (p. 264). Schools are institutions that can provide young people with the opportunity to reason with others with different views than their own (Hess & McAvoy, 2015). For example, young people from poor urban areas, like Jaden, are likely to have clarity about the issues that affect their neighborhoods and can provide a wealth of information and ideas to make positive changes in their communities (Hart & Kirshner, 2009), which young people from wealthier backgrounds, like Maisie, may not have considered. It is idealistic to believe that young people will carry out these conversations on their own, as findings in Chapter 5 demonstrate. Even teachers struggle to cultivate a safe space in the classroom for civil discussion, and some teachers have avoided civics entirely because they do not want to ignite hostility or discord in their classroom (Korbey, 2017). Civic education must recognize that students may have multiple and flexible identities (Ong, 1999), and also have experiences to share and voices to be heard.

Political efficacy is positively correlated with the opportunity to discuss controversial issues in the classroom (Hahn, 2010; Levy, 2011; Serriere,

2014; Torney-Purta, Lehmann, Oswald, & Schulz, 2001) and build perspective-taking skills. Given the hesitation that young people experience when thinking about discussing politics or issues of public concern with their friends, young people could benefit from opportunities to develop their perspective taking skills so that future digitally mediated interactions would be less daunting. Friendships are an effective way for young people to gain practice in perspective taking (Flanagan, 2013) and to test out their political opinions (Livingstone et al., 2007), but the participants in this study are most concerned that if they discover their friend has a view or opinion that differs from their own, they will lose that friendship. Kaitlyn and Addie demonstrate that for young people, it seems that sometimes friendship is more important than understanding what beliefs that friend holds: perhaps young people are also barriers to their own peers' voices being heard. Young people should encourage each other to take each other's perspectives and develop their own voices. Osler and Starkey (2018) suggest that when young people have skills for efficacy and the opportunity to practice those skills, they will then be able to use those skills to build a more cohesive and peaceful society. The more voices there are, the more young people could be amplified as a group, and their concerns would be heard.

Unmistakably, a sense of agency is key to civic identity and engagement (Watts & Guessous, 2006; Youniss & Yates, 1997). Increasing young people's sense of efficacy can be done by reinvigorating civic education and opportunities for engagement, and by carefully listening to the voices of young people. Young people have opinions and beliefs about politics, and listening to them can provide insight into what democracy will be like in the future (Linton, 2015) because young people *are* the future. One way for young people to start having a say is in their schools, where they can practice articulating their concerns at a more immediate and local level (Fielding, 2004). Young people are socially positioned to be experts on young people's experiences, and should be treated as authorities on these matters (Nasir & Kirshner, 2003). Young people need positive reinforcement—when they are asked to share their voice, and adults listen, young people will be more empowered to continue sharing their voice (Bandura, 2008). Civic education can have a positive impact on self-efficacy, primarily through providing young people with the skills and knowledge they need to feel able and equipped to make a difference in their family, school, and community (Keating et al., 2010). But, while educators must focus on efficacy, it is important to remember to nurture the awareness of how institutions work and what roadblocks they might face so that the red tape does not impact young people's efficacy (Kahne & Westheimer, 2006). Results from this study build on this finding, and demonstrate that societal roadblocks—society's positioning of young people as "just kids"—are a major factor in preventing young people from having a voice.

6.3.2   Civic Education for Digitally Mediated Civic Engagement

Technology has the potential to be a powerful tool for civic engagement when young people know how to use it for that purpose, as illustrated by the #NeverAgain movement. The young people of Parkland were able to circumvent societal roadblocks and harness their civic knowledge to make their voices heard. Scholars note that the Parkland students successfully created the #NeverAgain movement that gained traction on social media, but it was their civic education and the values of their school and school district that equipped them with the skills they needed to best interact with and pressure lawmakers to enact stricter gun control (Rousseau & Warren, 2018). In this section, I use the #NeverAgain movement to illustrate the importance of civic education, and how it can be reinvigorated for the digital era.

The student leaders at Marjory Stoneman Douglas High School were part of the school newspaper and broadcast journalism programs, and there is a school district-wide debate program that teaches public speaking to students from a young age (Lithwick, 2018), suggesting that the school values its students and their engagement with the wider world. Marjory Stoneman Douglas High School is committed to student voice, having invited Mary Beth Tinker, who had an important role in the *Tinker v. Des Moines* free speech Supreme Court case, to speak to students (Lithwick, 2018). The Black Lives Matter movement, as discussed in Chapter 5, and the #NeverAgain movement are similar in that they harness digital tools for amplifying the voices and experiences of those affected by the tragedies that sparked the movements. However, the #NeverAgain movement has the privilege of arising from a well-resourced high school and an affluent community (Lithwick, 2018), privileges which the students acknowledge and seek to use to attract national attention and advocate for policy reform to affect overall gun statistics. The young people who spearheaded the #NeverAgain movement do not want just white people or black people to be protected, they want everyone to be protected. This privilege and power have united them with other student-led gun-reform groups in Chicago and other cities riddled with gun violence (Alter, 2018). In summer 2018, the young people of Parkland launched a voter mobilization bus tour, called the Road to Change, that made over 50 stops in 20 states, with stops that included areas affected by gun violence and areas where there is a strong pro-gun culture (Booker, 2018). This voter registration effort came just before the 2018 midterm elections in the United States, to mobilize young voters to turn out to the polls to vote in elections that normally experience low youth voter turnout (Booker, 2018). But, recent analysis indicates that 31 percent of young voters aged 18 to 29 turned out to vote in the recent US midterm elections—up from 21 percent in 2014 (The Center for Information and Research on Civic Learning and Engagement (CIRCLE), 2018).

The young people of Parkland understood that they could reach a large audience through social media, which was used as a tool because they already possessed the knowledge of how government and special interest groups work. The young people who created the #NeverAgain movement harnessed the skills they had gained through their learning environment, and engaged their immediate network to begin what is now a widespread social movement. Civic engagement in the digital era arises from networks and learning environments (Middaugh & Kirshner, 2015). Young people in Parkland reached out to their community for support in digital mediated ways, but social media may have seemed like an afterthought because it was not *consciously* used as a tool for this specific civic purpose—social media were merely used to spread voice and awareness and spark change. In the future, civics curriculum must address how to harness these digital tools for civic purposes, in addition to focusing on the institutions of democracy and civic engagement—a recommendation that will be further explored in this section. While the Parkland activists demonstrate that it is not necessary to have formal knowledge of how to utilize technology for civic engagement, it is imperative to have knowledge about how government works and how to assert pressure on certain points in government to enact change. In contemporary society, many interactions with public officials are digitally mediated, and therefore civics curriculum must address these means of engagement.

It is evident that in contemporary society, young people have become civically engaged in digitally mediated ways. Young people access news information through newspapers and social media, and form their opinions by staying informed about current events and other's opinions, such as reading Tumblr posts like Tanesha does. Some young people, like Elsie and Imani, choose not to post political content on social media or share with their peers that they have been watching the news so as to conform to what adults think young people are doing. Young people also organize and participate in protests using communications through social media, as evidenced by the school walkouts and #NeverAgain movement. Scholars, civic activists, and technology designers are all interested in the "empowerment potential of social media" (Livingstone, 2010, p. 1), and interest in this area continues to grow. Schools are influenced by the social and political climate of the country (Hess & McAvoy, 2015), and as schools are influenced by external factors, there may not ever be a perfect time to engage in this type of education reform, but it must be done. In the digital era, technology is embedded in daily life, and therefore educators must address the ways in which young people are already engaging in the political world through digital means, and scaffold the skills that young people need to develop and share their voices.

A curriculum that combines digital skills and civic learning is key to preparing young people for civic engagement in contemporary society (Hodgin, 2016). Teachers already incorporate new media into learning activities in the classroom (Beach & O'Brien, 2012; Morrell, Dueñas, Garcia, & López, 2013; Ohler, 2011), so digitally mediated civic engagement could be added to this pre-existing curriculum. Educators must cultivate what Vilchis et al. (2015) call techno-social literacy: integrating digital skills and social emotional education into other areas in the curriculum, and civics can be embedded throughout. This might involve incorporating a civics portfolio, kept digitally as a blog, for all students, where they have a collection of their posted writing, videos, and reflections on their civic and political actions (Kahne, Ullman, & Middaugh, 2011). Such technologies can aid young people in developing their voice (Buckingham & de Block, 2007). Blogging can help young people develop and articulate their perspectives and opinions on civic issues with a sense of authority and ownership over their opinions (Schultz, Hodgin, & Paraiso, 2015). Jenkins (2008) argues that the production and circulation of this type of media is important in shaping wider public dialogue. When young people have the opportunity to practice this through blogging and creating media in school, young people can learn to find their own voices when they reach the public stage (Jenkins, Ito, & boyd, 2016). Moreover, within these collaborative exercises of creating original content and sharing with others, experienced students can help their less experienced peers acquire knowledge and skills to use the technology and become confident in sharing their opinions with a wider social network (Jenkins, 2009). Curriculum that explicitly develops the skills for productive digitally mediated dialogue and engagement helps students build confidence in sharing their perspectives and "appreciate feedback" from others when they voice their opinions (Middaugh, 2016, p. 3). Figure 6.2 illustrates how the recommendations presented above may inform and enhance young people's sense of efficacy and help them to develop their voice. Figure 6.2 also demonstrates how research in the three fields in which the study is situated have informed the recommendations for transforming

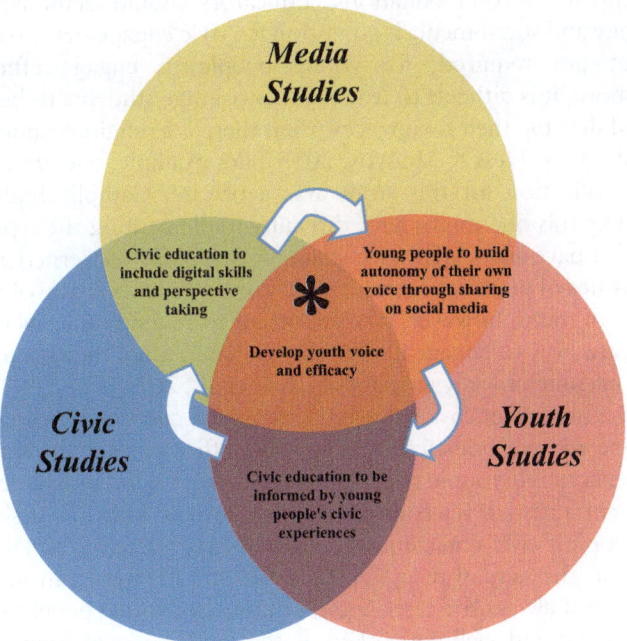

Fig. 6.2 Recommendations for improving youth voice and efficacy through civic education. Civic education should be reinvigorated for contemporary society and include schooling on digitally mediated ways of civic engagement that can improve perspective taking and overall efficacy. Civic education must be informed by the civic experiences of young people, as illustrated in the framework of civic identity presented in Figure 6.1

civic education with the aim of enhancing youth efficacy and voice in contemporary society.

There are, however, some caveats and cautions related to this type of civic education. If teachers elect to use social media platforms in schools, teachers must ensure they discuss Internet safety and privacy with students as a part of teaching them digital skills, and must consider the diversity of technology use among young people. It is important to highlight that schools cannot require all students to have their own device or turn to technology as a platform from which to share their voice, because some students might not be interested in or motivated to use it. It is also imperative that educators do not assume that all of their students have access to technology or the knowledge to utilize it in the ways discussed here and in other scholars' recommendations. Educators should demonstrate that technology and social media is an option for civic engagement that is available, but not required, for young people to engage efficaciously. Furthermore, it is difficult to teach and encourage students to be autonomous and develop their own voices when there is a religious underpinning to school values (Hess & McAvoy, 2015). For example, one of the settings for data collection for this study was a private, Catholic high school. Schools like this one might have difficulty implementing the type of civic education I have advocated for because they are also concerned about the sorts of issues of public concern in which their students are involved. With all of this in mind, however, it is important to reiterate that when young people learn how to engage in digitally mediated ways, they become more likely to become civically engaged (Kahne et al., 2011).

It is also important to acknowledge that these curriculum recommendations alone will not boost efficacy, and that efficacy is not the single solution to encourage young people to share their voice and increase civic engagement; rather, it is a contributing factor in the wider discussion about young people's civic engagement today. Society perceives that youth are engaging in the same way as the leaders of the #NeverAgain movement, but that is not always the case. A great number of young people are not as well-resourced and well-networked as the young people from Parkland. People from lower socioeconomic backgrounds find it challenging to feel a sense of efficacy, and will be able to change much less than those from wealthier backgrounds as they are not as civically engaged (Godfrey & Cherng, 2016; Levinson, 2010). These social class issues are highlighted in the case of the #NeverAgain movement, wherein the movement's organizers were from an affluent community and education system that valued civic education.

Community values and the attitudes of adults toward young people play a role in youth efficacy, as evidenced by the experiences of the participants in this study, and by the young people of Parkland. In addition to the curriculum recommendations mentioned throughout this book, communities and school districts must adapt their values to support young people in their development of civic identity and efficacy. The wider discussion about youth engagement and efficacy must come from a society that believes in and listens to the voices of young people.

References

Alter, C. (2018, March 22). The School Shooting Generation Has Had Enough. *TIME*.

Annette, J. (2008). Community Involvement, Civic Engagement, and Service Learning. In J. Arthur, I. Davies, & C. Hahn (Eds.), *The SAGE Handbook of Education for Citizenship and Democracy* (pp. 388–398). London, England: SAGE.

Bandura, A. (2008). An Agentic Perspective on Positive Psychology. In S. Lopez (Ed.), *Positive Psychology: Expecting the Best in People*. New York: Praeger.

Beach, R., & O'Brien, D. (2012). Using Apps for Learning with Literacy Across the Curriculum. Retrieved from http://usingipads.pbworks.com.

Bell, B. (2005). *Children, Youth, and Civic (dis)Engagement: Digital Technology and Citizenship*. CRACIN Working Paper, Canadian Research Alliance for Community Innovation and Networking.

Bennett, W. L. (2008). Changing Citizenship in the Digital Age. In W. L. Bennett (Ed.), *Civic Life Online: Learning How Digital Media Can Engage Youth* (pp. 1–24). Cambridge, MA: The MIT Press.

Booker, B. (2018, June 16). *Parkland Survivors Launch Tour To Register Young Voters and Get Them Out in November*. Retrieved June 20, 2018, from NPR https://www.npr.org/2018/06/16/620486174/parkland-survivors-launch-tour-to-register-young-voters-and-get-them-out-in-nove

Boston Public Schools, Office of Data and Accountability. (2015, September).

boyd, d. (2009, April 18). *Living and Learning with Social Media*. Symposium for Teaching and Learning with Technology. State College, PA: Penn State.

Brint, S. (2001). Gemeinschaft Revisited: A Critique and Reconstruction of the Community Concept. *Sociological Theory, 19*(1), 1–23.

Brubaker, R. (1992). *Citizenship and Nationhood in France and Germany*. Cambridge, MA: Harvard University Press.

Buckingham, D. (2013). *Beyond Technology: Children's Learning in the Age of Digital Culture.* Cambridge: John Wiley & Sons.

Buckingham, D., & de Block, L. (2007). Finding a Global Voice? Migrant Children, New Media, and the Limits of Empowerment. In P. Dahlgren (Ed.), *Young Citizens and New Media: Learning for Democratic Participation* (pp. 147–163). New York, NY: Routledge.

Camino, L., & Zeldin, S. (2002). From Periphery to Center: Pathways for Youth Civic Engagement in the Day-To-Day Life of Communities. *Applied Developmental Science, 6*(4), 213–220.

Cohen, C. J., Kahne, J., Bowyer, B., Middaugh, E., & Rogowski, J. (2012). *Participatory Politics: New Media and Youth Political Action.* YPP Research Network.

Colby, S. L., & Ortman, J. M. (2014). *Projections of the Size and Composition of the U.S. Population: 2014 to 2060.* United States Census Bureau.

Côté, J. E., & Levine, C. G. (2002). *Identity Formation, Agency, and Culture: A Social Psychological Synthesis.* Mahwah, NJ: Lawrence Erlbaum Associates.

Davies, C., & Eynon, R. (2013). *Teenagers and Technology.* London: Routledge.

Dias, T. S., & Menezes, I. (2014, June 2). Children and Adolescents as Political Actors: Collective Visions of Politics and Citizenship. *Journal of Moral Education, 43*(3), 250–268.

Dudley, R. L., & Gitelson, A. R. (2002). Political Literacy, Civic Education, and Civic Engagement: A Return to Political Socialization? *Applied Developmental Science, 6*(4), 175–182.

Erikson, E. H. (1968). *Identity: Youth and Crisis.* New York: W.W. Norton & Company.

Fielding, M. (2004). 'New Wave' Student Voice and the Renewal of Civic Society. *London Review of Education, 2*(3), 197–217.

Flanagan, C. A. (2013). *Teenage Citizens: The Political Theories of the Young.* Cambridge, MA: Harvard University Press.

Gardner, H., & Davis, K. (2013). *The App Generation: How Today's Youth Navigate Identity, Intimacy, and Imagination in a Digital World.* New Haven, CT: Yale University Press.

Gimpel, J. G., & Pearson-Merkowitz, S. (2009). Policies for Civic Engagement Beyond the Schoolyard. In J. Youniss & P. Levine (Eds.), *Engaging Young People in Civic Life* (pp. 81–101). Nashville, TN: Vanderbilt University Press.

Godfrey, E. B., & Cherng, H.-Y. (2016). The Kids Are All Right? Income Inequality and Civic Engagement Among Our Nation's Youth. *Journal of Youth and Adolescence, 45*(11), 2218–2232.

Goffman, E. (1959). *The Presentation of Self in Everyday Life.* Garden City, NY: Doubleday Anchor Books.

Goffman, E. (1978). The Presentation of Self to Others. In J. G. Manis & B. N. Meltzer (Eds.), *Symbolic Interaction: A Reader in Social Psychology* (3rd ed., pp. 234–244). London: Allyn and Bacon.

Goodman, S., Sirriyeh, A., & McMahon, S. (2017). The Evolving (Re) Categorisations of Refugees Throughout the "Refugee/Migrant Crisis". *Journal of Community & Applied Social Psychology, 27*(2), 105–114.

Gould, J. (2011). *Guardian of Democracy: Civic Mission of Schools.* The Leonore Annenberg Institute for Civics of the Annenberg Public Policy Center at the University of Pennsylvania. Philadelphia: University of Pennsylvania.

Hahn, C. L. (2010). Comparative Civic Education Research: What We Know and What We Need to Know. *Citizenship Teaching and Learning, 6*(1), 5–23.

Hall, T., & Williamson, H. (1999). *Citizenship and Community.* Leicester: Youth Work Press.

Hart, D., & Kirshner, B. (2009). Civic Participation and Development Among Urban Adolescents. In J. Youniss & P. Levine (Eds.), *Engaging Young People in Civic Life* (pp. 102–120). Nashville, TN: Vanderbilt University Press.

Hartmann, M., Carpentier, N., & Cammaerts, B. (2007). Democratic Familyship and the Negotiated Practices of ICT Users. In P. Dahlgren (Ed.), *Young Citizens and New Media: Learning for Democratic Participation* (pp. 167–186). New York: Routledge.

Hasebrink, U., & Paus-Hasebrink, I. (2007). Young People's Identity Construction and Media Use: Democratic Participation in Germany and Austria. In P. Dahlgren (Ed.), *Young Citizens and New Media: Learning for Democratic Participation* (pp. 81–101). New York, NY: Routledge.

Haste, H. (2004). Constructing the Citizen. *Political Psychology, 25,* 413–439.

Haste, H. (2005). *My Voice, My Vote, My Community: A Study of Young People's Civic Action and Inaction.* London: Nestle Social Research Programme.

Hess, D. (2009). *Controversy in the Classroom: The Democratic Power of Discussion.* New York, NY: Taylor & Francis.

Hess, D., & McAvoy, P. (2015). *The Political Classroom: Evidence and Ethics in Democratic Education.* New York, NY: Routledge.

Hodgin, E. (2016, June 27). Educating Youth for Online Civic and Political Dialogue: A Conceptual Framework for the Digital Age. *Journal of Digital and Media Literacy, 4*(1–2). Retrieved from http://tinyw.in/iAr8

Ignatieff, M. (1995). The Myth of Citizenship. In R. Beiner (Ed.), *Theorizing Citizenship* (pp. 66–72). New York: State University of New York Press.

Ito, M., Baumer, S., Bittani, M., boyd, d., Cody, R., Herr-Stephenson, B., et al. (2010). *Hanging Out, Messing Around, and Geeking Out: Kids Living and Learning with New Media.* Cambridge, MA: The MIT Press.

Ito, M., Horst, H., Bittan, M., boyd, d., Herr-Stephenson, B., Lange, P. G., et al. (2008). *Living and Learning with New Media: Summary of Findings from the Digital Youth Project.* The John D. and Catherine T. MacArthur Foundation Reports on Digital Media and Learning. John D. and Catherine T. MacArthur Foundation.

James, C. (2014). *Disconnected: Youth, New Media, and the Ethics Gap.* Cambridge, MA: The MIT Press.

204   J. K. VIOLA

Jenkins, H. (2008). *Convergence Culture: Where Old and New Media Collide.* New York: New York University Press.

Jenkins, H. (2009). *Confronting the Challenges of Participatory Culture: Media Education for the 21st Century.* Cambridge, MA: MIT Press.

Jenkins, H., Ito, M., & boyd, d. (2016). *Participatory Culture in a Networked Era: A Conversation on Youth, Learning, Commerce, and Politics.* Malden, MA: Polity Press.

Jennings, M., & Zeitner, V. (2003). Internet Use and Civic Engagement: A Longitudinal Analysis. *Public Opinion Quarterly, 67,* 311–334.

Kahne, J., & Middaugh, E. (2009). Democracy for Some: The Civic Opportunity Gap in High School. In J. Youniss & P. Levine (Eds.), *Engaging Young People in Civic Life* (pp. 29–58). Nashville, TN: Vanderbilt University Press.

Kahne, J., & Sporte, S. (2008). Developing Citizens: The Impact of Civic Learning Opportunities on Students' Commitment to Civic Participation. *American Educational Research Journal, 45*(3), 738–766.

Kahne, J., Ullman, J., & Middaugh, E. (2011). Digital Opportunities for Civic Education. *Civics 2.0: Citizenship Education for a New Generation.* American Enterprise Institute.

Kahne, J., & Westheimer, J. (2003). Teaching Democracy: What Schools Need to Do. *Phi Delta Kappan, 85*(1), 34–66.

Kahne, J., & Westheimer, J. (2006). The Limits of Political Efficacy: Educating Citizens for a Democratic Society. *PS: Political Science & Politics, 39*(2), 289–296.

Ke, L., & Starkey, H. (2014). Active Citizens, Good Citizens, and Insouciant Bystanders: The Educational Implications of Chinese University Students' Civic Participation via Social Networking. *London Review of Education, 12*(1), 50–62.

Keating, A., Kerr, D., Benton, T., Mundy, E., & Lopes, J. (2010). *Citizenship Education in England 2001–2010: Young People's Practices and Prospects for the Future: The Eighth and Final Report from the Citizenship Education Longitudinal Study (CELS).* Great Britain Department for Education.

Kennedy, K. J., Hahn, C. L., & Lee, W. (2008). Constructing Citizenship: Comparing the Views of Students in Australia, Hong Kong, and the United States. *Comparative Education Review, 52*(1), 53–91.

Knefelkamp, L. L. (2008). Civic Identity: Locating Self in Community. *Diversity & Democracy: Civic Learning for Shared. Futures, 11*(2), 1–3.

Korbey, H. (2017, April 20). *New Times Call for a New Civics.* From Edutopia. Retrieved from https://www.edutopia.org/article/new-times-call-new-civics-holly-korbey

Lagemann, E. C., & Lewis, H. (2012, March–April). Renewing Civic Education: Time to Restore American Higher Education's Lost Mission. *Harvard Magazine,* pp. 42–45.

Levine, P. (2008). A Public Voice for Youth: The Audience Problem in Digital Media and Civic Education. In W. L. Bennett (Ed.), *Civic Life Online: Learning How Digital Media Can Engage Youth* (pp. 119–138). Cambridge, MA: The MIT Press.

Levinson, M. (2010). The Civic Empowerment Gap: Defining the Problem and Locating Solutions. In L. Sherrod, J. Torney-Purta, & C. Flanagan (Eds.), *Handbook of Research on Civic Engagement in Youth* (pp. 331–361). Hoboken, NJ: John Wiley & Sons.

Levy, B. (2011). *Fostering Cautious Political Efficacy Through Civic Advocacy Projects: A Mixed Methods Case Study of a High School Class.* New Orleans, LA: American Educational Research Association.

Linton, A. (2015). Politically Engaged and Alienated Youth: Reevaluating 2010 UK Student Protests. In E. Middaugh & B. Kirshner (Eds.), *#youthaction: Becoming Political in the Digital Age* (pp. 191–207). Charlotte, NC: Information Age Publishing, Inc.

Lister, R., Smith, N., Middleton, S., & Cox, L. (2003). Empirical Perspectives on Theoretical and Political Debate. *Citizenship Studies, 7*, 235–253.

Lister, R., Smith, N., Middleton, S., & Cox, L. (2005). Young People Talking About Citizenship in Britain. In N. Kabeer (Ed.), *Inclusive Citizenship: Meanings and Expressions* (pp. 114–131). New York: Zed Books.

Lithwick, D. (2018, February 28). They Were Trained for This Moment: How the Student Activists of Marjory Stoneman Douglas High Demonstrate the Power of a Comprehensive Education. *Slate.*

Livingstone, S. (2010). Digital Learning and Participation Among Youth: Critical Reflections on Future Research Priorities. *International Journal of Learning and Media, 2*(2–3), 1–13.

Livingstone, S., Couldry, N., & Markham, T. (2007). Youthful Steps Towards Civic Participation: Does the Internet Help? In B. D. Loader (Ed.), *Young Citizens in the Digital Age: Political Engagement, Young People and New Media* (pp. 21–34). London: Routledge.

Marshall, T. H., & Bottomore, T. (1992). *Citizenship and Social Class* (Vol. 2). London: Pluto Press.

McLeod, J. M., & Shah, D. V. (2009). Communication and Political Socialization: Challenges and Opportunities for Research. *Political Communication, 26*(1), 1–10.

McMillan, D., & Chavis, D. (1986). Sense of Community: A Definition and Theory. *American Journal of Community Psychology, 14*(1), 6–23.

Mesch, G. S., & Coleman, S. (2007). New Media and New Voters: Young People, the Internet and the 2005 UK Election Campaign. In B. D. Loader (Ed.), *Young Citizens in the Digital Age: Political Engagement, Young People and New Media* (pp. 35–47). London: Routledge.

Middaugh, E. (2016, August 26). Social Media and Online Communities Expose Youth to Political Conversation, But Also to Incivility and Conflict. *USApp–American Politics and Policy Blog*. London School of Economics.

Middaugh, E., & Kirshner, B. (2015). Educating Powerful Citizens in a Changing World. In E. Middaugh & B. Kirshner (Eds.), *#youthaction: Becoming Political in the Digital Age* (pp. 1–8). Charlotte, NC: Information Age Publishing, Inc.

Montgomery, K. C. (2008). Youth and Digital Democracy: Intersections of Practice, Policy, and the Marketplace. In W. L. Bennett (Ed.), *Civic Life Online: Learning How Digital Media Can Engage Youth* (pp. 25–49). Cambridge, MA: The MIT Press.

Morrell, E., Dueñas, R., Garcia, V., & López, J. (2013). *Critical Media Pedagogy: Teaching for Achievement in City Schools*. New York: Teachers College Press.

Mossberger, K., Tolbert, C. J., & McNeal, R. S. (2008). *Digital Citizenship: The Internet, Society and Participation*. Cambridge, MA: MIT Press.

Nasir, N. S., & Kirshner, B. (2003). The Cultural Construction of Moral and Civic Identities. *Applied Developmental Science, 7*, 138–147.

National Council for the Social Studies. (2008). A Vision of Powerful Teaching and Learning in the Social Studies: Building Effective Citizens. *Social Education, 75*(2), 277–280.

Ohler, J. (2011). Digital Citizenship Means Character Education for the Digital Age. *Kappa Delta Pi Record, 47*, 25–27.

Ong, A. (1999). *Flexible Citizenship: The Cultural Logics of Transnationality*. Durham, NC: Duke University Press.

Osler, A., & Starkey, H. (2006). Education for Democratic Citizenship: A Review of Research, Policy and Practice 1995–2005. *Research Papers in Education, 21*(4), 433–466.

Osler, A., & Starkey, H. (2018). Extending the Theory and Practice of Education for Cosmopolitan Citizenship. *Educational Review, 70*(1), 31–40.

Raynes-Goldie, K., & Walker, L. (2008). Our Space: Online Civic Engagement Tools for Youth. In W. L. Bennett (Ed.), *Civic Life Online: Learning How Digital Media Can Engage Youth* (pp. 161–188). Cambridge, MA: The MIT Press.

Rheingold, H. (2008). Using Participatory Media and Public Voice to Encourage Civic Engagement. In W. L. Bennett (Ed.), *Civic Life Online: Learning How Digital Media Can Engage Youth* (pp. 97–118). Cambridge, MA: The MIT Press.

Riger, S., & Lavrakas, P. (1981). Community Ties: Patterns of Attachment and Social Interaction in Urban Neighborhoods. *American Journal of Community Psychology, 9*, 55–66.

Rousseau, S., & Warren, S. (2018, March 20). *Civic Participation Begins in Schools: Fostering a Robust Democracy in America Requires That We Create a*

Truly Democratic School Culture. (S. S. Review, Producer). Retrieved March 20, 2018, from Stanford Social Innovation Review https://ssir.org/articles/entry/civic_participation_begins_in_schools?mc_cid=cc4f6cc921&mc_eid=2480d25459\

Schlenker, B. (1985). Identity and Self-Identification. In B. R. Schlenker (Ed.), *The Self and Social Life* (pp. 65–99). New York: McGraw-Hill.

Schlenker, B. (2012). Self-Presentation. In M. R. Leary & J. P. Tangney (Eds.), *Handbook of Self and Identity* (2nd ed., pp. 542–570). New York: Guilford Press.

Schlozman, K., Verba, S., & Brady, H. (2010). Weapon of the Strong: Participatory Inequality and the Internet. *Perspectives on Politics, 8,* 487–509.

Schultz, K., Hodgin, E., & Paraiso, J. (2015). Blogging as Civic Engagement: Developing a Sense of Authority and Audience in an Urban Public School Classroom. In E. Middaugh & B. Kirshner (Eds.), *#youthaction: Becoming Political in the Digital Age* (pp. 147–168). Charlotte, NC: Information Age Publishing, Inc.

Serriere, S. C. (2014). The Role of the Elementary Teacher in Fostering Civic Efficacy. *The Social Studies, 105*(1), 45–56.

Shapiro, S., & Brown, C. (2018, February). *The State of Civic Education.* Retrieved from Center for American Progress: https://www.american-progress.org/issues/education-k-12/reports/2018/02/21/446857/state-civics-education/.

Steidley, T., & Colen, C. G. (2017). Framing the Gun Control Debate: Press Releases and Framing Strategies of the National Rifle Association and the Brady Campaign. *Social Science Quarterly, 98*(2), 608–627.

The Center for Information and Research on Civic Learning and Engagement (CIRCLE). (2018, November 7). *Young People Dramatically Increase Their Turnout to 31%, Shape 2018 Midterm Elections.* Retrieved November 8, 2018 from The Center for Information and Research on Civic Learning and Engagement (CIRCLE). Retrieved from https://civicyouth.org/young-people-dramatically-increase-their-turnout-31-percent-shape-2018-midterm-elections/

Torney-Purta, J. R., Lehmann, R., Oswald, H., & Schulz, W. (2001). *Citizenship and Education in Twenty-eight Countries.* Amsterdam, The Netherlands: The International Association for the Evaluation of Educational Achievement.

Vilchis, M., Scott, K., & Besaw, C. (2015). COMPUGIRLS Speak: How We Use Social Media for Social Movements. In E. Middaugh & B. Kirshner (Eds.), *#youthaction: Becoming Political in the Digital Age* (pp. 59–79). Charlotte, NC: Information Age Publishing, Inc.

Watts, R., & Guessous, O. (2006). *Civil Rights Activists in the Information Age: The Development of Math Literacy Workers.* Center for Information and Research on Civic Learning and Engagement.

Westheimer, J., & Kahne, J. (2004). What Kind of Citizen? The Politics of Educating for Democracy. *American Educational Research Journal, 41*(2), 237–269.

Young, I. (1995). Polity and Group Difference: A Critique of the Ideal of Universal Citizenship. In R. Beiner (Ed.), *Theorizing Citizenship* (pp. 175–207). New York: State University of New York Press.

Youniss, J., McLellan, J. A., & Yates, M. (1997). What We Know About Engendering Civic Identity. *The American Behavioral Scientist, 40*(5), 620–631.

Youniss, J., & Yates, M. (1997). *Community Service and Social Responsibility in Youth*. Chicago: University of Chicago Press.

Appendix A: Social Media Features and Affordances

© The Author(s) 2020
J. K. Viola, *Young People's Civic Identity in the Digital Age*,
Palgrave Studies in Young People and Politics,
https://doi.org/10.1007/978-3-030-37405-1

Table A1 Social media features and affordances

	Facebook (2004)	Twitter (2009)	Tumblr (2007)	Instagram (2010)	Snapchat (2011)
Common uses	Content sharing ranging from status updates, photographs, and videos, to links to news articles and YouTube video clips.	Sharing content via Tweets and Re-Tweets. Re-Tweet feature "empowers a user to spread information of their choice beyond the reach of the original Tweet's Followers" (Kwak, Lee, Park, & Moon, 2010). This allows the dissemination of information beyond the intended audience, broadening the reach of individual voices. Users can Follow other users, tag their Tweets, or search for other Tweets on a particular topic, by using the hashtag. A hashtag, which is written with a # symbol, is used to "index keywords or topics" on Twitter (Twitter, Inc., 2018).	Sharing original content, including text, images, and videos. Follow other blogs and topics in a similar manner to how it is done on Twitter, using hashtags. Re-blog other users' posts.	Post edited photographs and videos—with the help of the app's photograph filter features. Comment on other users' content.	Photo and video sharing. Texting.

	Facebook	Twitter	Tumblr	Instagram	Snapchat
Following and tagging	Began as a social networking website to connect individuals within a pre-existing social network in the context of their university. Today, Facebook includes features that allow people to connect with each other, brands, and news outlets.	Follow other users (using the @ symbol followed by the user's identifier) without reciprocation. Users are able to Follow people they know, people in the public eye, brands, and news outlets.	Follow other blogs and topics in a similar manner to how it is done on Twitter, using hashtags (Tumblr, Inc., 2018).	Users are able to Follow people they know, people in the public eye, brands, and news outlets in a similar manner to how it is done on Twitter, using hashtags (Instagram, Inc., 2018).	Friend connections are more intimate, beginning with existing contacts that users have in their smartphone contact list (Snapchat, Inc., 2018).
Unique features	Anyone aged 13 or over can join Facebook by creating a profile using their real name, not a username like some social networking websites allow (Fordham & Goddard, 2013).	Twitter allows communication in discrete bits, called Tweets, that were previously limited to 140 characters (Hosterman, 2012).	Blog customization with various fonts, colors, layouts, and usernames. Unlike Facebook, Tumblr allows for people to explore identity with their username and maintain an anonymous identity if they wish.	Focus on user-produced photography.	Photos and videos that are shared in individual messages disappear after the recipient views the message. Stories disappear 24 hours after they are posted.

(*continued*)

Table A1 (continued)

	Facebook (2004)	Twitter (2009)	Tumblr (2007)	Instagram (2010)	Snapchat (2011)
Affordances to young people and potential implications for civic identity formation	The Facebook Group feature allows young people to connect with others who have similar interests. Most commonly, young people belong to Facebook Groups for their sports teams and clubs at school. Groups are often the way that young people find out about their sports match schedule, or club meeting times. The Facebook Events feature allows users to create events, or find out about events happening in their area that they might be interested in. Young people may learn about protests (i.e., a school walkout) through a Facebook Event.	Allows young people to stay connected to their friends, their favorite celebrities and athletes, and current events. Twitter (theoretically) allows users to directly connect to anyone with an account, from their best friend to the President of the United States. Twitter news alerts on smartphones and tablets keep young people informed about political affairs and current events at the international, national, and local level.	Users can maintain an anonymous identity. Some users may take advantage of this anonymity to explore their political opinions and beliefs that they might not feel comfortable sharing with their friends and family, and others who know them, by starting their own blog or following the blogs of others to learn about diverse political opinions.	Young people often take to Instagram to post selfies and share photos from their daily lives. Young people can take to Instagram to share a selfie with a caption indicating a political message (i.e., "Black Lives Matter"), and can learn about current events by Following politicians' and news outlets' Instagram pages.	Parents and teachers cannot trace the message (unless the recipient is quick enough to take a screenshot of the message before it disappears), allowing for young people to have a sense of privacy to communicate with their friends. Young people can use Snapchat as a medium to communicate with their friends about current events.

Note: All of these social media websites and apps are starting to borrow features from each other—such as filters for photographs, and direct messaging features—and becoming more similar to each other over time

REFERENCES

Fordham, I., & Goddard, T. (2013). *Facebook Guide for Educators: A Tool for Teaching and Learning*. London: The Education Foundation.

Hosterman, A. R. (2012). Tweeting 101: Twitter and the College Classroom. In H. S. Al-Deen & J. A. Hendricks (Eds.), *Social Media: Usage and Impact* (pp. 93–110). Plymouth, England: Lexington Books.

Kwak, H., Lee, C., Park, H., & Moon, S. (2010, April). What Is Twitter, a Social Network or a News Media? In *Proceedings of the 19th International Conference on World Wide Web* (pp. 591–600).

Appendix B: Participant Descriptions

Table B1 Participant descriptions

Pseudonym	Age	Gender	Description
Kali	16	Female	Passionate and vocal student, who unabashedly shared her opinions and beliefs. Kali admires her mother, who raised Kali and her siblings as a single parent, and founded a non-profit organization. Kali's younger sister was shot and paralyzed at age 3, and her mother does outreach for victims of violence.
Veronica	15	Female	At first Veronica seemed timid, but as we continued talking, she comfortably revealed her thoughts and beliefs. A hard worker, Veronica skipped a year in school. While she is the youngest in her class, she is often called upon to tutor her classmates and help them succeed academically. Veronica highlighted her youth as an occasional barrier to opportunity.
Madeline	17	Female	A "happy, caring" person, Madeline is very active in her school and her church. Madeline views her social media profiles as a "billboard" of herself, and is careful to present herself online as accurately possible.
Laura	17	Female	Laura is very active in Live Action Role Play (LARP), but chooses to keep this passion of hers private and does not tell her school friends because it is "nerdy" and she does not want people to "judge" her. Laura is very involved in her church and often goes on church retreats with her father.
Jackie	16	Female	Very involved in sports and church youth group, of which she is a founding member. Active on social media, and her interest in sports prompts her to Follow sports news outlets.

(*continued*)

© The Author(s) 2020

J. K. Viola, *Young People's Civic Identity in the Digital Age*,
Palgrave Studies in Young People and Politics,
https://doi.org/10.1007/978-3-030-37405-1

Table B1 (continued)

Pseudonym	Age	Gender	Description
Hannah	16	Female	Down-to-earth with a sense of humor, Hannah enjoyed talking about the funny moments she recently shared with her friends. Hannah described her family as "political"—her father was a Marine, and her uncle was in the Army—and is well-informed as a result of following the news and having discussions about it at the dinner table with her family.
Naomi	16	Female	Energetic, and very interested in talking about politics. Naomi especially enjoys talking about politics with a particular friend who has opposing viewpoints.
Jane	14	Female	A newcomer to the school, Jane is excited to be involved in so many school sport activities. She is soft-spoken and loves drawing, and also enjoys video games.
Mira	15	Female	Mira has a peculiar sense of humor, and frequently inserted her sarcasm to our conversation. Mira's best friend is her former third grade teacher.
Grace	16	Female	Quiet student originally from China, with interesting comparisons between the idea of community in her homeland of China and her new home in the United States.
Kaitlyn	16	Female	Easygoing and talkative, but does not enjoy talking to her peers about politics. Kaitlyn prefers to not know whether her friends disagree with her point of view, as she is concerned that an argument of opposing viewpoints would jeopardize or terminate the friendship.
Allie	15	Female	Genuine and talkative, Allie shared her passion for school, her sports teams, and the fundraisers she participates in for local charities. Allie has been struck by the conflicts in the Middle East, particularly in Syria, and often reads news articles and talks to her friends about the issue.
Ava	16	Female	Feels a strong sense of community at her school, and demonstrates her community membership by participating in service activities.
Peter	17	Male	Gregarious and articulate, Peter described that his interests go beyond social media and technology. Due to his phone breaking and his girlfriend falling ill for several months, Peter noticed that he did not miss technology or social media while he focused on the "more important things in life."
Nora	15	Female	Nora is very shy, and expresses herself through dance. Humble, she did not share her impressive dance accomplishments until much later in the interview.
Aileen	15	Female	Very timid and shy in conversation, but very active on the ice with her hockey team.

(continued)

Table B1   (continued)

Pseudonym	Age	Gender	Description
Jillian	15	Female	Very talkative and engaged in performing arts. Her mother calls her "spirited." Jillian was not afraid to share her thoughts, beliefs, and opinions on any subject.
Carly	15	Female	A shy student, active with her sports teams and her church group.
Elsie	17	Female	A self-described "nerd," Elsie has attended several high schools. She is very interested in having thoughtful and productive conversations with others about political and social issues. Elsie often spends time on Tumblr, posting her thoughts anonymously, and reading the opinions of others.
Maisie	14	Female	Thoughtful, calculated speaker with wisdom beyond her years. Family chooses to not own a car to limit carbon footprint. At the time of our first interview, Maisie had removed herself from social media. Four months later, during our follow-up interview, Maisie told me she was back on social media.
Joelle	15	Female	Joelle's family has one car, and because her father works on the weekends, she often has difficulty going far beyond her home. While she uses technology and social media to entertain herself, she also follows the Black Lives Matter movement. As an African American, this movement is important to Joelle and her family.
Addie	14	Female	Addie has a bubbly personality, and is very well informed about political and social issues. She is very independent, and is unafraid to lead and guide her friends when they come to her for help. Addie recently decided to spend less time on social media, and finds she appreciates and pays attention to things that she did not notice before.
Imani	14	Female	Imani is attuned to what is happening on social media. She acknowledged that some people use social media as a way to "cause drama." Imani informed me about what "subbing" is: a public post that is directed at a specific person, without mentioning the name of that specific person.
Aidan	15	Male	Aidan is very involved in his community by doing "extra stuff," such as community service and academic enrichment activities. School is a central part of Aidan's life, and he believes that our school experiences shape us into who we are. For Aidan, school group projects are situations in which young people can exercise their leadership roles and "civic duty."
Camille	15	Female	Camille is active on social media, but does not believe that people behave the same way online and offline. Camille likes to text her friends to ask them what they think about current events.

(*continued*)

Table B1   (continued)

Pseudonym	Age	Gender	Description
Sean	15	Male	Very engaged in school and sports. Sean is very articulate and has carefully thought about many political and social issues.
Nadia	16	Female	Very active member in her community, specifically her citywide youth council. She advocates for the rights and education of the people in her age group, and was eager to discuss the projects with which she is involved.
Zelda	14	Female	A talkative, outgoing girl, Zelda is very active in sports. She considers herself to be better informed about current events than the rest of her family, and used Twitter to follow the presidential debates throughout the election cycle.
Selah	15	Female	Selah is very quiet, but very interested and passionate about her participation on the debate team at school. For Selah, participation on the debate team at school has opened her mind and kept her informed about current events.
Jaden	14	Male	Jaden describes himself as simultaneously "lazy and hardworking." He is active in online video games, and has met friends through the online game League of Legends.
Kenai	14	Male	Kenai is engaged in online video games, and has met friends through the online gaming system. He is interested in politics, but faces a complicated dynamic at home, in which his mother doesn't think he is old enough to have a discussion about politics, so deliberately excludes him from those discussions.
Robert	16	Male	Robert is a self-taught musician, and goes out of his way to help people. He has discussed politics and current events with his father, but perceives that his father has the "advantage" in those conversations because he is older.
Kevin	15	Male	While Kevin shows his outward self as funny, easygoing, and optimistic, he described his "dark" side that he keeps to himself ("I don't want people in the world to feel bad because I feel bad."). Well-informed about current events.
Habibah	16	Female	Habibah is funny, caring, and dependable. She is the youngest of 8 children, and firmly believes in the Golden Rule to treat others as you wish to be treated.
Damon	14	Male	Damon is "always cracking jokes and making people laugh." He will follow current events when they are local and may have a direct impact on him.
Bibiana	16	Female	Cheerful, shy, and an immigrant to the United States, Bibiana provided new perspective on the idea of citizenship, and what it means to be a citizen.
Sawyer	15	Male	Very driven, interested in improving his community through service and through civic action. Says he is "not good at current events," because he does not follow them.

(continued)

Table B1   (continued)

Pseudonym	Age	Gender	Description
Tanesha	16	Female	Tanesha did not use any adjectives to describe herself, because she doesn't like to put herself "in a box." Likes to express herself through her clothing and says she does "not know" who she is yet. Tanesha takes herself off social media at different intervals every few months to stay away from drama and focus on her schoolwork.
Bethany	14	Female	Generous, caring, and introspective. Keeps a journal and enjoys writing down her memories. Describes herself as "sociable" while also enjoying "silence and quiet."
Martin	15	Male	Thoughtful young man, concerned with how he presents himself to others. Wants to participate in Black Lives Matter movement, but worries for his safety and getting into trouble.
Stephen	14	Male	Plays a lot of video games and hopes to be a video game designer when he grows up. He perceives that he cannot be civically engaged until he reaches age 18.
Joseph	16	Male	A self-described "average high-schooler," Joseph does not show interest in politics and current events. However, he watches the news and learns about local events through social media.
Sachi	17	Male	Very civically engaged, and a member of a very civically engaged family. Keen to share experience of an 8-day trip during which he met government officials and other young people from all over the country.
Gwen	18	Female	Born in Cameroon and now a naturalized American citizen, Gwen has opposing views of citizenship in comparison with Bibiana.
Carol	17	Female	Outgoing, cares about school. Does not use social media much because she doesn't believe that the number of Facebook Likes one receives should determine one's happiness.
Keegan	18	Male	Only young person who specifically identified with ideals of the Republican Party. Described his viewpoints clearly and thoughtfully, and understood when he shifted his political beliefs.

INDEX[1]

[1] Note: Page numbers followed by 'n' refer to notes.

© The Author(s) 2020
J. K. Viola, *Young People's Civic Identity in the Digital Age*,
Palgrave Studies in Young People and Politics,
https://doi.org/10.1007/978-3-030-37405-1

CPI Antony Rowe
Eastbourne, UK
March 12, 2020